MODERN ENGLISH PLAYWRIGHTS

TO
"THE HELPERS AND THE SERVERS—
THEY MUST DO THEIR PART TOO,
IF IT IS TO BE OF ANY GOOD."

MODERN ENGLISH PLAYWRIGHTS

*A Short History of the
English Drama from 1825*

BY

JOHN W. CUNLIFFE, 1865 – 1946.

*Professor of English and Director of the School
of Journalism in Columbia University
in the City of New York*

KENNIKAT PRESS/PORT WASHINGTON, N. Y.

MODERN ENGLISH PLAYWRIGHTS

Copyright 1927 by Harper and Brothers; Copyright, 1955 by Guy S. Cunliffe
Reissued in 1969 by Kennikat Press by arrangement with Harper and Row, Inc.
Library of Congress Catalog Card No: 71-86009
SBN 8046- 0553-X

Manufactured by Taylor Publishing Company   Dallas, Texas

ESSAY AND GENERAL LITERATURE INDEX REPRINT SERIES

CONTENTS

PREFACE

From many years' experience of discussing modern literature both in the classroom and in print, I am aware of the provisional character of all judgments upon recent dramatic developments, and the opinions here presented, whether my own or other people's, are submitted with full reservation of the reader's right to re-adjust them to his own standard of values. I hope, none the less, that this connected account of what appears to me one of the most remarkable periods of English dramatic history will be of interest and of use.

I am obliged to the editor of the Series, Professor A. H. Quinn, whose view of recent dramatic developments is very different from mine, not only for the privilege of expressing my own opinions on controversial issues, but for many useful suggestions. I am indebted to Harper & Brothers for the use of copyright material in quotation from the text of recent plays; to Brentano's for permission to quote the excerpts from Bernard Shaw's plays; to Little, Brown and Co. for the citation from Sir Johnston Forbes-Robertson's *A Player under Three Reigns*; to Dodd, Mead and Co. for extracts from William Archer's *Playmaking* and *The Old Drama and the New*; to the Houghton Mifflin Co. for the lines quoted from John Drinkwater's *Abraham Lincoln*; to John W. Luce and Co. for quotations from J. M. Synge's *The Aran Islands* and *The Playboy of the Western World* and from Stanley Houghton's *Hindle Wakes*; to Martin Secker Ltd. for the passages quoted from St. John

Hankin's plays; and to G. P. Putnam's Sons for the passage from Lord Dunsany's *A Night at an Inn*.

Cordial thanks are also offered to the officers of the British Museum and the Bodleian Libraries, the New York Public Library, and the Columbia University Library for their unfailing courtesy and helpfulness. I wish to make special mention of the persevering skill of Mrs. Hitchcock, Librarian of the Columbia Journalism Library, and her staff, in running down for me dates and other elusive details as to which accuracy is a much prized virtue but one not easily attainable in the modern field.

CHAPTER I

INTRODUCTORY

THE nineteenth century brought the English theatre back to the people and the English people back to the theatre, but it took nearly the whole of the century to complete the reconciliation. In the early years of the Victorian era, an intelligent observer might well have thought that the prospects of the drama had not greatly improved since the Puritans closed the theatres in 1642; the Restoration had re-opened the theatre, but only to the most idle, the most frivolous, and the most debauched class of the nation —the Court and its hangers-on. When the Court became more respectable, the theatre lost its support without gaining that of the solid and industrious middle class which was slowly coming into power. The estrangement of the middle class from the theatre, resting upon a long-established tradition, was encouraged by the conditions under which plays were produced and by the kind of entertainment offered. Up to 1843 the performance of "legitimate" drama was restricted by law to two of the London theatres —Drury Lane and Covent Garden—under letters patent granted by Charles II at the Restoration, reinforced by Sir Robert Walpole's Licensing Act of 1737. But permission to present musical entertainments, partly dramatic in character, could still be obtained from the Lord Chamberlain for smaller theatres which were allowed to open during the summer months when the "patent" houses were closed. The success of the "summer" houses led the regular theatres

The "patent" theatres

1

to extend their winter season and to offer similar entertainments; the minor theatres retaliated by encroaching upon the winter months and the dramatic programmes which were supposed to be the monopoly of the regular houses. The usual bill of the smaller theatres, however, consisted of "pantomimes, ballets, farces, melodramas—all bearing the orthodox title of *burlettas*" with such occasional attractions as tight-rope dancers and performing dogs. The oldest of the minor theatres, Sadler's Wells, presented in 1825 the following programme, which has been preserved in Hone's *Every Day Book:*

The amusements will consist of a romantic tale of mysterious horror and broad grin, never acted, called the *Enchanted Girdles, or Winki the Witch, and the Ladies of Samarchand.* A most whimsical burletta, which sends people home perfectly exhausted from uninterrupted risibility, called *The Lawyer, The Jew, and The Yorkshireman,* with, by request of 75 distinguished families, and a party of 5, that never to be sufficiently praised pantomime, called *Magic in Two Colours, or Fairy Blue and Fairy Red, or Harlequin and the Marble Rock.* It would be perfectly superfluous for any man in his senses to attempt anything more than the mere announcement in recommendation of the above unparalleled representations, so attractive in themselves as to threaten a complete monopoly of the qualities of the magnet; and though the proprietors were to talk nonsense for an hour, they could not assert a more *important truth* than that they possess the only Wells from which you may draw wine, three shillings and sixpence, a full quart. Those whose important avocations prevent their coming at the commencement will be admitted for half price at half-past eight. Ladies and gentlemen who are not judges of the superior entertainments announced are respectfully requested to bring as many as possible with them who are. N. B.—A full moon during the week.

The special attraction at Sadler's Wells at this period was the "aquatic" drama, acted upon a gigantic tank; real ships floated upon real water, and the heroine fell in to be rescued by the hero or a Newfoundland dog. The home of the "equestrian" drama was Astley's Amphitheatre on the south side of the Thames, just across Westminster bridge. It was here that the famous rider Ducrow, celebrated by "Christopher North" in *Noctes Ambrosianæ*, gave his time-honoured injunction to the actors "Cut the cackle and come to the 'osses," adding, "I'll show you how to cut it. You say 'Yield thee, Englishman!' Then you (indicating the other) answer 'Never!' Then you say 'Obstinate Englishman, you die.' Then you both fights. There, that settles the matter; the audience will understand you a deal better, and the poor 'osses won't catch cold while you're jawing."

The successful competition of the minor theatres drove the "patent" houses in desperation to similar forms of entertainment, and it was the combination of tight-rope dances with a famous lion-tamer at Drury Lane that led the young Queen Victoria to pay the house the remarkable compliment of two special performances by royal command in 1839. By this time the monopoly of the "patent" houses had become an absurdity, and it was abolished by Act of Parliament in 1843. The extension of the privilege of playing Shakespeare and Sheridan to the smaller theatres was regarded with eager expectance, but only one of them, Sadler's Wells, under the management of Samuel Phelps, made any distinguished use of the opportunity. Whether it was the kind of entertainment offered that drove away the sober and educated sections of the population, or the character of the audience that prescribed the kind of entertainment necessary for financial success, the degradation of the stage in the first half of the nineteenth century is beyond question. Sir Walter Scott, in answer to a suggestion that he might do something for the London stage, could write in 1819: "I do not think the character of the audience in London is such that one could have the least pleasure in pleasing them. One half come to prosecute

"Cut the cackle

Queen Victoria at Drury Lane

3

their debaucheries, so openly that it would degrade a bag-nio; another set to snooze off their beef-steaks and port wine; a third are critics of the fourth column of the news-paper; fashion, wit, or literature there is not, and, on the whole, I would far rather write verses for mine honest friend Punch [the street 'Punch and Judy'] and his audience. The only thing that could tempt me to be so silly, would be to assist a friend in such a degrading task, who was to have the whole profit and the shame of it."

Professor
Henry
Morley

Nearly fifty years later Professor Henry Morley in the Prologue to his *Journal of a London Playgoer from 1851 to 1866* says: "The great want of the stage in our day is an educated public that will care for its successes, honestly inquire into its failures, and make managers and actors feel that they are not dependent for appreciation of their efforts on the verdict that comes of the one mind divided into fragments between Mr. Dapperwit in the stalls, Lord Froth in the side-boxes, and Pompey Doodle in the gallery. The playgoer who would find in our London theatres a dramatic literature, in which England is rich beyond all other nations, fitly housed, may be indignant at much that he sees in them. But what if Doodle, Dapperwit and Froth do clap their hands at pieces which are all leg and no brains; in which the male actor's highest ambition is to caper, slide, and stamp with the energy of a street-boy on a cellar-flap, the actress shows plenty of thigh, and the dialogue, running entirely on the sound of words, hardly admits that they have any use at all as signs of thought? Whose fault is it that the applauders of these dismal antics sit so frequently as umpires in the judgment of dramatic literature?"

Yet outside the theatre there were the multitudinous readers of Thackeray and Dickens, Charlotte Brontë and

George Eliot, Anthony Trollope and Thomas Hardy, the public which was brought, somewhat reluctantly, to appreciate the poetry of Tennyson and Browning. It was a public of marked prejudices and of limited sympathies, but it was not uneducated or unintelligent beyond the possibility of artistic appreciation. The theatre was neither respected nor respectable; people of education and refinement found nothing to break down their inherited prejudices save the occasional revival of a Shakespearean masterpiece by a leading actor, or the still rarer performance of Goldsmith's *She Stoops to Conquer,* or Sheridan's *School for Scandal.* Poets were called upon, as Browning was by Macready, to "write me a play and save me from going to America," but the result disappointed alike the audience, the actor, and the dramatist. The reasons for the failure are sufficiently obvious; the poets were held fast by the romantic tradition. They were still writing for the Elizabethan stage and chose subjects which permitted treatment in long, rhetorical speeches, and made no appeal to the interests of a modern audience. They did not know the theatre and they did not adapt their plays to the modern picture stage. Playwrights and actors were ill paid, and gained nothing in public esteem to make up for the lack of pecuniary reward. When Browning attended incognito the performance of one of his plays, he was bewildered by the question of the man in the next seat, "Is this Browning the author of *Romeo and Juliet?*"—a reference to a burlesque of the Shakespearean tragedy then popular. Undeterred by early failures, Browning made repeated attempts to capture the stage, but had ultimately to content himself with writing closet drama. Charming as some of the plays are for subtlety of characterization and occasional beauty of expression, the Browning admirer is bound to acknowledge that they have no theatrical life in them; and the same is to be said of the later attempts of Lord Tennyson and Stephen Phillips, in which fluent and graceful versification and gorgeous settings were offered as substitutes for plot and passion.

Another depressing element, arising perhaps inevitably out of the degradation of the drama, was the absence of any real criticism. The romantic criticism of Coleridge, Hazlitt and Lamb dealt with the Shakespearean drama as literature, but made little reference to the qualities even of these plays for dramatic representation. Indeed, Lamb wrote of Lear: "The Lear of Shakespeare cannot be acted. The contemptible machinery by which they mimic the storm which he goes out in, is not more inadequate to represent the horrors of the real elements than any actor can be to represent Lear; they might more easily propose to personate the Satan of Milton upon a stage, or one of Michael Angelo's terrible figures. The greatness of Lear is not in corporal dimension, but in intellectual; the explosions of his passion are terrible as a volcano; they are storms turning up and disclosing to the bottom that sea, his mind, with all its vast riches. It is his mind that is laid bare. This case of flesh and blood seems too insignificant to be thought on; even as he himself neglects it. On the stage we see nothing but corporal infirmities and weakness, the impotence of rage; while we read it, we see not Lear, but we are Lear."

The realization that Shakespeare's plays were written to be acted and were adapted to the stage for which they were written, was not reached till nearly the end of the nineteenth century, and has been noted as a contribution to the better appreciation of the theatre and its possibilities. The contemporary criticism of the plays actually

No real criticism

put upon the boards was conventional and perfunctory until the last quarter of the century, when William Archer and Bernard Shaw began to write for the London press. The mid-century critics cannot be entirely blamed for saying nothing worth while, for they had little that it was worth while to criticize.

The sensational melodramas of Lord Lytton (Sir Edward Lytton Bulwer) and of Dion Boucicault were popular, but they hardly offered material for serious discussion, although they may serve us very well as examples of the dramatic fare of the period. Boucicault was the Scribe of the English and American stage with 124 dramas to his credit. Born in Dublin in 1822 (his real name was Dionysius Boursecault) he leapt into fame before he was nineteen by the production of his first comedy, *London Assurance*, at Covent Garden Theatre. After making other plays, mainly borrowings from the French, some of them successes, some failures, for the London theatres, Boucicault at the age of thirty took to the stage as an actor and almost immediately transferred his activities to New York, where his earlier plays were already popular. More French adaptations followed—including *The Corsican Brothers*—and at the end of the 'fifties Boucicault had become the most conspicuous English dramatist, dividing his energies between London and New York. The success of the new Winter Garden Theatre season of 1859-60 was *The Octoroon*, Boucicault's first drama of American life, in which he himself took the part of the faithful Indian chief, Wah-no-tee. Attired in complete war paint and fully armed, Wah-no-tee at the end of the play confronts the villainous overseer, M'Closky, who with a bowie knife in his hand is trying to escape after setting fire to the steamer.

Dion Boucicault

The Octoroon

7

"Stand clear," cries M'Closky. "You won't—die, fool!" and we have the following stage direction:

> Thrusts at him—Wah-no-tee, with his tomahawk, strikes the knife out of his hand; M'Closky starts back; Wah-no-tee throws off his blanket, and strikes at M'Closky several times, who avoids him; at last he catches his arm, and struggles for the tomahawk, which falls; a violent struggle and fight take place, ending with the triumph of Wah-no-tee, who drags M'Closky along the ground, takes up the knife and stabs him repeatedly; George enters, bearing Zoe in his arms—all the Characters rush on—noise increasing —the steam vessel blows up—grand Tableau, and Curtain.

The Colleen Bawn

This was presented in London in 1861 as a picture of "life in Louisiana" and kept the stage up to the end of the nineteenth century, but Boucicault's more permanent reputation rests upon the series of Irish dramas beginning with *The Colleen Bawn*, first put on the New York stage in 1860, and during the following season acted by Boucicault and his wife (Agnes Robertson) 360 times at London and provincial theatres. When *The Colleen Bawn* was revived at the London Princess's Theatre in 1896, it attained the dignity of a three column notice by Bernard Shaw, then dramatic critic for the *Saturday Review* (afterwards included in Volume I of his *Dramatic Opinions and Essays*). Naturally the main part of the article is more about the stage Irishman than about the play, but the following paragraph throws some light on the stage conditions then prevailing:

> I have lived to see *The Colleen Bawn* with real water in it; and perhaps I shall live to see it some day with real Irishmen in it, though I doubt if that will heighten its popularity much. The real water lacks the translucent cleanliness of the original article, and destroys the illusion of Eily's drowning and Myles na Coppaleen's header to a quite amazing degree; but the spectacle of the two performers taking a call before the curtain, sopping wet,

and bowing with a miserable enjoyment of the applause, is one which I shall remember with a chuckle whilst life remains.

Even more popular than *The Colleen Bawn* was its successor *Arrah-na-Pogue*, first put on in 1864-5 in Dublin and London, and speedily reproduced in "all the principal cities of England, America, and Australia." The great scene is the escape of the hero Shaun from his condemned cell to "music, mostly tremolo." The stage direction reads further, *"Wall descends,"* and as the wall descends, the audience has a glimpse of Shaun climbing up it, amid the ivy. *"All is worked down. Gas up."* We see the heroine (played by Mrs. Boucicault) singing on a set bank, unconscious that Shaun (Boucicault himself) is climbing up to her. Michael Feeny ("first Low Comedy"), maddened by Arrah's rejection of his suit, interposes to hurl Shaun to his doom, but Shaun opportunely seizes him by the ankles, and it is Feeny, not Shaun, who falls into the lake a hundred feet below. At that very moment, Shaun's pardon arrives, and all ends happily, for Feeny is none the worse for his wetting. *Arrah-na-Pogue* was given in London by amateurs for charity in 1893, but it survived in New York (after an absence of twenty years) till 1903 and in Philadelphia till 1908, as given by Andrew Mack, "the singing comedian," supported by a mixed chorus of "comely girls and stalwart men," who sang "The Wearing of the Green" and other Irish songs, some of them new, and one of them Mack's own composition. Mack took his company round the world, and in Australia and New Zealand had an enthusiastic reception.

A French version of *Arrah-na-Pogue* held the stage for 140 nights in Paris, and when in 1865 Joseph Jefferson reached London on his way back from his Australian tour, it was naturally to Boucicault that he turned to make over an old play in his repertory, *Rip van Winkle*. It was Boucicault's version that was presented by Jefferson to the London public in that year and was "accepted without hesitation as one of the finest works of modern dramatic art." As the piece had been re-written by Jefferson's half-brother, Charles Burke, and made over by Jefferson himself before he handed the MS. to Boucicault, this play seems to belong to the history of the American drama rather than here. Boucicault wrote many plays for London theatres and even took a lease of Covent Garden with a stage-struck English peer, who lost many thousands of pounds by the transaction, "but the spectacular display was admitted to be the finest ever seen in London." After twelve years in England Boucicault returned to New York and made his home there, paying only occasional visits to England, until his death in 1890; in that year he was still writing plays and one of his most recent efforts was on the stage, but of this later period the only drama that *The Shaughraun* seems to call for mention is *The Shaughraun* (1874), in which Boucicault, both at Drury Lane, London, and at Wallack's Theatre, New York, took the part of Conn, "the soul at every Fair, the Life of every Funeral, the First Fiddle at all Weddings." Conn is the centre of the humorous business of the play, but its plot is concerned with the fortunes of a gallant young Fenian, Robert Ffolliott, who has returned to Sligo after escaping from penal servitude in Australia. An equally gallant young Englishman, Captain Molineux (played at Drury Lane by that excellent English actor, Terriss) is directed to capture him, and in searching for him falls in love at first sight with his sister, Claire Ffolliott; all are ignorant that "Her Majesty has been pleased to extend a full pardon to the

Fenian prisoners, but as Robert Ffolliott has effected his escape, the pardon will not extend to him unless he should reconstitute himself a prisoner." Ffolliott, taking refuge at Father Dolan's house and being tracked there by Captain Molineux, unwittingly fulfils the condition of his own pardon by giving himself up in order to save the priest from telling a lie—a, situation used half a century later by Galsworthy in *Escape*. The two villains of the play, to whom alone the fact of Ffolliott's pardon is known, plot to rob him of the advantage by inducing him to break prison and be picked up by a boat off the coast. They intend to shoot him as he escapes, but hit the Shaughraun by mistake. Conn is only slightly wounded, but he feigns death and is so able to assist at his own wake—one of the most popular scenes of the play. After many vicissitudes, the villains are defeated, Ffolliott's pardon is discovered, his sister accepts Captain Molineux, and the Shaughraun is united to the girl of his heart, the audience being appealed to for surety that he will give up drinking, poaching and all the merry tricks that have endeared him in the course of the action. Boucicault's son Aubrey revived the play in 1896, taking his father's part, and in his hands it kept the stage for some years. In 1922 it was made into a movie under the title *My Wild Irish Rose*, and the films may be still keeping Boucicault's memory green.

Among the other plays which kept the stage, with dwindling respect, might be mentioned *Virginius* (1820) and *The Hunchback* (1832) by Sheridan Knowles; the latter was revived by Viola Allen in 1902, and in the earlier years of this century James O'Neill was still playing *Virginius*, outside of New York and to diminishing audiences. Even longer lived were Lord Lytton's early Victorian melo- Lord dramas, *The Lady of Lyons* (1838) and *Richelieu* (1839). Lytton

11

Of the former the London *Times* records a successful revival at the Scala in 1919, and in 1918 *Richelieu* still formed part of the repertory of Robert Mantell. But at the revival of 1898 by Kyrle Bellew and Mrs. Brown Potter, the

The Lady of Lyons

London *Daily Chronicle* spoke of *The Lady of Lyons* as "that sentimental product of a bygone age," and the *Illustrated London News* dismissed it as "preposterous and tawdry rubbish, with its tedious rhodomontade and its banal insincerity." In connection with the somewhat earlier revival by E. H. Sothern and Virginia Harned the New York *Evening Post* described the play as a brilliant imposture, welcome to thé hardened theatregoer for its many pleasant associations in spite of its bombast and gush, its shady morality, its shallowness, extravagance, and utter artificiality. But for the half century after its first production by Macready at the Theatre Royal, Covent Garden, in 1838, *The Lady of Lyons* was the best known work of its kind and constantly on the boards. The veteran Victorian actor, Henry Howe, in the course of his career embodied in turn every male part the drama contains, beginning with young Major Desmoulins, "the third officer," and finishing up with old Deschappelles. One remembers that Sir Henry Irving was very impressive as the old Richelieu and less effective as the young Claude Melnotte. It hardly seems worth while to recall the extravagance of the plot or the absurdities of the dialogue. A few lines from the reconciliation scene of *The Lady of Lyons* will be sufficient as a sample:

PAULINE

Oh!

My father, you are saved—and by my husband!
Ah! blessed hour! (*she embraces Melnotte*)

12

INTRODUCTORY

MELNOTTE

Yet you weep still, Pauline!

PAULINE

But on thy breast—*these* tears are sweet and holy!

M. DESCHAPPELLES

You have won love and honour nobly, sir!

MME. DESCHAPPELLES

I am astonished!
Who, then, is Colonel Morier?

DAMAS

You behold him!

MELNOTTE

Morier no more after this happy day!
I would not bear again my father's name
Till I could deem it spotless! The hour's come!
Heaven smiled on conscience! As the soldier rose
From rank to rank, how sacred was the fame
That cancell'd crime, and raised him nearer thee!

MME. DESCHAPPELLES

A colonel and a hero! Well, that's something!
He's wondrously improved! (*crosses to him*) I wish
you joy, sir!

MELNOTTE

Ah! the same love that tempts us into sin,
If it be true love, works out its redemption!
And he who seeks repentance for the past
Should woo the Angel Virtue in the future.

(*Curtain*)

13

If these were the masterpieces of the early and mid-Victorian drama, it is difficult to conceive how bad it may have been at its worst, but the reminiscences of Sir Johnston Forbes-Robertson, *A Player under Three Reigns*, give us some idea of the enormities of which it was sometimes capable. Even in the palmy days of the Lyceum, London's leading theatre, in 1879, the company of which Forbes-Robertson was then a member, produced a serious drama called *Zilla or the Scar on the Wrist*, of which he gives the following account:

A Victorian horror

> How intricate and disjointed the plot was, may be gathered from the fact that one of the actors, J. H. Barnes, then known as "Handsome Jack", asked me at the third or fourth rehearsal what the play was about. I told him I did not know; this information appeared to give him much relief! The whole company was terribly in earnest, but, on the first night, whatever we said or did was received by pit, gallery, boxes and stalls with shouts of laughter. One of the characters, played by Frank Tyars, was supposed to be slain in the middle of the second act, and there the body lay a long time while other matters were toward. At last the dead man had the scene to himself, upon which, to the amazement of the audience, he rose and uttered a fatal line. "Ha! a light strikes in upon me, I see it all!" "Do you, b'God?" said a voice from the gallery! . . .
>
> During the progress of the play I had to rescue the heroine from the villain's castle, and to do so it was necessary to climb to a high window and carry her through. Now the heroine was playing a dual rôle, a princess and a gipsy, which entailed many rapid changes of costume, and when I dropped with her on the other side of the scene, I found myself in utter darkness caused by some flats having been adjusted immediately under the window at the back, that the lady might change at once from the princess to the gipsy. Protesting voices of mistress and maid came out from the gloom, saying, "Go away, you can't stay here, go away." But there was no going away, as the screens had been firmly tied together and to the back of the scene, the stage hands having

left no way for me to escape. I became vaguely conscious that the virgin princess was being stripped, and was much embarrassed by the indignant voices, now growing more insistent, "You cannot remain here; how dare you, etc." At last one of the stage hands realized my highly improper situation, and made an opening for me to slip through.

The gipsy, I need hardly say, had to die before the end of the play, but in order to be able to change to the princess to finish the piece, she, surrounded by her weeping friends, sweetly passed away on a couch, the back of which was so arranged that she might be tipped out, and a very obvious waxen figure take her place. Unfortunately the carpenters had failed to join the end of her couch with the wings, the result being that the poor lady was seen escaping on her hands and knees from the back of the couch to the wings, to the great delight of the audience.

In the last act some important title-deeds had been hidden in a well-bucket hanging very conspicuously in the centre of the market-place. I, as the good genius of the play, was hunting for these title-deeds, and looking for them in even more unlikely places than in the bucket, when a voice from the front shouted: "For Heaven's sake, Robertson, look in the bucket and finish the piece!"

We can hardly be surprised that George Henry Lewes, a diligent student of the contemporary drama in the 'sixties and 'seventies, finding the critic's office "something of a sinecure" in London, went off to see what he could find on the Continent—without receiving much encouragement. He accounted for the universal degradation of the stage, as it appeared to him, as follows (*On Actors and Acting*, Chapter XIII):

George
Henry
Lewes

The Drama is everywhere in Europe and America rapidly passing from an Art into an Amusement; just as of old it passed from a religious ceremony into an Art. Those who love the Drama cannot but regret the change, but all must fear that it is inevitable when they reflect that the stage is no longer the amusement of the cultured few, but the amusement of the uncultured and miscultured masses, and has to provide larger and lower appetites with food. For one playgoer who can appreciate the beauty of a verse, the delicate humour of a conception, or the exquisite adaptation of means to ends which give ease and harmony to a work of art, there are hundreds, who, insensible to such delights, can appreciate a parody, detect a pun, applaud a claptrap phrase of sentiment, and be exhilarated by a jingle and a dance; for one who can recognize, and recognizing, can receive exquisite pleasure from fine acting, thousands can appreciate costumes, bare necks, and "powerful" grimace; thus the mass, easily pleased, and liberally paying for the pleasure, rules the hour.

Matthew Arnold

Matthew Arnold, writing a few years later (1879), says: "In England we have no drama at all. Our vast society is not homogeneous enough, not sufficiently united, even any large portion of it, in a common view of life, a common ideal capable of serving as basis for a modern English Drama." Even in the 'eighties, in spite of the advent of Jones and Pinero, things did not immediately improve to any marked extent. H. G. Wells recalls in *The World of William Clissold* the days of the late 'eighties and early 'nineties, when he and his hero were in their early twenties and Bernard Shaw was still merely an unsuccessful novelist, better known as a pamphleteer and musical critic; his recollections take form (in 1926) as follows:

H. G. Wells

> Those were the absurd days of the British theatre; Barrie and Shaw had yet to dawn upon us; even the mockery of Wilde's *Importance of Being Earnest* had not relieved the pressure of the well-made play, and two leaden masters, Henry Arthur Jones and Pinero, to whom no Dunciad has ever done justice, produced large, slow, pretentious three-act affairs that were rather costume shows than dramas, with scenery like the advertisements of fashionable resorts, the reallest furniture and the unreallest passions and morals it is possible to conceive.

16

INTRODUCTORY

Perhaps there is a touch of malicious exaggeration in Wells's review of the past; but such a sober critic as the late A. B. Walkley of the London *Times* says in *Drama and Life:* "It is impossible to think of the early Victorian theatre without a yawn, so 'unidea'd' was it, so ephemeral, so paltry and jejune. One shrinks from dwelling on this tedious theme." It was not until after the turn of the century (1904, to be exact) that Walkley was able to be a little more cheerful: "There is a small minority of the playgoing public which shows symptoms of discontent. Its artistic conscience, if not deeply stirred, is, at any rate gently pricked. It signs manifestoes, writes to the newspapers, and in other futile ways gives vent to its suspicions that something ought to be done. But what precisely ought to be done nobody knows. Meanwhile the theatres, music-halls in everything but name and an atmosphere of tobacco-smoke, have it all their own way. The vast majority of the public takes its theatrical amusement, as it takes its newspaper information, in snippets. It is a public without patience, without the capacity for sustained attention, and, like Lady Teazle when she married Sir Peter, it has no taste. To speak of the drama as an art to such a public as this is to talk a language which it does not understand, and has no inclination to learn. *Vox clamantis in deserto.*"

It is evident that the depressing conditions outlined above prevailed through the greater part of the nineteenth century and were not entirely overcome at the end of it. About midway in the Victorian era T. W. Robertson made a valiant effort to provide the public with dramatic fare of a light and wholesome character—an effort important enough to demand fuller notice in the next chapter, but this was almost a false dawn, it faded so quickly. It took a long time to dispel the atmosphere or disrepute and con-

A. B. Walkley

T. W. Robertson

17

tempt in which the theatre was enveloped. The efforts of Irving and Tennyson, though they did little or nothing toward the revival of modern English drama, helped to make the theatre respectable, and the efforts of John Hare, Charles Wyndham, the Bancrofts and the Kendals, were similarly helpful in this regard, especially when their respectability was duly recognized by the bestowal of knighthoods. "Mrs. Kendal," says H. Burton Baker, the historian of the London stage, "was proficient from top to toe; equally at home in the brightest comedy and the deepest pathos of domestic drama, though not in the poetic. Yet this does not quite explain the secret of her popularity; it is rather that she is the representative of all the proprieties of private life, the wife, the mother, the champion—with a very loud trumpet—of the respectabilities; in fine, it is as the matron of the British drama that the *pater* and *mater familias* of the middle classes especially patronize her, rather than for her talent."

The influence of the popular and innocuous operas of Gilbert and Sullivan told in the same direction. Gilbert is on record as saying: "When Sullivan and I determined to work together, the burlesque stage was in a very unclean state. We made up our minds to do all in our power to wipe out the grosser element, never to let an offending word escape our characters, and never to allow a man to appear as a woman or *vice versa*." With the exception of objections to *Ruddigore* on account of its title (for reasons which may mystify a modern reader) and to *The Mikado* on account of its supposed international inopportuneness, Gilbert succeeded in keeping clear of the rocks and quicksands of Victorian prejudice, but the dangers were there and they were not easy to get by, much less to overcome. When the manager of the first Gilbert and Sullivan opera

Gilbert and Sullivan

engaged George Grossmith for the first production, that popular comic entertainer said: "Look at the risks I am running. If I fail I don't believe the Young Men's Christian Association will ever engage me again, because I have appeared on the stage, and my reputation as a comic singer to religious communities will be lost for ever!" Apparently this objection was quite serious, for Grossmith asked three guineas a week extra as insurance against the risk mentioned, although he was persuaded to forego it after the manager had treated him to an unusually good luncheon.

From all these considerations it is obvious that the revival of English drama in the nineteenth century was a task of enormous difficulty, and it is not surprising to find that the earlier efforts were tentative and compromising in character. *The Second Mrs. Tanqueray* may appear to the present generation neither particularly skilful from a technical point of view, nor particularly courageous as a discussion of a social problem, but when it was first produced in 1893 there was a hot debate as to whether it was "the greatest play of the century" or "the most immoral production that has ever disgraced the English stage." It would be easy to dismiss it as neither, but we cannot arrive at an understanding of the masterpieces of English drama in the twentieth century without due consideration of the pioneer work done in the nineteenth, which made the masterpieces possible.

The Second Mrs. Tanqueray

The social prejudices against the theatre in the Victorian era were strongly entrenched, arising partly from the past history of the theatre itself, partly from the prevailing Puritanism of the English middle class, then at the height of its social and political influence. There was little, either by way of pecuniary reward or of public esteem, to induce young authors to devote their talents to learning enough stagecraft to make successful production possible or to put into a play the amount of thought and work necessary to give it permanent value. Tennyson, George Meredith, Henry James and others were conscious of the general opportunity the stage offered, and were willing to write for it, but with them all it was a side issue; they found their natural and remunerative opportunity of appeal to the public and of self-expression in either fiction or poetry. They may not have had dramatic genius, but one suspects that Dickens had it, if the way of fame and fortune had opened itself to him in that direction. As things were, he very naturally preferred to supply the British and American public with melodrama (and much else) which they read in comfort and quiet at their own firesides, without the sacrifice of their inherited and conventional prejudices.

CHAPTER II

The Victorian Transition

I. T. W. ROBERTSON (1829-1871)

THE Shakespearean tradition weighed heavily upon nineteenth-century English drama in more ways than one. Shakespearean drama is not merely romantic but rhetorical. The Elizabethan stage, projecting well into the auditorium, encouraged the dramatist to write and the actor to make speeches, which were indeed in character, but were actually delivered to the audience. This encouraged all the actors of the old régime to cultivate a rhetorical and somewhat artificial style, and it encouraged the dramatist to fill his play with speeches which were in accordance with the romantic tradition but were far removed from the speech of ordinary men and women. When the platform gave place to the picture stage, the platform tradition remained. This is the fault of all the romantic dramas of the nineteenth century from Browning through Tennyson and Swinburne to Stephen Phillips. So far as they were written for the stage at all, they were written for the platform stage of Shakespeare, which had long ceased to exist; and the sense of removal from popular speech led to a choice of themes removed from present-day interests, which adds to the impression of artificiality. The actors of mid-nineteenth century England almost prided themselves on the rhetorical fashion in which they delivered set speeches on romantic themes and spoke disdainfully of the "trou-

The platform stage tradition

sers" or "cup and saucer" drama, which dealt with every-day life in the language of the day.

The first and most obvious reform came precisely from the actors in this despised "trousers" or "cup and saucer" drama. Browning and Tennyson, Swinburne and Stephen Phillips were all on the wrong track; they were harking backward to the Elizabethan age, not dealing with the present or looking forward to the future. The romantic drama, resting on its claim of appealing to the imagination, could content itself with tawdry scenery and shabby dresses, belonging to any period or to none. The actors in the trouser drama insisted on having good trousers, well cut and well pressed; they insisted that doors should have handles, that windows should open, and that the furniture in a scene representing a gentleman's drawing-room should not look as if it came out of a third-rate back office. The equipment of modern comedies with dignified and refined settings led to a similar improvement in the staging of the romantic and the Shakespearean drama. Henry Irving won fame by his Shakespearean spectacles and his example was followed by Beerbohm Tree and others on both sides of the Atlantic. They did a great deal for the stage, but very little for the drama. Irving was a great producer, a great stage manager, a keen psychologist and a considerable Shakespearean critic, but not a great actor, and not really interested in the development of the drama as an art in touch with modern conditions and expressing the national consciousness. The plays he put on were almost without exception great spectacles, Shakespearean or other, or romantic melodrama. When Henry Arthur Jones was asked why he did not write a play for Irving, he said, "Irving does not want a dramatist around his theatre." There is a touch of personal bitterness in the remark, but

"Cup and saucer" drama

it was true.   The development of the spectacular side of the drama was of dubious advantage from the artistic point of view.   But Irving, if not a great actor, was a gentleman and a scholar, and he made his profession respectable and respected.   He became Sir Henry Irving, as John Hare became Sir John Hare; the Bancrofts, Sir Squire and Lady Bancroft; Wyndham, Sir Charles Wyndham; Forbes-Robertson, Sir Johnston Forbes-Robertson; Beerbohm Tree, Sir Herbert Beerbohm Tree; and Benson, Sir Frank Benson.   Oxford graduates and society beauties (such as Mrs. Patrick Campbell and Mrs. Langtry, the first with talent, and the second without) made the stage fashionable.   The dresses and manners continued to improve, until the stage was better dressed than the house; people went to the theatre to see what the actresses had on, and the matinée-idol became "the glass of fashion and the mould of form."   It was an advance of a sort, but entirely on the material side.   The most important improvements were in the naturalness of the acting: the gentlemen and ladies were still gentlemen and ladies when they acted on the stage.   The plays improved, but they did not show a corresponding improvement. *[Stage knighthoods]*

The scenery, the dresses, the natural tones and gestures of the actors were the changes which impressed themselves upon the contemporary admirers of T. W. Robertson, whose comedies on modern subjects led the English stage back to nature about midway in the Victorian period.   His first success in this style, after many failures and disappointments, was *Society* (1865), but a more enduring interest attaches to *Caste*, acted by the Bancrofts and John Hare in 1867 and still capable of representation on the modern stage, though it has begun to have an old-fashioned flavour and when last acted in London was given with mid- *[Caste]*

Victorian costumes. It has more than a touch of mid-Victorian sentimentality and mid-Victorian caricature. Esther and Polly Eccles are hardly the types of the ladies of the ballet who marry into the English aristocracy, nor is the picture of domestic bliss exhibited to us in the play the usual consequence in real life. And if the Eccles girls and the gallant dragoons are sentimentalized, old Eccles and Sam Gerridge and the Marchioness are caricatured. No English lady, even in mid-Victorian times, ever recited long passages from Froissart in praise of her ancestors. Sam Gerridge is a comic plumber and belongs entirely to the stage. Old Eccles is a comic drunkard and is equally comic as a labour agitator. Sam's speech about old Eccles was quite likely to win approval from a middle-class audience— it might even yet in more remote centres, but a modern cosmopolitan audience would regard it as "old stuff." Polly's next speech is equally mid-Victorian in tone and sentiment. There is obvious exaggeration in the amusing scene in which old Eccles steals the baby's coral to pawn it for drink, and equally obvious melodrama in Esther's speech which follows close upon it. The technique throughout is of a childish ingenuousness, with a profusion of "business," openly fabricated for stage effect. But there is real humour and real pathos in the third act, and one forgives the author the touches of caricature and tawdry or exaggerated sentiment, without accepting the shallow lesson of the play that brains may break through the barriers of caste, and "what brains can break through, love may leap over." Love may leap over the barriers, but is more than likely to come a cropper on the other side. There is more truth and real feeling in the final interchange between Hawtrey and old Eccles: "Don't you think that, with your talent for liquor, if you had an allowance of about two pounds a week, and went to Jersey, where spirits are cheap, you could drink yourself to death in a year?"—*Eccles.* "I think I could—I'm sure I'll try."

II. W. S. GILBERT (1836-1911)

As has been already noted, W. S. Gilbert was careful not to offend Victorian prudishness, but under the shelter of Sullivan's melodious airs and his own clever rhymes, he was able to accustom the public of the later nineteenth century to a criticism of their cherished institutions which, in spite of its apparent good humour, was not without the sting of satire. His earlier comedies of the '70's were of no permanent significance, but the light operas of the '80's made a distinct impression and were revived forty years later with conspicuous success both in London and New York. No doubt the charm of the music and the pretty dances, costumes, and settings counted for a great deal in this sustained popularity, but one has only to compare Gilbert's text with that of his successors in the same *genre* to realize his immense intellectual and artistic superiority; his apparently easy and light-hearted rhymes have more than superficial intention. He avoided the difficulties of the sex question by making his heroines conventionally correct in their observance of the obligations of marriage or engagement to marriage—sometimes to the point of absurdity—though they are seldom so sentimental as not to have an open eye for the advantages of wealth, rank, or fashion. But he is not afraid to poke fun at the Victorian deference to established political institutions, from the throne downwards. The Pirates of Penzance, victorious in a conflict with the Police, give in at once to the summons to yield in Queen Victoria's name, "because with all our faults,

Gilbert's political satire

we love our Queen," and proceed to take their places in respectable society because:

> They are no members of the common throng;
> They are all noblemen who have gone wrong.

The General chimes in:

> No Englishman unmoved that statement hears,
> Because, with all our faults, we love our House of Peers.
> Resume your ranks and legislative duties,
> And take my daughters, all of whom are beauties.

The last speaker is "the very model of a modern major-gineral," in "matters vegetable, animal and mineral," but his military knowledge has only been brought down to the beginning of the nineteenth century. Similarly the Rt. Hon. Sir Joseph Porter, K. C. B., has become First Lord of the Admiralty without ever seeing a ship.

> I grew so rich that I was sent
> By a pocket borough into Parliament.
> I always voted at my party's call
> And I never thought of thinking for myself at all.
> I thought so little, they rewarded me
> By making me the Ruler of the Queen's Navee!

Private Willis, on sentry in Palace Yard, outside the House of Commons, soliloquizes:

> When in that house M. P.'s divide,
> If they've a brain and cerebellum too,
> They've got to leave that brain outside
> And vote just as their leaders tell 'em to.
> But then the prospect of a lot
> Of dull M. P.'s in close proximity,
> A-thinking for themselves, is what
> No man can face with equanimity.
> Then let's rejoice with loud fal, lal, la!
> That Nature wisely does contrive (fal, lal, la!)

> That every boy and every gal
>   That's born into the world alive
> Is either a little Liberal
>   Or else a little Conservative,
>   Fal, lal, la!

The House of Lords comes equally under the lash. The Duke and Duchess of Plaza-Toro may be described as Grandees of Spain, but their ways of getting on were not (and are not) unknown in London:

DUKE

> I sit, by selection,
> Upon the direction
>   Of several Companies' bubble—
> As soon as they're floated
> I'm freely bank-noted—
>   I'm pretty well paid for my trouble!

DUCHESS

> I write letters blatant
> On medicines patent—
>   And use any other you mustn't—
> And vow my complexion
> Derives its perfection
>   From somebody's soap—which it doesn't!

In a time of confident patriotism, Gilbert had the courage to bring this conventional sentiment under the fire of ridicule,—indirectly in *The Mikado:*

> But if patriotic sentiment is wanted
>   I've patriotic ballads cut and dried;
> For where'er our country's banner may be planted,
>   All other local banners are defied!
> Our warriors, in serried ranks assembled,
>   Never quail—or they conceal it if they do—
> And I shouldn't be surprised if nations trembled
>   Before the mighty troops of Titipu!

Similarly with direct reference to his own country in *H. M. S. Pinafore*, in which the hero's boast, "I am an Englishman" is re-echoed:

> For he might have been a Roosian
> A French, or Turk, or Proosian,
>   Or perhaps Itali-an!
> But in spite of all temptations
> To belong to other nations,
>   He remains an Englishman!
>   Hurrah!
> For the true-born Englishman!

Lightly as these popular ditties were heard, hummed, and sung by the Victorian middle class which the Gilbert and Sullivan operas had brought back to the theatre, the public was not so unintelligent, or so hidebound in its prejudices, as not to catch a gleam of the writer's deeper intention. When the younger generation scoffs at Victorian conventionality, smugness and hypocrisy, it is well to remember that the Victorians listened with good humour and applause to these outspoken criticisms of their weaknesses and follies. It is a long cry from W. S. Gilbert to Bernard Shaw, but the earlier satirist had made a beginning; first by securing the attendance of a middle-class audience at the theatre, and then by winning their approval, he had opened the way for the more profound criticism of national life and character on the stage by his more richly gifted successor.

III. HENRY ARTHUR JONES (1851-   )

When Henry Arthur Jones visited the United States in 1906, he met an American millionaire and bibliophile who laid before him on the table three little books—first editions of *The Rivals, The School for Scandal,* and *She Stoops to Conquer,* with the remark, "That's all the harvest of your British drama for the last two hundred years." The American millionaire was a little out of his count, but if he had put back the final date of observation by a dozen years or so, he would not have been far from the truth, though he might still have been thought lacking in politeness to his guest, to say nothing of contemporary dramatists. Jones wrote "a great drama" in 1867, and produced his first play at Exeter in 1878. But the time of these early productions and the conditions of the drama at the time must not be lost sight of. Jones's own remark to Barrett H. Clark is apposite: "Don't forget that when I began it was the day of Robertson and H. J. Byron. They were my only models." Nor were the personal circumstances of Jones's early life at all favourable to dramatic production. The son of a Buckinghamshire farmer, he had a brief education at a local Grammar School, went into business in the North of England at 13, and earned his living as a commercial traveller until he was 30. He gives a striking picture of the alien conditions under which he began to interest himself in dramatic composition. "I became a dramatist because I couldn't help it. I was born in the country among the strictest people, who thought that dancing and playgoing were the devil's own work. In my boyhood I never saw a play or heard any talk about such subjects. I never was in a theatre until I was 18 years old, but two years before that, all alone and discouraged, I had written a great drama of my own."

The success of that once popular melodrama *The Silver King* (1882), done in collaboration with Henry Herman, released Jones from the trammels of business and definitely established his position as a dramatist, but it cannot be considered seriously as a work of art, and was not so considered by our author. He began about this time a series of essays and lectures which were published in volume form in 1895 under the title, *The Renascence of the English Drama*. In 1884, again in collaboration with Mr. Herman, Jones attempted to turn Ibsen's *A Doll's House* into a "sympathetic play" in an adaptation to mid-Victorian tastes called *Breaking a Butterfly*—a performance the adapters would, no doubt, be glad to forget. Jones's work at this time shows little trace of Ibsen's influence, but it is interesting to notice the momentary contact.

In this same year 1884 Jones made an attempt at serious drama in *Saints and Sinners*, published in 1891 (after the passage of the American Copyright Act which protected English authors from American performances of their plays without payment of royalties) with a preface in which Jones deplored the decay of the British drama, and pointed the way to better things by insisting that playwriting should be not merely "the art of sensational and spectacular illusion," but "mainly and chiefly the art of representing English life." *Saints and Sinners* was a gallant but not altogether successful attempt to put these principles into practice. Its inspiration probably came not so much from Ibsen as from George Eliot's studies of English middle-class life, which were at the time exceedingly popular. Matthew Arnold was interested by the play's attack on "the middle-class fetish," and the unsympathetic representation of Puritan morality provoked a discussion to which the author himself contributed in an article in the *Nineteenth Century*. The play was "hooted" by the first-night audience, "condemned by nearly all the London press," and quickly withdrawn. Jones's own account is that he was so discouraged that he weakly sold

Saints and Sinners [side note]

himself to the "dull devil of spectacular melodrama to which he remained a bondslave for many years." To a modern reader, *Saints and Sinners* will appear fearfully sentimental and melodramatic, and even Jones's admiring American editor, Clayton Hamilton, stamps it as "old fashioned and unquestionably crude," but Jones should be given credit for his good intentions, and a well meant effort as early as 1884 is worthy of record.

The melodramas which followed need no further condemnation than the author himself has given them, but one cannot help deploring the loss of the opportunity of which Jones was himself conscious. The time was ripe for change. Ibsen, first introduced to the British public in a *Fortnightly Review* article by Edmund Gosse in 1873, began to appear in translation in 1876, and the cheap little volumes of the Camelot Classics containing his plays in English had a wide circulation in the later 'eighties and early 'nineties. William Archer, who had begun a lifelong career of able and intelligent work as a dramatic critic in 1879 on the *London Figaro*, in that year published his translation of *A Doll's House*; in 1880 his version of *Pillars of Society* was produced at the Gaiety Theatre. "As I look back to 'seventy-nine and the early 'eighties," he reflected some forty years later, "I confess I am puzzled to conceive how anyone with the smallest pretension to intelligence could in those years seriously occupy himself with the English theatre;" but at the time he was sufficiently aware of the opportunity presented, not only to devote his energies to dramatic criticism and translation, but to collaborate with Bernard Shaw (as early as 1885) on the play which afterwards developed into *Widowers' Houses*. Shaw's *Quintessence of Ibsen* was published in 1891, and the same year *Ghosts* was privately

Ibsen's plays in England

performed at the Independent Theatre in London to the dismay and disgust of the older critics. But it was not Jones but Pinero who swung into the new current of opinion with *The Second Mrs. Tanqueray* in 1893.

The Case of Rebellious Susan   Jones followed in 1894 with *The Case of Rebellious Susan*, more than capably presented at the Criterion Theatre by Wyndham and Mary Moore. Though the author's preface indicates that the "case" presented was "perhaps a tragedy" rather than a light comedy, the dramatist makes no attempt in the play to deal with anything deeper than the polite surfaces of life. The heroine's rebellion is not serious, and in the upshot, after receiving much worldly advice about bowing the neck as well as the knee to Mrs. Grundy, (to whom the preface is dedicated), she is consoled by her errant husband's promise to take her to Bond Street and buy her all the jewels she desires.

Michael and His Lost Angel   *Michael and His Lost Angel* (1896) was a more courageous attempt to treat a serious subject seriously. It was "booed" by a first-night audience at the Lyceum, and, to quote the author, "again I met with the general condemnation of the press;" it was equally a failure in New York. In the author's and his editor's opinion, it is the highest of Jones's achievements; but if it failed at the time because it was too much in advance of public opinion, it failed to secure the respect of the next generation because the problem was not faced with sufficient courage on the part of the dramatist. The forward-looking eye of Bernard Shaw marked this at the time, and the dramatist himself acknowledged defeat by returning to polite comedy, dealing only with the surfaces of life, such as *The Liars* (1897) and *Mrs. Dane's Defence* (1900), excellent in their superficial way, but attempting nothing beyond the provision of a conventional evening's entertainment. *The Lie* was put

on the New York stage in 1914, but did not reach London *The Lie*
till 1923, with Sybil Thorndike in the leading part. At
the latter date it was cruelly stigmatized by James Agate
as "in the manner of 1860." "This is the old world where
strong men are fearful of meeting one another, or even
their womenfolk, face to face, and prefer the postman;
where a hero, who can be trusted to dam the Nile single-
handed, has to have his love affairs managed for him by
somebody else; where men of engineering genius, who would
not take thrust or pull on trust, believe incredible things
of a fiancée at the merest whisper."

"The 1860 manner" is hyperbole, but it is none the less
true that Jones, in spite of valiant efforts, never succeeded
in shaking himself free from the dramatic technique and
the point of view of the earlier Victorian period in which his
first efforts at dramatic composition were made.

IV. ARTHUR WING PINERO (1855-   )

Sir Arthur Pinero was more fortunate than H. A. Jones, Pinero's
not only in being born at a later date in London, but in early stage experience
passing before he was twenty from his father's law office
to the stage; varied experience in London and the provinces
as an actor, including a five years' engagement with Irving
at the Lyceum, gave him a familiarity with the conditions
of theatrical production which served him in good stead
during a career of dramatic composition extending well on
toward half a century.

Pinero's versatility was as remarkable as his stagecraft,
and, beginning to produce in 1877, he had put a score or
so of plays to his name before a successful plunge into mid-
Victorian sentiment (*Sweet Lavender*, 1888) gave him
fame and fortune and left him free (to use his own phrase)

"to write great plays regardless of the predilections of the public." His first attempt in this laudable crusade was apparently *The Profligate* (1889), which deals somewhat

The Profligate

superficially with the punishment of a dissolute man about town who has married an innocent schoolgirl, not, as one might expect, by his disappointment in the schoolgirl, who turns out all that his fancy painted her, but in the unfortunate recurrence of another lady who turns up persistently at railway stations and Italian villas with protestations about outraged virtue. One can hardly take this play seriously, because the author himself did not take it seriously. After condemning the profligate to suicide in the original version, he accepted the suggestion of John Hare, the actor-manager who produced the play, and let the sinner off with a happy ending. So that instead of being a reproof of vice, the play, as acted, was really an encouragement of it, and the profligate, instead of being a horrible example, suggested rather the possibility of making the best of both worlds.

We had better accept (at any rate so far as Pinero is concerned) the assurance of the editor of his collected plays, Clayton Hamilton, that the modern English drama began when *The Second Mrs. Tanqueray* was acted for the

The Second Mrs. Tanqueray

first time on the stage of the St. James's Theatre in London on May 27th, 1893. We should pay heed to his further remark that Pinero was encouraged to compose the play "by the exhibition of Ibsen's *Ghosts* in London in 1891." Clayton Hamilton also reminds us, and it is a useful reminder, that while the impulse to write a serious play, dealing seriously with a serious subject, came to Pinero from Ibsen, Pinero did not take over the Ibsen technique. He contented himself with the easier and more theatrical manner devised by Scribe and improved by Dumas.

The Second Mrs. Tanqueray made a success beyond the author's expectation, partly owing to the successful acting of Mrs. Patrick Campbell as the wicked heroine, and partly owing to the fact that Pinero was not so much in advance of his public as he thought. His subsequent experience and that of the younger men who came later, (whether they followed in his footsteps or not is another question), showed that by this time the British public, or at any rate a small section of it, had become sufficiently educated to appreciate this kind of play.

What kind of play is it? Well, in the first place, it is a play presenting an idea or thesis or problem, though not a very involved or weighty one. Aubrey Tanqueray has taken as his second wife a lady, one can hardly say of doubtful reputation, for her reputation was beyond all doubt. She has led a life of open irregularity, not merely with one man, but with several, and Aubrey Tanqueray knows when he marries her that she will not be received by his friends. The progress of the play shows not merely the impossibility of their social position, but the impossibility of his wife's domestic position, especially in relation to his innocent young daughter, who, immediately on her release into the world, falls in love with a young officer who has previously conducted a liaison with her stepmother. Paula, on the eve of her marriage, had offered her husband a complete list of her various intrigues, but he had generously burned it without reading it, and it is she who prevents the marriage of Captain Ardale to her stepdaughter by the revelation of his previous relation to herself. After this she commits suicide, but these three actions are the only evidence of uprightness or even of common sense shown by Paula Tanqueray in the course of the play. Otherwise she is neurotic, ill-tempered, with none of even the superficial attraction which women of the upper ranks of her profession are supposed to exercise. When (after staying away for two months, it is true,) one of her husband's former friends—an influential married lady living near—is induced to make the necessary social advance of calling, Paula shows quite inexcusable ill-temper and rudeness; and her husband begins to see, a little late in the day perhaps, that he has not acted wisely in bringing his young and innocent daughter into contact with "poor Paula's light, careless nature."

Now of course it is excellent morality that the leopard cannot change her spots, and that a woman who has once led an irregular life will remain forever after absurdly jealous, incapable of controlling herself or even of exercising her wits for her own advantage, but is it true? There is general agreement, even on the French stage, which is more liberal than ours in these matters, that the lesson Pinero wishes to teach is a sound one, and that it is an act of supreme folly for a man to attempt to project into regular society a lady whose life has been notoriously irregular. The trouble with Pinero's presentation is not that it is unconvincing, but that it is too convincing. It proves too much, and offers a painful contrast in this respect with several treatments of the same theme on the French stage by Augier and others, and with the very different treatment of the same issue in fiction by Meredith in *One of our Conquerors*. In the latter novel, the lady, although in an irregular position, is entirely sympathetic, but she is unable to overcome the defects of her social position and breaks under the strain. In Pinero's play the lady is entirely unsympathetic. She has absolutely nothing and does absolutely nothing to commend herself to us. In fact she brings her fate entirely on her·own head, everybody else having acted with the greatest possible consideration for her.

The claim made by Clayton Hamilton and other admirers of Pinero that this is the first masterpiece the English stage can show after the production of *The School for Scandal* in 1777 is one that cannot be accepted. It is true the play made a great sensation in England at the time, but if it is put to the test of continental standards, it must be admitted that in subject, in thought, and in technique, it was already old-fashioned at the time it was written, and the lapse of years has served only to reveal its essentially conventional trivialities.

From the technical point of view the action is well devised according to the traditions of the well-made play. The author has selected a number of possibilities and combined them ingeniously so as to provide effective stage situations. Granted a man foolish enough to marry a woman of Paula's character, it is possible that his young daughter, who has hitherto stayed away from him, should propose to return to him (end of Act I) ; it is possible that having returned, she should not get on well with her stepmother, and that she should be sent away to Paris; it is possible that the first man she meets there should be one of her stepmother's old lovers and that she should fall in love with him; it is possible that they should all return to her home and that they should arrive unannounced; it is possible that the stepmother would reveal to her husband her former relation to the young officer to whom her stepdaughter is engaged, and that having revealed it, she would commit suicide; all this is possible, but it is far from inevitable; it is hardly probable, though perhaps it is probable enough for the purposes of an evening's entertainment on the stage. It is, of course, inevitable that Paula Tanqueray should be unhappy in her enforced seclusion; it is inevitable that her husband should be unhappy with her; but the engagement of her former lover to her stepdaughter is invented for the purposes of the play to bring about a conventional ending of suicide. The treatment by means of the older Scribe technique of a subject no doubt suggested by Ibsen is fatal to the permanent reputation of the play as a work of art. It is a transition play and is only of interest from that point of view.

Pinero within the play never showed the slightest reason for his original assumption—that Aubrey Tanqueray would marry a woman not merely of Paula's reputation but of Paula's character. Why should he? He makes no pretence of a mad passion; he is between forty and fifty, a man with a daughter almost grown up (nineteen) and with a knowledge of the world; he describes his feelings for Paula as "a temperate, honourable affection," and looks forward to a life of happiness and good repute, though he admits he is building on a miserable foundation. Evidently the justification for the marriage was to be provided by the personal charms of the actress taking the part, and Pinero was excellently served by Mrs. Patrick Campbell, an actress of admirable talent and fashionable reputation. She made the play and gave it such verisimilitude as it possesses.

The Notorious Mrs. Ebbsmith Pinero tried again two years later (1895) in *The Notorious Mrs. Ebbsmith*, which was evidently written for Mrs. Patrick Campbell. The character was a more ambitious undertaking, both for actress and playwright, and Pinero told Clayton Hamilton that he considered Mrs. Ebbsmith the most interesting woman he had created. She is a young widow who has made herself prominent in

Socialistic agitation and has earned the nickname of "mad Agnes." After a career of severe hardship she has taken refuge in a hospital and from being a patient has become a nurse—a transition which is glossed over rather too easily. As a nurse she rescues from a severe illness a young English M. P., a grass widower who has been travelling on the Continent, and they have set up house together at Venice. His wife and his relatives come to Venice and urge him to conduct his amours with greater discretion for fear of injuring his public career. The interest of the play lies in the efforts of Agnes Ebbsmith to defeat the attempt to detach her lover from her—which she at first succeeds in doing—and in her failure to maintain their free union on the high level she has planned. She has in mind for the future an intellectual comradeship, devoid of passion, in which they would work together openly for the regeneration of humanity. He wants to eat his cake and have it— to enjoy her personal charm and the solace of her companionship and to keep his old place in the world. For a while, she yields for the sake of keeping him, but ultimately, after throwing the Bible into the fire, she drags it out again and takes refuge in the household of a clergyman to pray for the husband she has misled, and the wife she has wronged. This idea does not occur to her—or to anyone else—till the very end of the play, and her repentance is so contrary to common experience of Socialistic ladies who console deserted husbands that the public rather sniffed at it. The repentance was too sudden and too complete to be convincing.

In the same year was produced *The Benefit of the Doubt*, but in this there was no question of doing anything but covering up the indiscretion of a married lady who had been too frank under the influence of two glasses of cham-

The Benefit of the Doubt

pagne. A benevolent bishop was introduced in the last act to take the erring lady under his social wing, and as it is merely a question of saving her face, all ends happily.

After a play or two written in what Clayton Hamilton calls Pinero's "vacational intervals," in which he "rests his inventive mind," the author stiffened his intellectual sinews for the problem of *The Gay Lord Quex* (1899)—acted with enormous success by John Hare and Irene Vanbrugh both in London and New York and successfully revived in 1917-18. It is undoubtedly a very cleverly devised play; its bedroom scene, around which the whole structure is built, is perhaps the very best of bedroom scenes, and might have been thought to exhaust that particular situation if the experience of the New York stage since the revival had not been to the contrary. But, except as an evening's entertainment, the play has no interest and no significance. The only question at issue is whether the old roué Quex will succeed in marrying the silly little society girl he has set his heart on, and except as a sporting proposition this issue is of no possible interest to anyone. The characters exist only for the sake of a very cunningly devised situation—the bedroom scene—and when this is over the play is done. It was worth the money as an intellectual excitement when it was new, but one cannot imagine anybody wanting to see it—must less to read it—twice. Yet in the opinion of many critics it shows Pinero at his best—*i. e.*, exercising to perfection his peculiar talent.

The Gay Lord Quex

Pinero's plan of making a play is, according to his own statement, to imagine his characters and then construct the plot, but one can hardly believe that *The Gay Lord Quex* was built by this method. In no play up to this point had Pinero taken a character and allowed him—or her—to work out an inevitable destiny. He always interposes the long arm of coincidence in order to make the clash more obvious and effective. His next play *Iris* (1901) has been put forward by his admirers as fulfilling the exacting requirements of permanent art, but it does not do so altogether and on the stage it was not a success. It is, however, an eminently readable play if we make the author a few concessions. Iris Bellamy is a young widow whose late husband has left her a fortune which she loses if she marries—not an altogether unenviable position, some might think—but she is of a soft, luxurious, self-indulgent nature, and her natural inclination to remarry is divided between a young amateur artist (Trenwith) without a penny, whom she is fond of, and a rich Jewish financier whom she finds only just tolerable. We first see her at a dinner party at her own house, at which she has accepted the millionaire Maldonado, but after the party is over she feels he is impossible and withdraws her word in order to take the young artist abroad with her as her lover—in secret, for if he is openly her lover, he must go off to British Columbia to earn a living for both of them in lieu of the forfeited inheritance. They are still living in a fool's Paradise on the Italian Lakes when the inheritance conferred by the dramatist upon the heroine is lost by the dishonesty of her trustee, and her lover goes to British Columbia accordingly, while she retires to an obscure pension to live on her small remaining income in the meantime. Maldonado, piqued at his rejection and angry at her acceptance of young Trenwith, cloaks his passion under the guise of friendliness, and induces her to accept financial help, which, with her habitual extravagance, she soon finds insufficient. She realizes her dependence on him and makes a despairing effort to get on without it. In her lowest straits he offers her a refuge—on conditions—and she becomes his mistress.

Iris

They are unhappy together, but he is still attached to her and offers to make her his wife. She is half inclined to accept, but asks for a week's respite in the hope of her lover's return from British Columbia. And of course he does return—that very evening. Iris receives him at her flat—Maldonado's flat—tells him her story, and he leaves her for ever, though the log-hut in British Columbia is now ready for its occupants. But the meeting has been suspected and watched by Maldonado, who, mad with jealousy and rage, bursts in upon the deserted woman to turn her with brutal violence out of her last refuge into the street. William Archer said (and it appears probable) that Pinero intended to end the play with Maldonado throttling Iris, but he eventually decided on the preferable expedient of turning Iris out and rang the curtain down on Maldonado smashing up the furniture of the flat. In spite of some minor improbabilities and coincidences *Iris* is the best of Pinero's serious plays. It is a conscientious and artistic study of character, exhibiting the ruin of a weak and vacillating woman under the stress of circumstance. If Iris had the courage to marry Maldonado in the first instance or to share Trenwith's poverty in British Columbia, she would doubtless have been unhappy, but she would not have come to irretrievable ruin. She was right in thinking that she was unfitted for anything but a life of luxury; if she could have combined love with it, she would doubtless have been a model wife and a very successful hostess. It may be that the virtue of other successful hostesses and model wives stands on no more secure foundation, and that we take them for what they are because they have not been tried. They are the more fortunate on that account, but we cannot waste any bitter tears on Iris, who, after all, gets only what she deserved. As a rule, things have to be paid for in this life, and the lesson of the play, if somewhat obvious, is a wholesome one.

Pinero's later work would hardly seem worthy of detailed examination if it were not for the extravagant claims made by his admirers on its behalf. Clayton Hamilton, writing in 1922, claims that *The Thunderbolt* and *Mid-Channel* may be regarded as "the two greatest plays of British authorship that have been given to the world in the first two decades of the twentieth century." Technically, he considers *The Thunderbolt* "the ultimate monument of intensive artistry in the modern drama" and "is willing to risk the statement that *Mid-Channel* is a greater play than *Hedda Gabler* or *A Doll's House*." This is certainly a tremendous risk, and Mr. Hamilton is on safer ground when he claims that these two plays represent Pinero's mind "at its most completely characteristic moment." Pinero, he reports, wrote them "to please himself," and was not taken aback when the English public failed to appreciate them. *The Thunderbolt* presents itself as a study in provincial life: four families are offered for our inspection, James Mortimore and his wife, Stephen Mortimore and his wife, Thaddeus Mortimore and his wife and children, Rose Ponting (*née* Mortimore) and her husband; they are all eager to divide the estate of their deceased brother Edward, and to do as little as possible for his illegitimate daughter, Helen Thornhill. As he appears to have died intestate, Helen is at their mercy until it is disclosed that Mrs. Thaddeus Mortimore has secretly destroyed, just before Edward's death, a will in which he left his fortune to Helen Thornhill, who thereupon offers to divide the estate with them in equal shares. Apart from the excitement of a well-constructed plot, the interest of the play lies in the revelation of the small-mindedness of these petty provincial magnates, their jealousies and snobberies, and the contrast between their hectoring attitude to Helen when they have the whip hand of her and their cringing when it becomes clear that she has the whip hand of them. Only in the case of Thaddeus and his wife does Pinero allow any alleviation of the dark colours in which he paints English provincial society; James and Stephen are monsters of greed, hypocrisy, and vulgarity; Colonel Ponting and his wife add to these vices a foolish pretentiousness. As a representation of contemporary English society claiming historical accuracy they are absurd. Clayton Hamilton chooses this play as the best example of Pinero's power to "distinguish the natural key of unpremeditated conversation from the more formal key of studied and premeditated prose." Well, as a sample of the "unpremeditated conversation" of a little girl, take the following consecutive utterances of Joyce Mortimore, interrupted only by the exclamations of Helen:

Grandfather was a grocer, Helen—a grocer. Oh, mother has suffered terribly through it—agonies. We've all suffered. Sometimes it's been as much as Cyril and I could do to keep our heads up; but we've done it. The Singlehampton people are beasts. If it's the last word I ever utter—beasts. And only half of it was grocery—only half. It was a double shop. There were two windows; the other half was bottles of wine. They forget that; they forget that!

In the same scene the curate invites the ladies to go out in these terms:

Ladies, I have reason to believe that several choice specimens of the *Dianthus Caryophyllus* refuse to raise their heads until you grace the flower-show with your presence.

This might be defended as the curate's "premeditated prose," but his off-hand conversation (and he is a "sympathetic" character, obviously intended to pair off with the heroine in good time) is in much the same tone:

> My dear Miss Thornhill, to show you how little I regard myself as worthy of the privilege of lecturing you; to show you how the seeds of selfishness may germinate and flourish even in the breast of a cleric—may I make a confession to you. I want to confess to you that the circumstances of your having been left as you are—cast adrift on the world, unprotected, without means apart from your own talent and exertions—is one that fills me with—hope.

This is not the conversational style of any provincial curate; it is the stage style of Sir Arthur Pinero.

Mid-Channel, as interpreted by Ethel Barrymore in the United States, ran for over a year, but in London, even with the valiant help of Irene Vanbrugh, it was much less successful, both at its original production in 1909 and on its revival in 1922. It is amusing to contrast the verdict of a London critic (Sydney W. Carroll) on the latter occasion, with the encomiums of Clayton Hamilton, quoted above and penned about the same date—"only so much lumber of the past . . . a muck-heap of drawing room débris . . . There are other ways of making people suffer *mal de mer* than through marriage. Watching comedies like this is one of them." The "theme" of the play (again to quote Clayton Hamilton, "eternally important to every member of the theatre-going public") is the folly of people who marry with the determination not to have any children. The wife consoles herself with a collection of "tame robins," and when she becomes so much entangled with one of these that she loses both her husband and her lover, she commits suicide. Husband and wife are alike in their lack of ordinary respect for themselves or each other, their manners are even worse than their morals, and one would be

Mid-Channel

sorry for any children committed to their charge; it would have ruined the children without saving the parents. In spite of the deep human issues involved, the play deals entirely with the superficies of life, and the wordy sermons of the conventional *raisonneur*, Peter Mottram, are insufferably tiresome. This character is, as Sydney Carroll puts it, a warning to the younger generation against the folly of "allowing interfering old gentlemen to make themselves such conspicuous nuisances, giving advice and passing observations that can only lead to the discomfort and suicide of the people to whom they are given."

Summary   Pinero is little more than a skilful stage craftsman, admirable as a contriver of a lively drawing-room comedy, but holding no permanent place in dramatic literature. He is well worth study by those who seek to acquire familiarity with the technical devices of the modern stage; he has nothing to say to those who look to the drama for a revelation of human life and character by artistic means. Professor Ludwig Lewisohn's judgment upon him, though undoubtedly severe, is just: "His is a conventional mind under the impact of a world in the throes of moral protest and readjustment; his, a conventional technique under the impact of a nobler and a plainer art. In the direction of that finer art his progress has been less than moderate. With the intellectual dilemma he has dealt by pleading for certain exemptions from the full rigour of the social law. Except in *Iris* he has always treated the problem of sex as one of social, rather than of personal, reality and conflict. In that emphasis upon the external social order his art is akin to that of the French stage, but he lacks the latter's passion, its keen intelligence, its conviction, and its style. The extraordinarily high position which he holds in the world of the English drama is sure to decline rapidly with the introduction of such critical standards as are un-hesitatingly applied in every other department of imaginative literature."

v. OSCAR WILDE (1854-1900)

Oscar Wilde was a phenomenon whose significance belongs rather to literary history than to the exposition of the development of modern English drama. As the leader of the decadent school of the naughty 'nineties, his work attracted an amount of attention which was out of all proportion to its merits, or even its demerits, and the scandal of his fall, which for a time put a ban on the production of his plays, after a while enveloped the author's personality with a kind of satanic aura.

Of his romantic dramas, the only one which demands even passing mention is the one-act *Salomé*, originally *Salomé* written in French and extraordinarily successful in Germany, where Richard Strauss used it for the libretto of his opera, now better known than the original play. The four comedies, all produced between 1892 and 1895, are brimful of epigram and paradox, and no doubt helped to brighten the dialogue of the drawing-room plays of the next two or three decades. The first three are marred by shallow and tawdry sentimentalism, and the characters are often as lacking in humanity as the episodes are lacking in probability. One of Wilde's favourite epigrams was: "The first duty of life is to be as artificial as possible," and he seems to have conceived this as also the first duty of the dramatist. But his comedies have kept the stage, and it is impossible to overlook them altogether in estimating the factors which contributed to the revival of English drama at the end of the nineteenth century.

Lady Win-
dermere's
Fan

It would be futile at this date to point out the improbabilities and inconsistencies of *Lady Windermere's Fan* or
the impudent unnaturalness alike of its characters and its
dialogue. It was an old-fashioned play when it was born,
and contemporary critics were quick to point out its glar-
ing imperfections. The veteran nineteenth century critic
of the London drama, Clement Scott, writing in the *Daily
Telegraph* immediately after the first performance at St.
James's Theatre, said: "The story is of the slightest
consequence; plot, intrigue, interest, are beneath his
consideration; character-painting, creation, and development result in an amusing crowd of Oscar Wildes . . . .
The play is a bad one, but it will succeed. No faults of
construction, no failure in interest, no feebleness in motive,
will weigh in the scale against the insolence of its caricature." On the first performance in New York the critics
were equally prompt in condemnation. The *Herald* said:
"It is ingeniously constructed; it is sufficiently supplied
with striking situations; it is written in fluent and often
pungent dialogue, and it moves steadily and rapidly to a
climax. The form of it manifests artistic talent and pleases
the sense of symmetry. At that point its worthiness ceases.
The substance of it is false and the spirit of it is pert. No
such persons exist as those that populate its scenes, nor is
there anywhere such a state of society extant as Mr. Wilde
has suggested. The characters are a hybrid collection and
the plot a rigmarole of impossible incidents." Wilde
affected to despise newspaper criticism, and he was annoyed
by the suggestion that the change at the end of Act I by
which he let the audience into the secret of Lady Windermere's relationship to Mrs. Erlynne at an earlier point in
the play than he had originally intended, was owing to
newspaper comment. His letter to the *St. James's Gazette*

at the time is a characteristic production and is worth quoting:

> Allow me to correct a statement put forward in your issue of this evening to the effect that I have made a certain alteration in my play in consequence of the criticism of some journalists who write very recklessly and very foolishly in the papers about dramatic art. This statement is entirely untrue and grossly ridiculous.
>
> The facts are as follows. On last Saturday night, after the play was over and the author, cigarette in hand, had delivered a delightful and immortal speech, I had the pleasure of entertaining at supper a small number of personal friends; and as none of them was older than myself, I naturally listened to their artistic views with attention and pleasure. . . . All my friends, without exception, were of the opinion that the psychological interest of the second act would be greatly increased by the disclosure of the actual relationship existing between Lady Windermere and Mrs. Erlynne—an opinion, I may add, that had previously been strongly held and urged by Mr. Alexander.
>
> As to those of us who do not look upon a play as a mere question of pantomime and clowning, psychological interest is everything, I determined, consequently, to make a change in the precise moment of revelation. This determination, however, was entered into long before I had the opportunity of studying the culture, courtesy, and critical faculty displayed in such papers as *The Referee, Reynolds'* and *The Sunday Sun.*

With the exception of *The Importance of Being Earnest,* none of the Wilde plays had a "good press;" the author ascribed it to the fact that in one of his stories he had made a character say: "All the dramatic critics are to be bought, but to judge by their appearance they cannot be very expensive." The real reason of the critical condemnation of Wilde lay, of course, in the plays themselves, and not in any personal quarrel with the dramatist, whose conviction and imprisonment while *The Importance of Being*

The Importance of Being Earnest

Earnest was still in its first London run led to the disappearance of his name from the playbills, though not to the disappearance of the play from the boards of the St. James's Theatre. The professional critics were irritated by the careless craftsmanship of the earlier comedies, their insolent admixture of sentimentalism and cynicism, their superficial glitter, and the evident contempt of the author for both the theatre and the audience. They praised *The Importance of Being Earnest*, because, though its plot and characters are obviously absurd, there is more in it of the genuine Wilde which lay behind all his poses. Max Beerbohm, speculating, some years after Wilde's fall, on the loss to the stage incurred by his disgrace, wrote in the *Saturday Review* (November 26, 1904):

> His mind was essentially a fantastic mind. Into his last play, *The Importance of Being Earnest,* he poured much of this essence, treating the scheme of a commonplace farce in an elaborately fantastic spirit, and thus evolving an unrelated masterpiece which has often, and never passably, been imitated. I fancy that his main line of development would have been from this play. Abandonning the structure of commonplace farce, he would have initiated some entirely new kind of fantastic comedy—comedy in which the aim would have been not to represent men and women, but to invent them, and through them to express philosophic criticisms of the actual world.

St. John Hankin, in a *Fortnightly Review* article published in May, 1908, came to a similar conclusion:

> Paradoxical as it may sound in the case of so merry and light-hearted a play, *The Importance of Being Earnest* is artistically the most serious work that Wilde produced for the theatre. Not only is it by far the most brilliant of his plays considered as literature. It is also the most sincere. With all its absurdity, its psychology is truer, its criticism of life subtler and more profound, than that of the other plays. And even in its technique

it shows, in certain details, a breaking away from the conventional well-made play of the 'seventies and 'eighties in favour of the looser construction and more naturalistic methods of the newer school.

These judgments have been borne out by the subsequent history of the comedies on the stage. When *The Importance of Being Earnest* was revived at the Actors' Theatre, New York, in May, 1926, it was noted that the play had more life in it than its predecessors, carelessly built on a combination of the models of Sheridan and Scribe. Wilde had considerable dramatic gifts, but he lacked the will power to make the best of his talents. He wanted money, and he saw in the play an opportunity of making it by an exercise of his turn for epigram; this, combined with a large dose of sentimentalism, which was as insincere as the small dose of cynicism was genuine, and an insolent borrowing of old stage tricks, was enough to win a temporary success; it was not enough to win critical approval or to ensure a permanent place for his work in dramatic literature. His contribution to the development of English comedy was confined to the encouragement of the Sheridan tradition of sparkling dialogue; his influence on the artistic form and social or intellectual significance of the drama was exceedingly slight.

PLAY LISTS

Principal plays only are cited

T. W. ROBERTSON

1864 *David Garrick.*
1865 *Society.*
1866 *Ours.*
1867 *Caste.*
1869 *School.*

W. S. GILBERT

1875 *Trial by Jury.*
1877 *The Sorcerer.*
1878 *H. M. S. Pinafore.*
1880 *The Pirates of Penzance.*
1881 *Patience.*
1882 *Iolanthe.*
1884 *Princess Ida.*
1885 *The Mikado.*
1887 *Ruddigore.*
1888 *The Yeomen of the Guard.*
1889 *The Gondoliers.*

H. A. JONES

1882 *The Silver King* (with Henry Herman).
1884 *Saints and Sinners.*
1889 *The Middleman.*
1890 *Judah.*
1891 *The Dancing Girl.*
     The Crusaders.
1894 *The Masqueraders.*
     The Case of Rebellious Susan.
1896 *Michael and His Lost Angel.*
1897 *The Liars.*
1900 *Mrs. Dane's Defence.*
1913 *Mary Goes First.*
1914 *The Lie.*

THE VICTORIAN TRANSITION

A. W. PINERO

1885 *The Magistrate.*
1888 *Sweet Lavender.*
1889 *The Profligate.*
1893 *The Second Mrs. Tanqueray.*
1895 *The Notorious Mrs. Ebbsmith.*
1898 *Trelawney of the "Wells".*
1899 *The Gay Lord Quex.*
1901 *Iris.*
1903 *Letty.*
1906 *His House in Order.*
1908 *The Thunderbolt.*
1909 *Mid-Channel.*
1911 *Preserving Mr. Panmure.*
1912 *The "Mind-the-Paint" Girl.*
1922 *The Enchanted Cottage.*

OSCAR WILDE

1892 *Lady Windermere's Fan.*
1893 *A Woman of No Importance.*
1895 *An Ideal Husband.*
      The Importance of Being Earnest.
1896 *Salomé.*

CHAPTER III

George Bernard Shaw (1856-   )

BERNARD SHAW is beyond question the central figure of the revival of the modern drama in England. It is difficult to say whether his reputation will remain at the high level it has now reached, but as it has grown slowly, there seems no reason to anticipate an immediate decline. The story of the author's determined struggle to make himself heard on the contemporary stage is worth telling in some detail; the rebuffs he encountered justified his jibe in *You Never Can Tell* (written in 1896 but not acted till 1900) that in its intolerance of modern views the theatre of the last decade of the nineteenth century was many years behind other institutions—more retarded even than the Church. Shaw had used both voice and pen as a militant Socialist before he became a dramatist, and as he regarded the stage primarily as a pulpit for the propagation of his opinions, it was not altogether surprising that it took time for the public to realize his genuine gift for comedy. There had to be concessions on both sides, and Shaw had to learn to present his views in a dramatic form which appealed to the audience's sense of art and humour, before he was able to communicate his message effectively.

It is Shaw's dramatic career with which we are here concerned, and it seems unnecessary to go over the familiar ground of his birth in Dublin of English Protestant stock, his uneventful life there up to the age of twenty, his

Bohemian struggle for existence and education in London, whither he had followed his talented mother, and his early efforts as a novelist and journalist, culminating in his book *The Quintessence of Ibsenism* (1891) and his appointment as dramatic critic for the *Saturday Review* in 1895. His dramatic ambitions had sought vent ten years before the latter date in an attempt to collaborate with William Archer in a "well-made play" for which the original suggestion was taken from Augier's *La Ceinture Dorée,* but only two out of the three acts were completed owing to Archer's amazed disapproval of what his scenario had become in the hands of Shaw. It was not until J. T. Grein, who had established the Independent Theatre in London in 1891 and was on the lookout for native talent, gave Shaw his opportunity, that the play was completed under the title of *Widowers' Houses,* and duly put on the stage in 1892. Shaw was already known as a Socialist stump orator and pamphleteer, and the production enjoyed a momentary *succès de scandale,* but the play was speedily withdrawn. Shaw himself described it afterwards, with unflinching accuracy, as "a grotesquely realistic exposure of slum landlordism, municipal jobbery, and the pecuniary and matrimonial ties between it and the pleasant people of 'independent' incomes who imagine that such sordid matters do not touch their own lives." The hero and heroine, whose love affair supplies what little of plot there is, are singularly unromantic and unsympathetic, and though the dialogue shows occasional flashes of the wit that was to delight Shaw's twentieth-century admirers, the rejection of the play by the audience of 1892 gives no ground for surprise.

The Philanderer, written in 1893, was an elaborate satire on the pseudo-Ibsenites (Ibsenism being about that time a

Widowers' Houses

popular craze in London), but Grein thought it beyond the capacity of his company, and it waited for production until 1907, when a New York audience found itself even less able to understand its significance than a London company could have been fourteen years before.

Mrs.
Warren's
Profession

The next play, *Mrs. Warren's Profession*, (written 1894) was prohibited by the Censor, and when it was put on eight years later in New York, the performance was interrupted by the police. The aggressively "unpleasant" character of its criticism of contemporary social and industrial life would have made any Victorian audience "sit up," as it did the Censor in the 'nineties, though the Censor of thirty years later, when it was actually produced at the Regent Theatre in London, found nothing to object to beyond the casual mention of the name of the Duke of Beaufort in connection with Tintern Abbey, of which he was and is still the owner. A crowded audience gave the play a warm welcome and the London critics were keenly appreciative. Evidently, in the lapse of thirty years, times had greatly changed. St. John Ervine was probably right in his suggestion that *Mrs. Warren's Profession* marked the point at which Shaw's zeal for reform and propaganda reached its height. "After that he began to let artistry temper his reforming spirit." Shaw himself described it in 1924 as "a terrible play, written thirty years ago, when I was a young tiger, fearing neither God nor man." Apart from the propaganda, it shows an increased power of construction and dialogue, as compared with the two previous efforts, but the virulence of the attack upon established institutions was such as to damn it with any London audience within a decade of its composition, if the Censor had allowed it to reach the stage.

Arms and the Man, written and produced in 1894, makes

much greater concessions to the theatre and to the public; it is a definite endeavour to write a "pleasant" instead of an "unpleasant" play, and as such it succeeded. Shaw's own account of its composition, written in 1898, is, as usual, worth quoting: "In 1894, some public-spirited person, then as now unknown to me, declared that the London theatres were intolerable, and financed a season of plays of the 'new' order at the Avenue Theatre. . . . I, having nothing but 'unpleasant' plays in my desk, hastily completed a first attempt at a pleasant one, and called it *Arms and the Man*. It passed for a success: that is, the first night was as brilliant as could be desired; and it ran from the 21st April to the 7th July. To witness it the public paid precisely £1777.5.6 . . . the loss to the Avenue management was not far from £5000. . . . What the feelings of the unknown benefactor of the drama were . . . I do not know." It was subsequently revealed that the unknown benefactor was Miss Horniman, and the loss incurred was not sufficient to discourage her from subsidizing the Abbey Theatre in Dublin and the Gaiety in Manchester with the same object in view. But to the outside public at the time Shaw appeared to have scored a success, and the play was inoffensive as well as witty enough to be popular. It furnished the libretto of a favourite light opera of the time, *The Chocolate Soldier*, and it has been frequently revived, both by amateur and professional companies, notably at the Guild Theatre, New York, in the fall of 1925, when it had a long and successful run.

In 1895, with his appointment as dramatic critic for the *Saturday Review*, Shaw seemed to be on the highroad to success, and his second attempt at a "pleasant" play ought to have had no difficulty in securing a favourable hearing, but luck was against it. Richard Mansfield, who had made a hit with *Arms and the Man* in the United States by his impersonation of Captain Bluntchli, had the offer of the new play, and went so far as to put it in rehearsal, but had not the courage to produce it, and so passed on the opportunity of making theatrical history to Arnold Daly, whose New York production of *Candida* in the season of 1903-4 marks the real beginning of the Shaw vogue. Meanwhile the author had to content himself with the addition of *Candida* to the Independent Theatre repertory merely for the purpose of a propagandist tour through the provinces—"to the great astonishment of its audiences," Shaw testifies, adding grimly that "the drunken scene" in it "has been much appreciated, I am told, in Aberdeen." This was in 1897.

Candida

Richard Mansfield also rejected *The Man of Destiny*, written "in an idle moment in 1895," and it was hastily performed at Croydon in 1897 to secure its stage rights before publication. Cyril Maude, then manager of the Haymarket Theatre, heard of it and made inquiry about it from the author; Shaw, with his usual self-confidence, replied that it would not suit the Haymarket, but he would write a play that would. This was *You Never Can Tell*, intended to satisfy "the popular demand for fun, for fashionable dresses, for a pretty scene or two, a little music, and even for a great ordering of drinks by people with an expensive air from an—if possible—comic waiter." Shaw restrained his impulse to propaganda within the limits of an occasional fling at Victorian ideals of love and marriage, the relations between parents and children, and so on. Presumably it was the propagandist speeches that puzzled the actors and resulted in the failure to produce the play. Shaw has left his own account of the circumstances, incorporated under Maude's name in the latter's

You Never Can Tell

book, *The Haymarket Theatre;* the kernel of fact in the midst of a deal of ironical jesting is that Allan Aynesworth complained "of the number of speeches he had to deliver, whereupon Mr. Shaw cut out no less than seventeen of them." What actually happened was told by John Harwood, then stage-manager of the Haymarket, in a letter to the *New York Times,* dated April 12, 1922:

> The members of the company had not the faintest idea of what they were talking about, and I suppose Shaw was either too lazy or too pained to tell them, and the climax came when Allan Aynesworth and Winifred Emery said to Shaw, "Why don't you cut these parts?" "Right!" replied Shaw. "A rehearsal for cuts at 11 o'clock tomorrow." The next morning Allan Aynesworth walked on to the stage with the largest blue pencil I have ever seen. God knows where he had got it, but it was about eighteen inches long and about three in circumference. With a beatific smile on his face, he strolled down to Shaw and, handing him his part, said, "You said you would cut my part, Mr. Shaw; here is a pencil." Shaw took the part, glanced at the pencil and without batting an eye took the pencil with a "Thanks, very much, I've left mine at home," and deliberately made a downward stroke on every page of the part. There were snickers and muttered conversation all round. Rehearsal was dismissed. Harrison, Maude, and Shaw retired to the office. One hour after Cyril Maude said to me with great glee: "We're not going to produce the play; ain't that a bit of luck!" Just about three weeks after that I met Ailsa Craig (daughter of Ellen Terry) on the street. She said: "Hello; your management has turned down the best play written for years!"

This was in the winter of 1897, and Shaw had already determined on the use of the printing press to give the reading public access to the seven plays above mentioned, of which only one had been successfully produced and three had not even reached the stage. The two volumes of *Plays Pleasant and Unpleasant,* furnished with elaborate stage directions and prefaces as "first aid to critics," had a wide circulation, and did much to establish Shaw's reputation as a dramatic author; but they did not secure success on the stage. *The Devil's Disciple* (written 1897) and *Cæsar and Cleopatra* (written 1898), though they later proved exceedingly popular, were both produced in 1899 without success, and were accordingly printed along with *Captain Brassbound's Conversion* (written 1899 but not produced till 1902) as *Three Plays for Puritans* (1901).

Just when the dramatist seemed to be relaxing his efforts, success came in full tide. This may be definitely dated in the New York season of 1903-4, of which the most striking feature was the production of *Candida, The Man of Destiny*, and *You Never Can Tell* by Arnold Daly and the revival of *Arms and the Man* by Richard Mansfield. Granville-Barker, allying his efforts with J. E. Vedrenne at the Court Theatre in London, gave over 700 performances of Shaw plays in three seasons, beginning in 1904. About the same time German translations of some of the early plays, made at the instance of William Archer, were successfully performed at Vienna, Frankfort, Dresden, and Berlin; translations into Swedish, Danish, Magyar, Polish, Russian, and Dutch speedily followed, and the dramatist's European reputation was established almost simultaneously with the acknowledgment of his supremacy in England and America.

Man and Superman, written in 1901 and published in 1903, was the success of the season in 1904-5, both in London and New York, and for the next decade Shaw's plays were produced as soon as they were written, in spite of occasional troubles with the Censor. *John Bull's Other Island*, written for the Irish National Theatre, proved more acceptable in London, and by way of revenge *The Shewing-*

Man and Superman

up of Blanco Posnet, prohibited in London, passed into the repertory of the Abbey Theatre in Dublin, where the Lord Chamberlain's writ did not run. It was successfully produced by the Irish players in the United States, and apparently had some unforbidden performances by them in England before the Censor's ban was formally removed half a dozen years ago. *Pygmalion* (1912) had the distinction of being first performed at the Hofburg Theatre in Vienna and afterwards at the Lessing Theatre in Berlin before it reached England or America.

With the outbreak of the War in 1914, Shaw's energies were diverted, disastrously so far as his dramatic work was concerned, to his old love of pamphleteering, and for a time his popularity with the theatre-going public suffered an almost complete eclipse. The more intelligent theatregoers to whom he appealed were too busy with other things, and the flappers whom the soldiers temporarily in London on leave took to a "show" had no mind either for wit or wisdom. His *Playlets of the War* and his one serious play dealing with war issues, *Heartbreak House*, were hardly *Heartbreak* calculated to conciliate British public opinion, which had *House* been gravely offended by his pamphlets about the War, and at the suggestion of St. John Ervine negotiations were set on foot with the New York Theatre Guild for the production of the last-mentioned play, though Shaw doubted whether there existed in New York a management "bold enough and clever enough to know that the alternative to pleasing an audience for two hours is to put the utmost strain upon their attention for three and send them home exhausted but impressed." *Heartbreak House* was produced in November, 1920, at the Garrick Theatre by the Guild, and its members stood the strain. Emboldened by its success, the Guild in January, 1921, requested permission to produce the monumental *Back to Methuselah, A Metabiological Pentateuch,* extending in five episodes from B. C. 4004 (*In the Garden of Eden*) to A. D. 31,920 (*As Far as Thought Can Reach*), and making, when it was printed with a long preface, a fat volume of over 350 pages. It was for this reason that Shaw cabled in reply to the request, "You are quite mad but go ahead," and in **Back to Methuselah** February, 1922, *Back to Methuselah* had its first production at the Garrick Theatre, New York, at a loss of $20,000, for which Shaw consoled them by the remark that there was really a clear profit of $10,000 as they expected to lose $30,000. The play was first presented in England at the Birmingham Repertory Theatre in October, 1923, and did not reach London till the fall of 1924.

The New York Theatre Guild enjoyed a similar priority **Saint Joan** in the production of *Saint Joan* at the Garrick Theatre on December 28, 1923, with Winifred Lenihan in the title part; the first performance in London was on March 26, 1924, in the New Theatre with Sybil Thorndike as the Saint. The Guild was rewarded by Shaw for its enterprise with a grant of control of the production of his plays in New York, and opened its new Guild Theatre on April 19, 1925, with a performance of *Cæsar and Cleopatra,* followed in September by a "season" of Shaw plays, which, at the time of writing, has not come to an end.

London, meanwhile, though suffering from severe financial depression, which had its repercussion on theatrical audiences, was recovering its fondness for Shaw. As early as February, 1921, the London *Observer* records, apropos of a Shaw season at the Everyman Theatre, Hampstead, that "Bernard Shaw, in theatrical parlance, is booming." In October, 1924, we have the note: "There is a boom in Mr. Shaw: *St. Joan* at the New; *Man and Superman* at the Regent; *The Devil's Disciple* at the Everyman; ana *Mrs. Warren's Profession* about to be put on." In May, 1925, the *Observer* was driven to accuse Shaw of "an unusual mood of modesty" because he reckoned all the readers of his books and newspaper articles and all the spectators of his plays at "not less than a million people." Upon this "Observator" was moved to the comment: "Seeing that his name has been a household word on the Continent for twenty-five years and in this country for ten; that it must be a poor week in which half-a-dozen of his plays are not running in one European town with another; that his published works number between thirty and forty; and that for many years he was a regular contributor to the daily and weekly Press, one might safely multiply the figure many times."

This change in the public attitude toward Shaw was accompanied by a change in the tone of critical appreciation. One can hardly say that the critics produced the change in public opinion, and it would be needlessly harsh to say that they followed it. The issue may be left as Shaw put it himself in a recent article in the *Saturday Review* (November 7, 1925): "I cannot pretend to consider my own reception as a playwright by my quondam colleagues as, on the whole, a critical success. But critics must be judged by their normal activities, and not by their convulsions when a new departure upsets them." Shaw took a good-natured fling at contemporary criticism in the prologue to *Fanny's First Play* in 1911, and again in the preface to *Saint Joan* (1924). His final and considered judgment is given in the *Saturday Review* article quoted above. On the whole, he admits an improvement: "The theatre . . . is beginning to educate its critics, whereas in the old days it stultified them. I have no space left in

Shaw and the critics

which to describe how completely the theatre used to be divorced from the national life. It was more secluded than any modern convent, and much more prudish. It knew nothing of religion, politics, science, or any art but its own. It had only one subject, which the censorship did not allow it to mention." In the Preface to *Back to Methuselah* Shaw dates the reform of criticism from the triumph on the stage of *Man and Superman* in 1905 and the discussion that took place about the published play at that time: "Since then the sweet-shop view of the theatre has been out of countenance; and its critical exponents have been driven to take an intellectual pose which, though often more trying than their old intellectually nihilistic vulgarity, at least concedes the dignity of the theatre, not to mention the usefulness of those who live by criticizing it. And the younger playwrights are not only taking their art seriously, but being taken seriously themselves. The critic who ought to be a newsboy is now comparatively rare."

Shaw's own criticism Shaw himself made important contributions to dramatic criticism in his four years on the *Saturday Review* (1895-98) but his more important service to criticism, as to the drama itself, was in enlarging the scope of dramatic interest from the one subject of "clandestine adultery" to the many issues of modern life. A new generation of theatregoers and a new generation of critics arose who were alive to these interests, and Shaw did his full share in educating the new public. He had to fight his way through the thick brush of Victorian prejudice, and though he did not do it single-handed, he took a leading part—perhaps the leading part—in the struggle.

As the result of all this movement—certainly one of the most remarkable in the development of English thought—the attitude of both critics and public to Shaw underwent a complete change. Regarded at first as a negligible jester and fabricator of paradoxes, he came to be tolerated as a rational but destructive critic of contemporary institutions; when it was realized that he had substantive as well as negative opinions to promulgate, he was appreciated as an original thinker, but not a dramatist; later, the critics were forced to admit that his claim to unusual comedic talent could not be denied; and finally he was acclaimed as the intellectual force which has revolutionized modern English drama and made an indelible mark upon its history.

As the public has come to agree with Shaw in regarding him primarily as a propagandist, it seems reasonable to ask what principles he devoted so many years of his life to advocating on the stage. As this period, beginning with the first two acts of *Widowers' Houses* in 1885, has already covered over forty years—perhaps the most crucial in English history—it is natural to suppose that the opinions of so active-minded a man as Shaw underwent some change, and that this change reflected itself in the dramas which were, for the last thirty years of the period, his principal medium of expression. In the first group of plays, gathered together for publication as *Plays Pleasant and Unpleasant* in 1898, his main object of attack is romantic idealism, in social or political affairs, ethics or religion. "In spite of a Liberal Revolution or two," he says in the preface to the second volume, "I can no longer be satisfied with fictitious morals and fictitious good conduct, shedding fictitious glory on overcrowding, disease, crime, drink, war, cruelty, infant mortality, and all the other commonplaces of civilization which drive men to the theatre to make foolish pretences that these things are progress, science, morals, religion, patriotism, imperial supremacy, national greatness and all

Shaw's opinions

the other names the newspapers call them." Of these seven plays, three— *Widowers' Houses, Mrs. Warren's Profession,* and *Candida*—are definitely socialistic in temper, resting ultimately on the conviction that the evils of the competitive and capitalistic system can be remedied only by the adoption of a basis of equality of income. "All roads in Mr. Shaw lead, and all roots dig down to, Communism," says James Agate, and this is no doubt true of his last drama as of his first, but one notices after the first group a change of emphasis, a variety of interests, due only in part to the necessity of making plays that were entertaining enough to be acceptable to the public. In the last play of the early group, *You Never Can Tell,* in one of Valentine's speeches, ("Nature was in deadly earnest with me when I was in jest with her"), and in the final description of him as "the captured Duellist of Sex," we get a hint

The Life Force

of the doctrine of the Life Force which received its first full presentation seven years later in *Man and Superman.* Six years of service on the St. Pancras Borough Council convinced Shaw that "we have yet to see the man who, having any experience of Proletarian Democracy, has any belief in its capacity for solving great political problems, or even doing ordinary parochial work intelligently and economically." He saw further that "man will return to his idols and cupidities, in spite of all 'movements' and all revolutions, until his nature is changed. . . . The only fundamental and possible socialism is the socialization of the selective breeding of Man: in other terms, of human evolution." Evolution takes a long time, and although in 1911 Shaw declared himself still theoretically in favour of "a system of society where all the income of the country is to be divided up in exactly equal proportions," it is evident that this had become a pious belief which held in his mind a very different position from that of the period of youthful enthusiasm when he thought that "a fortnight would be ample" to get Socialism into working order. He jokingly connected this growing moderation in his views with the success of *Arms and the Man* in 1894, when, he says, "I opened a very modest banking account, and became comparatively Conservative in my political opinions." But as a matter of fact Shaw realized the impossibility of at once putting the Socialistic programme into force about ten years earlier than that, through his work during the early years of the Fabian Society (founded 1884), and the realization of the difficulties and the time needed to overcome them naturally increased with Shaw's maturity. Speaking at a meeting of the Independent Labour Party in May, 1924, Shaw expressed his approval of the moderate policy of the Labour Government and spoke as follows:

The Labour Party

> I am an old Communist, but I am perfectly respectable, legally married, and my wife is respectable. I am a perfectly respectable landlord and a capitalist, and can speak feelingly about the condition of the landlord and the capitalist. I am of a quiet and simple life, a vegetarian, a teetotaller, and non-smoker. My wants are very few. A nice little flat in the West End of London, a pleasant country house not too far from London, a couple of motorcars, three or four thousand pounds pocket money, and there is no more contented man in England than Bernard Shaw. Multi-millionaires describe me as a poor devil, but I get on very comfortably. This is the simple, plain position I should like to see every man and woman in this country occupy.

Speaking more seriously at a dinner given by members of the Parliamentary Labour Party in celebration of his seventieth birthday on July 27, 1926, Shaw said nothing more revolutionary than that the present government was always interfering with capitalism and making all sorts of regulations which were breaking up their own system. If private property stood in the way of distribution it would have to go. They must get seriously to work to get a technique of government so that they would know their business and be ready when the time came.

The predominant dramatic interest of Shaw's later years was no longer Socialism but religion—the new creed of Creative Evolution, which the Vitalists and the French philosopher Bergson had brought to the front. Shaw's first attempt to present this new gospel (not metaphysical, but metabiological) was in the Third Act of *Man and Superman;* in its printed form the play was further provided with a direct setting-forth of the new doctrine in *An Epistle Dedicatory,* the *Revolutionist's Handbook,* and *Maxims for Revolutionists.* But Forbes-Robertson, whose performance made the play popular, omitted the Third Act, containing the dramatic parable of creative evolution, and the audiences both in New York and London were content to enjoy the fun of the setting without inquiring further as to the ultimate intention of the author. As Shaw put it some years later: "Being then at the height of my invention and comedic talent, I decorated it too brilliantly and lavishly." It is significant of the change of view about Shaw outlined above that when some twenty years later the play was put on as a whole at the Regent Theatre, London, (the performance began at 5 p.m. and lasted about six hours), the decoration had become "a mere unnecessary coating of jam to a highly delectable pill," and the three-cornered debate, with Donna Anna holding a watching brief, seemed "skies higher in interest and power than the rest." (*Observer,* October 25, 1925.)

For the time being, however, Shaw's effort to provide the twentieth century with a new religion passed almost un-

Religion

noticed. In *Major Barbara* (1907), *The Shewing-up of Blanco Posnet* (1909), *Fanny's First Play* (1911), and *Androcles and the Lion* (1912) there are passages which show his continued interest in the subject of religion, and the last mentioned, with its elaborate preface, is devoted entirely to an exposition of Primitive Christianity, as Shaw saw it; but again his comedic talent got in the way: the comic Androcles and still more comic Lion (taken over from *Sandford and Merton*) and the comic martyrs who sing "Onward Christian Soldiers" on their way to the Arena, prevented the few serious passages of the play from being taken seriously, though in the final conversation between Lavinia and her handsome Captain there is a deeper note struck which was afterwards to be sounded again, more effectively and more effectually, in *Back to Methuselah* and *Saint Joan*.

The end of the War found Shaw over sixty years of age, and beginning to feel that the sands of life were running out. In a new mood of modesty, he reviewed his past achievements and the issues he had attempted to deal with —slum landlordism in *Widowers' Houses;* doctrinaire Free Love (pseudo-Ibsenism) in *The Philanderer;* prostitution in *Mrs. Warren's Profession;* militarism in *Arms and the Man;* marriage in *Candida* and *Getting Married;* history in *The Man of Destiny* and *Cæsar and Cleopatra;* current politics in *John Bull's Other Island, Major Barbara,* and *Press Cuttings;* natural Christianity in *The Shewing-up of Blanco Posnet* and *Androcles and the Lion;* national and individual character in *The Man of Destiny, Cæsar and Cleopatra, John Bull's Other Island, Fanny's First Play* and *Great Catherine;* paradoxes of conventional society in *You Never Can Tell, How He Lied to Her Husband, Misalliance,* and *Pygmalion;* husband-hunting in *Man and*

Shaw reviews his achievements

Superman; questions of conscience and professional delusions and impostures in *The Doctor's Dilemma.* A man of smaller intellectual energy and courage might have surveyed the record with an inclination to rest and be thankful, in view of the turn of the tide of popular success in his favour, but Shaw found that he had not adequately presented the most important topic of all—that of religion—

Back to Methuselah in which he himself was most interested. He therefore laid aside the professional cap and bells, and pleaded the garrulity of age as an excuse for setting forth his religious views at length in a form, it is true, more or less dramatic, but in a shape in which he could hardly hope for performance on the commercial stage. We have seen that the enterprise of the New York Theatre Guild and the Birmingham Repertory Company gave this strange play or collection of plays a hearing, and it is in parts not without considerable dramatic qualities, but as a whole it is obviously impossible of reproduction under ordinary commercial conditions. It is Shaw's religious testament to his generation—his "beginning of a Bible for Creative Evolution," and he says with unaccustomed humility that while he hopes younger hands will do better, "I am doing the best I can at my age."

As a contribution to the modern Bible, *Back to Methuselah* is, it must be owned, neither particularly helpful nor particularly encouraging. The final prospect of becoming a vortex of pure thought, without bodily parts, is not alluring to the vast majority of intelligent mankind, as their conception of the victory of the mind over matter is something quite different: it is one thing to learn all about matter and make it subject to the human will; it is another thing (to most people quite inconceivable) to abolish matter altogether. Few men and fewer women would make the effort required to live three centuries or more, if the time were to be spent continuously in mathematical contemplation; the life of a mathematical professor, always engaged in study, without sleep and without holidays, would be, to the average intellectual, so far as we have known him, an intolerable bore. The "men like Gods" of the Utopia of H. G. Wells, who retain their delight in natural beauty and vary physical research with intervals of social intercourse and love-making, seem much more attractive, and nearer the future possibilities of mankind.

Shaw suggests in the preface that we enormously exaggerate the periods required for the pre-natal acquirement of habits and that the future swing of opinion may be nearer Archbishop Usher's count of six thousand years from Creation to the present time than to the modern geologist's and astronomer's demand for millions of years. But in the matter of time he is pretty generous with himself and not very heartening to his disciples. According to his forecast, the Burge-Lubin who is President of Great Britain in 2170 A. D. combines the silliness and weaknesses of Lubin and Burge, who were successively Prime Ministers of England a century and a half before. Even when the telescope is moved on another thousand years into the future, the improvement is still very limited: the higher civilization is confined to a body of select spirits who keep themselves secluded in the British Isles, while the rest of the world, including North America, with the exception of a few American exiles, is given up to the old crimes, follies and frivolities—political jobbery and humbug, endless and devastating wars, week-end riverside hotels on the Euphrates, minstrels and pierrots on the sands of the Persian Gulf, toboggans and funiculars on the Hindoo Koosh. In thirty thousand years from the date of the play, mankind has got rid of its functions of digestion and reproduction, has cut down the period of childhood to four years, is well on the way to losing its sense of natural beauty and abolishing the arts, spends its adult centuries in abstruse mathematical calculations, and is looking forward to the time when, matter having been entirely suppressed, life will be all thought—with apparently no one to think and nothing to think about. It is not an exhilarating prospect.

While the aim held out to mankind is one little likely to commend itself, the means by which the end is to be attained, although sufficiently simple, have small guarantee of adequacy for less weighty reforms than are here proposed. According to Shaw, all humanity needs to do is to will to live for three hundred years, and the rest will follow. But his assertion that the desire for long life will secure longevity is contradicted by human experience and scientific investigation; the Lamarckian principle on which it depends, if it has not been disproved, is certainly very far from being proved, and as Shaw applies the principle, it is a pure assumption. St. John Ervine, who was profoundly impressed by the beauty of the play, in spite of its repetitions and irrelevances, could not bring himself to accept its central idea. "Our actions are not conditioned by our prospects of life, but by the nature inside us, and that nature is not appreciably affected by the length of our years. If the Savvys of twenty years' existence will not learn anything, neither will the Savvys of a thousand years' existence. Longevity in itself is of no particular service to mankind . . . I see nothing in human life to justify the belief that a flighty-minded person will become a serious-minded person merely by the prolongation of his existence."

At the same time St. John Ervine was deeply moved by Shaw's passionate sincerity and religious fervour, as expressed in the Garden of Eden scenes, and in the recall of the Ghosts of the earliest characters at the end of the play. The critics have agreed with the audiences in their appreciative response to the emotional appeal of the final speech of Lilith:

> I am Lilith: I brought life into the whirlpool of force, and compelled my enemy, Matter, to obey a living soul. But in enslaving Life's enemy I made him Life's master; for that is the end of all slavery; and now I shall see the slave set free and the enemy reconciled, the whirlpool become all life and no matter. And because these infants that call themselves ancients are reaching out towards that, I will have patience with them still; though I know well that when they attain it they shall become one with me and supersede me, and Lilith will be only a legend and a lay that has lost its meaning. Of Life only is there no end; and though of its million starry mansions many are empty and many still unbuilt, and though its vast domain is as yet unbearably desert, my seed shall one day fill it and master its matter to its uttermost confines. And for what may be beyond, the eyesight of Lilith is too short. It is enough that there *is* a beyond.

Saint Joan is more completely imbued with the religious spirit as Shaw understood it than *Back to Methuselah*. It was of course impossible to keep evolution out of it (at any rate out of the preface) for the force behind evolution was to Shaw what ordinary people call God. He is enough of a mystic (for one may be a mystic without accepting any of the revealed religions) for Joan's voices not to trouble him any more than he is upset by the Daimon of Socrates; they are to him merely personifications of her own intelligence and insight. He is not concerned, as Anatole France professed to be, as to whether Saint Catherine, Saint Margaret and Saint Michael ever really existed and could have appeared in bodily form to Joan, as she believed. He takes it for granted that Joan was in many ways subject to the ordinary beliefs and superstitions of her time, as we

Saint Joan

all are, more or less, to the ordinary beliefs and superstitions of our time, for he sees that mankind is still far from achieving the absolute truth. What interests him in her is the power she possessed of penetrating, by sheer common sense, beyond the accepted beliefs and institutions of the Middle Ages to a foresight of human needs and aspirations, which was entirely unrecognized by herself and was to be revealed to the common consciousness only by the political and social developments of the next two or three centuries. To make this clear he has endowed Cauchon, Lemaître and Warwick with an intelligence they probably never possessed and with a realization of the significance of the organizations they served which they certainly never had. This is justifiable as a dramatic expedient to bring home to the audience the very different surroundings, not only material and physical, but intellectual and spiritual, in which Joan lived and of which she was in a sense the victim, though it may be that Shaw, for the purposes of his argument, has minimized the ordinary human motives of self-interest and love of power which in all ages count for more in the lives of men of action than abstract principles. In the discussions between Warwick and Cauchon, between Cauchon and Lemaître, there is obvious anachronism and exaggeration, but Shaw did not wait for the critics to point it out—he forestalled them by acknowledging it. The historical Cauchon, Lemaître, and Warwick "were part of the Middle Ages themselves, and therefore as unconscious of its peculiarities as of the atomic formula of the air they breathed"; dramatically they are represented as "saying the things they would actually have said if they had known what they were really doing." Joan's Protestantism, her claim to the right of individual judgment ("What other judgment can I judge by but my own?"), her assertion that God must be served before the Church, must be regarded in the same way, as what was implicit in her attitude rather than what was clear to her consciousness; but when every deduction has been made, Shaw probably came nearer to the realization of Joan's extraordinary personality than any of the poets, historians and biographers who preceded him; and the task of interpreting Joan to a twentieth-century audience was no light one. In spite of his interest in intellectual questions such as toleration, nationalism, and democracy, which arise naturally in connection with any consideration of feudalism and the authority of the Church, he has succeeded in making Joan a living figure, sympathetic and understandable to a modern audience through communicated emotion as well as through the ideas that, often without her own knowledge, she stood for. She appealed to Shaw, not as a national heroine, still less as a military leader, but as one of the pure spirits who strive to bring justice and mercy on the earth without much regard for the conventional standards of their own time. He uses her national and military ardour effectively for dramatic purposes, but in the end all these fall away from her, and she is revealed as one who has fought, not altogether in vain, to hasten the coming of the kingdom of heaven. Her last cry, "O God that madest this beautiful earth, when will it be ready to receive thy saints? How long, O Lord, how long?" echoes, as does the whole trend of *Back to Methuselah* and *Heartbreak House*, Shaw's final conviction of the human limitations which are bound to make any real progress of mankind a very long and painful business. The mass, and the ordinary leaders chosen by the mass, will always be hampered by their natural stupidity and their acquired prejudices; the hope of the future lies in the very few who have the wit and the courage to do their own thinking and to outstep the conventional boundaries set by their education and surroundings. In a sense, these last plays are Shaw's *Apologia pro vita suâ*.

There will probably always be people to doubt whether Bernard Shaw was the inspired prophet of his time, but there is general agreement that he is the most gifted writer of comedies produced in the British Isles, not only during the last century but possibly a century or two before that. There seems no need to labour the point, and a few examples of contemporary criticism will be enough to illustrate the final stage of the attitude toward Shaw of which the curious changes have already been noted. The younger critics are not a little bewildered at the hostile or cool reception given by their predecessors to Shaw's earlier and middle-period plays. In a notice of the production of *Man and Superman* for the first time in its entirety in 1925, we read: "In attempting to report on it I feel like a junior subaltern called upon for a précis of the campaign with the roar of the guns still in my ears. At five o'clock the battle began, and it was well after eleven before the Life Force triumphed. For most of that time the greatest of living rhetoricians not only held the packed audience at the Regent in their seats, but kept their enthusiasm at shouting pitch."

Plays such as *The Man of Destiny*, *The Doctor's Dilemma* and *Misalliance*, which could once get themselves produced with difficulty and met with a very critical appraisement when they were acted, are now acclaimed at revivals with such phrases as "a superb play," "a rare entertainment," "little short of a masterpiece," and so on. The chorus of praise for *Saint Joan* was practically unanimous. But even before *Saint Joan*, Walter Prichard Walter Prichard Eaton Eaton, the *doyen* of American dramatic critics, reviewing Shaw's contributions to the stage up to *Back to Methuselah*, wrote (in the New York *Freeman*, of March 29, 1922):

Shaw has proved his easy mastery of the peculiar technique required to set imaginary characters on a stage and cause them to hold the interest of an audience. Indeed, his mastery is so easy that it makes the masters of the "the well-made play" look like straining schoolboys. To this sheer theatrical skill he has added a pungent wit, a racy satire, and the driving force of a restless mind that questions, revolts, disturbs, harasses. It is a fact rather ignored by critics that his output of stage plays for the past quarter-century has been huge, considering their quality (about one a year for an average), and that their percentage of success in the popular theatre has been extraordinarily high. There is probably no other dramatist of our day whose works, over anything like an equal period of time, have seen so many performances. His reputation as an intellectual has obscured his solid success as a man of the theatre. But it is through the theatre that he has driven his ideas into the minds of his fellows; it is the theatregoers who have made him the figure he is.

Similarly John Corbin, then the dramatic critic of the John Corbin New York *Times*, wrote a little later (May 6, 1923): "In purity of type and perfection of form *Candida* is a little masterpiece . . . *Cæsar and Cleopatra* verges by turns upon melodrama, upon farce, upon musical comedy; but, by and large, it is the most richly coloured, most profoundly psychologic and most potently atmospheric play in the modern drama." St. John Ervine brought away from the St. John Ervine first public performance of *Mrs. Warren's Profession* on September 28, 1925, the conviction that "even at his crudest, Shaw is immeasurably better than any living dramatist. The vitality of this piece is astounding."

The final discovery of those who had long recognized Shaw's supremacy as a writer of witty dialogue and a genius in the dramatic presentation of his ideas, is that he also "has a heart." It is a surprising discovery in view of the fact that for over thirty years Shaw had shown himself a master of humour as well as of wit, and one cannot create humorous characters without feeling kindly toward them and communicating this feeling of kindliness to the audience. The fact that the waiter in *You Never Can Tell* seems to have a distant relationship with characters in Dickens should have been enough to warn the critics that Shaw was by no means devoid of emotional sympathy, as some of them were fond of saying up to a comparatively recent date. It must be admitted that this vein in his work grew richer with his advancing maturity and experience of the stage. There are touches of real feeling in *Cæsar and Cleopatra, Man and Superman, The Shewing-up of Blanco Posnet* and *Fanny's First Play*—to mention only a few— but up to 1911 Shaw's characters are mainly conceived in the spirit of satire. Androcles is, however, a genuinely humorous character in that he is conceived not in the spirit of satire but in the spirit of sympathy, for at bottom Shaw profoundly approved of the attitude of the Greek tailor toward life, however quaintly this attitude is expressed. It is evident also that the creator of Alfred Doolittle has a genuine liking for this humorous rogue, though his morals no more commended themselves to Shaw than to the average Philistine. Take, for instance, Doolittle's introduction of himself:

Humour and pathos

What am I, Governors both? I ask you, what am I? I'm one of the undeserving poor: that's what I am. Think of what that means to a man. It means that he's up agen middle-class morality all the time. If there's anything going, and I put in for a bit of it, it's always the same story: "You're undeserving; so you can't have it." But my needs is as great as the most deserving widow that ever got money out of six different charities in one week for the death of the same husband. I don't need less than a deserving man: I need more. I don't eat less hearty than him; and I drink a lot more. I want a bit of amusement, 'cause I'm a thinking man. I want cheerfulness and a song and a band when I feel low. Well, they charge me just the same for everything as they charge the deserving. What is middle-class morality? Just an excuse for never giving me anything.

When Doolittle is condemned to respectability by a legacy from an American millionaire, his transformation from a dustman into a silk-hatted incarnation of English middle-class respectability is no less amusing than his own lamentation over his misfortunes:

What I'm complaining of is that he has made a gentleman out of me. Who ever asked him to do that? I was happy. I was a free man. I have got money out of pretty nearly everyone, just as I got it out of you, Henry Higgins, when I needed it. Now I'm hedged in, bound hand and foot, and everyone gets money out of me. You ought to congratulate yourself, says my lawyer. You mean that you ought to congratulate yourself, I tell him.

When I was a poor man and needed a lawyer because somebody found a baby carriage in my cart, he argued my case for nothing and then saw to it that he was free of me as soon as possible. The same way with the doctors. They used to shove me out of the hospital before I could stand, without making me pay a penny. Now they have discovered that I'm not healthy and can't live if they don't examine me twice a day. I don't dare lift a finger in my own house, but somebody else must do it for the good money I have to pay him. I'm only allowed to live for others—instead of for myself.

That is middle-class morality for you. A year ago I didn't have a single relative in the whole world outside of two or three people who wouldn't have a thing to do with me. Now I have fifty. And not one of them has a decent salary.

In his latest plays, *Back to Methuselah* and *Saint Joan*, the satiric element, though still present, is warmed by a current of kindly humour. There is often deep feeling in the Garden of Eden episodes, as well as deep thought, and the politicians in the next three sections are, with the exception of the militarist, represented as silly rather than noxious; they are not unlikeable. The young people in the last section are altogether charming—much more so, in fact, than the purely intellectual ancients. In *Saint Joan* Shaw indulges his tendency to satire in the figure of Stogumber—Shaw is never tired of taking a fall out of the English, perhaps because they do not seem to mind it—but even Stogumber sees the light, and ends up as an entirely kindly though half-witted village rector. Dunois, the born man-at-arms, the Archbishop, Warwick, Cauchon, the Inquisitor and the weak-minded King—all characters with whose view of life Shaw had little intellectually in common —are given at any rate moments of kindliness and emotional understanding, and Joan, though not at all a conventional heroine, is a real heroine by virtue of her devotion, high-mindedness, and supreme common sense.

Shaw's influence on drama The influence of Shaw on modern English drama was enormous. He lifted it out of the terrible rut into which it had fallen, and opened up to it the manifold issues of our complex modern life. In these paths many have followed him and they have learnt much from him in breadth of outlook, brilliance of dialogue, and deftness of presentation. But none of his successors has been able to come near him in originality of ideas, or skill in the creation of character and incident, which is the essential quality of dramatic genius. Not only will the period of his active connection with the theatre come to be known as the Shaw period, but he seems likely to occupy as pre-eminent a position in it as

Shakespeare does in the Elizabethan drama. No other English dramatist at any period has received during his lifetime the critical and popular appreciation accorded to Bernard Shaw in America and on the European Continent, and the award of the Nobel Prize in 1926 was merely a recognition of solid and successful literary achievement to which abundant testimony had already been given in other ways.

PLAY LIST

1892 *Widowers' Houses,* wr. 1885-1892, pub. 1893.

1894 *Arms and the Man,* wr. 1894, pub. 1898.

1897 *Candida,* wr. 1894-5, pub. 1898.

The Man of Destiny, wr. 1895, pub. 1898.

1899 *The Devil's Disciple,* wr. 1897, pub. 1901.

Cæsar and Cleopatra, wr. 1897, pub. 1901.

1900 *You Never Can Tell,* wr. 1896, pub. 1898.

1901 *The Admirable Bashville.*

1902 *Captain Brassbound's Conversion,* wr. 1899, pub. 1901.

Mrs. Warren's Profession (in New York; in London, 1925), wr. 1894; pub. 1898.

1904 *Man and Superman,* wr. 1901 and pub. 1903.

1904 *John Bull's Other Island,* pub. 1907.

1905 *Major Barbara,* pub. 1907.

1905 *How He Lied to Her Husband,* wr. 1904, pub. 1907.

1906 *The Doctor's Dilemma,* pub. 1911.

1907 *The Philanderer* (New York), wr. 1893, pub. 1898.

1908 *Getting Married,* pub. 1911.

1909 *Press Cuttings.*

The Shewing-up of Blanco Posnet, pub. 1911.

1910 *Misalliance,* pub. 1914.

The Dark Lady of the Sonnets, pub. 1914.

1911 *Fanny's First Play,* pub. 1914.

1913 *Androcles and the Lion,* wr. 1912, pub. 1914.

Over-ruled, wr. 1912, pub. 1914.

Pygmalion, wr. 1912, pub. 1914.

Great Catherine, wr. 1912, pub. 1914.

1917 *O'Flaherty V. C.,* pub. 1919.

The Inca of Perusalem, pub. 1919.

Augustus Does His Bit, pub. 1919.

1918 *Annajanska, the Bolshevik Empress,* pub. 1919.

1920 *Heartbreak House* (New York), pub. 1919.

1922 *Back to Methuselah* (in New York; in Birmingham, 1923; in London, 1924), pub. 1921.

1923 *Saint Joan* (in New York; London, 1924), pub. 1925.

CHAPTER IV

J. M. Barrie (1860-   )

BARRIE has had two successful careers, and the second has almost obliterated the first in the mind of the present generation. His first career, terminating conveniently with the nineteenth century, brought him from Kirriemuir via Edinburgh University to be a striving young journalist in the English Midlands, and from Nottingham to London to be the most popular novelist of the Scottish sentimental group known in its time as the "kailyard School." Of his earlier literary work all that need here be said is that it revealed that curious division between realism and romance, satire and sentiment, truth to fact and whimsical fancy which by a combination of opposites gave his later dramas their characteristic charm. His dramatic period, strictly considered, begins in the earlier 'nineties, but up to 1900 he had made so little mark on the stage that in that year J. A. Hammerton, his enthusiastic admirer, could write, "Barrie is not, and is not likely to be, a serious factor in the contemporary drama." In 1921 Bernard Shaw, in a letter to J. T. Grein congratulating him on the achievements of the Independent Theatre, gave credit to Barrie for "the final relegation of the nineteenth-century London theatre to the dust-bin." In the interval between Hammerton's prophecy and Shaw's historical retrospect, a good deal had happened, and probably what the latter had in mind was the successful run of *The*

Admirable Crichton in 1902—the year before Shaw himself finally captured the London stage.

In excuse for the slighting reference to Barrie's dramatic powers by his first biographer, it should be said that his earlier plays were not of a kind to ensure a favourable verdict from a conscientious critic. He began (in collaboration with H. B. Marriot-Watson) with a romantic drama dealing with the misfortunes of the eighteenth-century Bohemian and literary hack, Richard Savage. In the same year (1891) he made a stage version of *Vanity Fair* and wrote a burlesque of Ibsen's plays, which were then striving for a hearing on the London boards. In none of these early fumblings was there anything that won—or deserved to win—the favour of the public or the attention of the critics. *Walker, London,* Barrie's next attempt, was a popular success, largely because of the opportunity it gave for J. L. Toole, an actor with a firm hold on the affections of the Victorian public, to exploit his comic powers in the portrayal of a London barber on a holiday, thrown by chance into acquaintance with a house-boat party on the Upper Thames and accepted by them in his assumed character of an African explorer. A pretty setting and smart dialogue made up for a tenuous plot and superficial characterization, and the innocent amours in which the hero involved himself were safely ended by the receipt of an imaginary telegram and his flight, leaving the address "Walker, London." Collaboration with Conan Doyle in the libretto of a comic opera (*Jane Annie,* 1893) followed, and then came the two great appeals to popular sentiment —*The Professor's Love-Story* and *The Little Minister,* the latter a dramatization of Barrie's own novel by the same name which had already gained very wide success. These two plays won for Barrie the ready applause of large audi-

Beginnings as a dramatist

84

ences on both sides of the Atlantic, but did not conciliate the critics who were already sated with Victorian senti-mentality. Possibly *The Wedding Guest*, written in the satirical vein which is as much a part of Barrie's genius as his pathos, was intended as amends to a more intelligent and exacting public, but it did not succeed, and Barrie returned to develop his turn for delicate and tender senti-ment in *Quality Street*. The period of the play is thrown back to a time a century or so ago when sentiment was in vogue, and the antique grace of the characters is admira-bly maintained, so that the critics were mollified by this con-cession, and the public was pleased; the simple charm of this elegant trifle was enough to ensure its successful revi-val twenty years later, when sentiment was supposed to be quite out of fashion, but it could not be regarded as in any sense a great play.

The Wedding Guest

Quality Street

Contrary to the newly-established practice of most of his contemporaries, Barrie withheld most of his plays from publication for years after they had successfully estab-lished themselves on the stage. *The Admirable Crichton*, acted in 1902 and immediately hailed as a masterpiece, waited for publication till 1915. The delay was doubtless due to Barrie's feeling that without the setting, the dresses, and the whole life and movement of the stage, the bare text was not sufficient to convey an adequate impression to the reader, and to supply this lack required time. He has sup-plied it in such a way as almost to create a new form of literature—half novel, half drama. His stage directions supply the deficiency with so much skill that a very compe-tent critic, Barrett H. Clark, goes so far as to doubt "whether the imaginative reader loses much by not seeing the plays on the stage." Professor Allardyce Nicoll, on the other hand, condemns this "only too fatally easy de-

The Admirable Crichton

vice" as once more leading the play away from the theatre, and points as an example to a final scene "entirely unsuited for stage performance." The answer to this is that Barrie's plays have been successfully performed before publication, and if by the device of a narrative setting the dramatist can reach a larger audience, it seems a gain rather than a loss, so long as the deftness of the dramatic author is sufficient to leave us a play and not a novel or short story in the shape of a dialogue with occasional interpolations of description and characterization. Barrie's skill in this respect is extraordinary, and he carries over into his narrative setting not only his peculiar whimsical charm, but also the spirit in which the particular play is conceived. Thus, in the printed version of *The Admirable Crichton*, the brief descriptions with which the characters are introduced add point to the satire of the leisured classes which is the main purpose of the play. The Hon. Ernest Woolley, who has just been released from the University of Cambridge without a degree, "is almost a celebrity in restaurants, where he dines frequently, returning to sup, and during this last year he has probably paid as much in them for the privilege of handing his hat to an attendant as the rent of a workingman's flat. He complains brightly that he is hard up, and that if somebody or other at Westminster does not look out, the country will go to the dogs." Similarly: "Young Lord Brocklehurst is nothing save for his rank. You could pick him up by the handful any day in Piccadilly or Holburn, buying socks—or selling them."

According to Harry Furniss, the suggestion of a Radical Peer, who once a month brings the servants' hall up to have tea in the drawing-room, came through stories brought by him from Canada of the attempts made by Lord and Lady Aberdeen, during their occupancy of the

Viceregal seat at Ottawa, to democratize the social customs of Rideau Hall. There were certainly such stories current in Canada at the time, and Furniss was doubtless right in his recollection that he repeated them to Barrie, but Barrie is no doubt equally right in his disavowal of the need of any such prompting and certainly of any intention of a personal reference. Lord Loam is evidently a freak of Barrie's fancy, too altogether foolish to have been taken from life; either when attempting to make a speech in his own drawing-room or playing the concertina in the servants' hall, this fantastic aristocrat is almost never in touch with reality, and when Barrie adds, "He is really the reformed House of Lords which will come some day," it is merely a characteristically cruel whimsy.

The desert island idea is as old as *Robinson Crusoe* and probably older. Ludwig Fulda had used it in 1896 for *Robinson's Eiland*, with which Barrie may—or may not— have been acquainted. In the earlier play we have not a butler, but the private secretary of a Kommerzienrat, (Arnold), who organizes and leads a shipwrecked company of his nominal superiors so well that he is hailed by them the Prince of Robinson's Island. On their return to civilization all fall back into their former ranks and stations, but Arnold is sent out to colonize the Island and Lydia, the Kommerzienrat's niece, goes with him. There are resemblances and differences between the German play and Barrie's, but the earlier treatment is much less humorous and less significant, and it is in the many original and humorous touches with which Barrie has invested an old idea that the excellence of his play consists. The helplessness of the three aristocrats (though it was before the days of Boy Scouts) is perhaps as much exaggerated as the remarkable enterprise and efficiency of the butler Crichton, whose feat of establishing an electric light supply (it is not explained how) is certainly without precedent in previous cast-away romances. But the bitterest satire is reserved for the return to England in Act IV: not only are the real achievements of Crichton consigned to a footnote in the book published about the party's adventures, but the fictitious prowess of Lord Loam and the Hon. Ernest Woolley (especially of the latter, who is the author of the book) are lauded to the skies. They lie through everything, and they lie meanly. Fishing, hunting and exploring are recognized temptations to exaggeration, but when a man not only exaggerates his own exploits, but takes to himself the credit due to another man, whose record he suppresses, all limits of decent conduct, either on a desert island or in London society, are overpassed. The aristocratic characters are represented, not merely as drawing the long bow to excess, but as deliberately lying, cheating, deceiving for their personal advantage, and every tradition of sportsmanship and fair play is cast aside. If this is Barrie's real opinion of the English upper class and of English society as at present organized, it does reveal "a very queer, very unhappy conception of the world and of human nature."

In the ending of the play as first acted, according to the report of A. B. Walkley, Crichton goes off contentedly to marry the underkitchenmaid and keep a public house on the Harrow Road. When the play was revived during the War, the original ending was changed in a way that Walkley recalls in strong terms of indignation:

The Harrow Road "pub" has been dropped out. Crichton glares at his old island subjects, and they cower with reminiscence. He glares at the formidable Lady Brocklehurst, and she, even she, quails. Lady Mary reminds him of the past, and even a *redinte-*

gratio amoris is hinted at. In short, the author "hedges"—
"hedges" against his old irony, that perfect thing. This *is* a
butler, he seems to say, but remember, Oh, please remember, he
was a superman. As though we should forget it!

And Crichton is even made to be wise after the event. He
foresees the late war, and predicts that if England should ever
hear the roll of the drums, then all the Bill Crichtons will get
their chance. With more about England, etc., Crichton, our imperturbable *homme fort,* turned mouthing, sentimental "patriot"!
Good heavens!

In the printed versions of the play (1915 and 1918)
there is no mention of the "pub" in the Harrow Road and
there is no patriotic outburst at the end. "Poor Tweeny"
in both versions is deprived (by a stage direction) of any
expectation of joining Crichton in married bliss as a London landlady, and Crichton's ultimate fate is left in doubt.
In the earlier printed version he is allowed to snub Lady
Mary just before the final curtain; in the later one, he
remains the imperturbable butler to the end, and simply
assures her that he has not lost his courage.

The same low estimate of human nature is suggested in
What Every Woman Knows, but it is combined with fantastic humour and superb deftness in stage handling, which
completely veiled the deeper significance of the play from
delighted and enthusiastic audiences in London and New
York. The opening scene and its setting in the printed
version are a triumph of Barrie's peculiar art. Only Barrie could have conceived or would have ventured to put on
the stage the extravagant figure of a Scotch railway porter
who practises burglary in order to get access to the
unused library belonging to his well-to-do middle-class
neighbours; and when we have been induced by a hundred
clever touches, humorous or pathetic, to accept this situation, the further step of bribing this enterprising youth to

What Every Woman Knows

pledge himself to marry the plain-looking daughter of the house seems almost probable. The subsequent political career of the railway porter (now transformed into a member of Parliament) is less successfully managed. It is a curious fact that the quaint personalities created by Barrie's fancy from his recollections of the humble Scotch families he had known in his youth are far more natural and lifelike than the purely conventional figures introduced by him into the latter part of the play. The stammering Lady Sybil, the French Comtesse, the political whip—sawdust drops out of them at every step; they have neither blood nor brains. Maggie, who has charm without knowing it, but is quite aware of her superior intelligence, was a far more difficult character to create, but she is living, and on the New York stage Maude Adams made her a touching and sympathetic personality. The "Scotchman on the make," endowed only with dogged energy and a complete lack of any sense of humour, seems less human. He lacks not only humour but feeling and intelligence, and (except in the world of fancy to which Barrie's art lends a certain verisimilitude) it is inconceivable that so wooden a hero could have won the affections of both the sensible Maggie and her aristocratic rival. Maggie's device for getting her rival out of the way is all very well on the stage; in real life there are emotional as well as intellectual factors in such a problem which Barrie finds it convenient to ignore. The final suggestion that every man who is high up owes his success mainly to his wife, and that she has to fool him into believing that he has done it all himself is a very pretty bit of sentiment; but the underlying hint that every successful man is in reality a fool and that his wife has to spend most of her energies in preventing him from finding it out is not so flattering to either sex. Maggie certainly

90

deserved all possible credit if she made anything out of Shand, as Barrie has depicted him.

In *The Twelve-Pound Look* this rather cynical view of masculine egotism and absurdity is extended by Barrie from the exceptional cases of a class or an individual to mankind at large. Harry Sims is even more fatuous than John Shand and has none of Shand's redeeming qualities. In the opening sentence of the play as printed the reader is told as directly as possible: "You are to conceive that the scene is laid in your own house, and that Harry Sims is you. . . . It pleases us to make him a city man, but (rather than lose you) he can be turned into a K. C., fashionable doctor, Secretary of State, or what you will." The inevitable inference from the play itself is that only the lack of economic independence keeps the average man's wife at his fireside: if "those machines" really guaranteed freedom from marital tyranny, the average household would break up as soon as the wife made sure that the door to liberty was open. Barrie concludes with an irony almost bitter: "We have a comfortable feeling, you and I, that there is nothing of Harry Sims in us." *The Twelve-Pound Look*

The Will again shows us "a beast of a world." A bright young fellow with a dear pretty wife, "such a happy pair," is shown turned by commercial success from romantic unselfishness to vulgar grasping egotism; the son, after a most expensive education, is "a rotter" who has to be shipped out of the country to escape from a criminal prosecution; the daughter has run away with the chauffeur; the simple little wife becomes an over-dressed, self-seeking, hardhearted woman without a spark of generous feeling; the husband has devoted his whole life to making money and does not know what to do with it. It would be difficult to *The Will* imagine a more appalling picture of success in life as it is ordinarily understood.

Dear Brutus leads to the same grim conclusion. For "dear Brutus" we are to read "dear audience" in the lines:

> The fault, dear Brutus, is not in our stars,
> But in ourselves, that we are underlings.

In Purdie's prose: "It's not Fate. Fate is something outside us. What really plays the dickens with us is something in ourselves. Something that makes us go on doing the same sort of fool things, however many chances we get." The hope of a second chance, which would have made everything different, is a delusion born of human weakness; superior circumstances, a better education, the right mate instead of the wrong one, would have left us the same in ourselves, and that is what counts. This hard, bitter kernel of truth is delivered to us in an attractive covering of humour and pathos, sometimes tenderly sentimental, always imaginative, often whimsical and even fantastic; when the play is seen on the boards, it is quite possible that the fantasy will distract attention from the central truth, and that only an unusually penetrating critic will discern in the significance of a Barrie play, apparently half humorous and the other half sentimental, a *tertium quid* which reveals "a clear cruelty, a strong hint of sneering."

In some of Barrie's plays the playful or pathetic elements are supreme, and the tang of satire is entirely absent. His masterpieces in this kind are *Peter Pan*, *A Kiss for Cinderella*, and *The Old Lady Shows Her Medals*, and they are deservedly popular, though they have induced continental and American critics to describe Barrie as "simply a purveyor of maudlin sentimentality"; even Bernard Shaw, in spite of his general appreciation of Barrie's genius, has sometimes deplored his flight from the solid ground of everyday experience to the thin clouds of whimsy. With notable exceptions (A. B. Walkley in England and William Lyon Phelps in America) the critics have been less kind to Barrie than the public. Barrie has many gifts, and he succeeds sometimes by dint of one, sometimes of another, in his best plays by a well-balanced combination of very various ingredients. In *Shall We Join the Ladies?* he succeeds by sheer cleverness of stage handling, laying aside all his other powers with the exception of an occasional stroke of satirical humour. His usual method of treatment is one of extreme delicacy, and there is always the danger of falling over into mawkishness or grotesque exaggeration; at his worst he is terrible and dismays even his most cordial admirers. For perhaps one-third of the plays he has put on the stage, one must implore the kindly hand of oblivion, and he has shown a becoming modesty in refusing to give to most of these the permanence of print. At his best he is unique, and his peculiar charm will probably always hold a certain public. The critics may continue to discuss whether his satire is deliberately intended or merely incidental to a view of life essentially playful and even superficial; the public will be content to accept his humour and pathos without inquiring too closely as to his ultimate purposes. In the heart of the average theatre-goer, whose mind is not troubled by subtleties, Barrie's place is secure.

PLAY LIST

1891 *Richard Savage* (with H. B. Marriot-Watson).
    Becky Sharp.
    Ibsen's Ghost.
1892 *Walker, London.*
1893 *Jane Annie* (with Conan Doyle).
1894 *The Professor's Love-Story.*
1897 *The Little Minister.*
1900 *The Wedding Guest.*
1902 *Quality Street.*
    The Admirable Crichton.
1903 *Little Mary.*
1904 *Peter Pan.*
1905 *Alice-Sit-by-the-Fire.*
    Pantaloon.
1906 *Josephine.*
    Punch.
1908 *What Every Woman Knows.*
1910 *The Twelve-Pound Look.*
    A Slice of Life.
    Old Friends.
1912 *Rosalind.*
1913 *The Legend of Leonora.*
    The Will.
    Half an Hour.
1914 *Der Tag.*
1915 *The New Word.*
    Rosy Rapture.
    The Fatal Typist.
1916 *A Kiss for Cinderella.*
1917 *The Old Lady Shows Her Medals.*
    Dear Brutus.
1918 *Barbara's Wedding.*
    A Well-Remembered Voice.
1920 *Mary Rose.*
    The Truth about the Russian Dancers.
1922 *Shall We Join the Ladies?*

CHAPTER V

JOHN GALSWORTHY (1867-   )

GALSWORTHY, like Barrie, had established his position as a successful novelist before he attempted to make a place for himself on the stage, and he had none of Barrie's early dramatic experiments and failures. Fortunate in his birth (he was the son of a leading London lawyer) and in his education (at Harrow and Oxford, followed by a year's travel), he was fortunate also in the moment at which he arrived at dramatic production. The pioneer work by Jones and Pinero, Shaw and Barrie, had been done, and the new movement was in the swing of a full tide. Granville-Barker was managing the Royal Court Theatre in London, and it was here that Galsworthy's first play, *The Silver Box*, had its original production with a *The Silver* more than competent company (Norman McKinnel as *Box* Jones, and Irene Rooke as Mrs. Jones) on September 25, 1906. Galsworthy acknowledged his indebtedness to Barker by dedicating to him the volume containing his earliest plays, and more than paid the debt by the services he was able to render to the modern British drama. Preeminently English (he was born in Surrey, not in Dublin or Kirriemuir), he was able to bring to the drama a firsthand acquaintance with the upper half of English society and the detachment springing from a superior social position, combined with a gentleness and refinement, partly natural, partly the result of education and association with gentlepeople. He has none of Shaw's ardent socialistic propagandism on the one hand nor of Barrie's whimsically humourous view of the lights and shadows of humble life on the other. To Galsworthy the plight of the poor is not humorous; it is pathetic, and his pathos is at times dangerously near to sentimentality, from which he is saved only by his keen and resolute insight and his artistic sense of balance and proportion. There is no more genuine exponent of the modern humanitarian desire that the best possible should be done for the waifs and strays of modern industrialism, but he sees limits to the possibilities. No one realizes more profoundly the inadequacy of modern social organization, but in his view the people who seem to control the vast machine are as much the victims of social forces as the more obvious sufferers. He does not romanticize his vagabonds beyond recognition or represent the working-man as the incarnation of all the virtues or the capitalist as a hard-hearted tyrant. He shows us society as it is, with an extra touch of sympathetic understanding for the under dog. The submerged classes, and the submerged sex (as it still existed in England at the beginning of the century) evoked from him a degree of passionate resentment which in a less balanced mind would have warped the judgment, but he was constantly on the watch to see that the other side got fair play. He has no villains and few heroes— just ordinary human beings such as one may meet every day, pushed this way or that by economic necessity, or traditional feeling, or class or national prejudice. No other dramatist has given us as unbiassed and complete a picture of England as it was before the War and after; and as, in addition to being a careful and sensitive observer, he was also a delicate and subtle artist, the pictures of English life he has drawn (in his plays as well as in his novels) have an abiding value beyond the time and place by which they were conditioned.

At the outset of his dramatic career, Galsworthy made up his mind quite definitely as to what he wanted to do on and with the stage. Secure in the possession of private means and a good income from his already successful novels, he was saved from the pressure of commercial necessity, and as a conscientious artist, more than usually free from personal ambition—during the War he served quite unassumingly as a masseur in a French hospital—he was able not only to work quietly and slowly, but to carry out, through good fortune and bad, the dramatic design he had set before himself. He outlined his dramatic programme as early as 1909 in a *Fortnightly Review* article which, with characteristic modesty, he entitled "Some Platitudes concerning Drama." The article was afterwards included in the volume of essays called *The Inn of Tranquillity;* it has taken its place among the significant pronouncements of the purposes of the modern drama and is, of course, especially interesting as a revelation of Galsworthy's own aims and methods. A short examination of this essay and of his principal plays will show that though he has made advances in technique, he has adhered with singular fidelity to the design he originally proposed to himself.

In a few trenchant sentences at the opening of the essay Galsworthy sets forth his view of the purpose of any serious drama: "A drama must be shaped so as to have a spire of meaning. Every grouping of life and character has its inherent moral; and the business of the dramatist is so to pose the group as to bring that moral poignantly to the light of day." By this moral he does not mean "the triumph at all costs of a supposed immediate ethical good over a supposed immediate ethical evil"—far from it. This

"A spire of meaning"

practice has been the most common and successful device of the popular dramatist in the past, and its ordinary procedure is to present to the public, by a distortion of plot and character, the views and prejudices which the public has already accepted. Another course, demanding much more originality and skill, is that of Bernard Shaw— though Galsworthy is careful not to mention him by name —that is, to present to the public those views and codes of life in which the dramatist himself believes, the more effectively if they are the opposite of what the public wants. The third course, that which Galsworthy regards as his own ideal, is "to set before the public no cut-and-dried codes, but the phenomena of life and character, selected and combined, *but not distorted*, by the dramatist's outlook, set down without fear, favour or prejudice, leaving the public to draw such poor moral as nature may afford." This is the hardest of the three methods suggested, for it requires a certain detachment, sympathy with things for their own sake, and the far view. For this subtle and delicate appeal to the moral and artistic sensibilities of the public, Galsworthy was peculiarly qualified by nature, circumstances, and education. His inclination to see both sides of a question, his love of humanity, his eagerness to understand and appreciate people with temperaments and views alien to his own, the skill in psychological analysis he had already acquired as a novelist, his sympathy for the downtrodden and the outcast—all these found scope and natural expression in the type of drama here outlined. It must not be didactic; it must not be propagandist; but it must have *a spire of meaning* which will develop itself as naturally from the drama as a spire completes the structure of a Gothic church. The public must get this meaning, not through a coarse melodramatic opposition of vil-

lain and hero, not through any intellectual argument, but
through emotional sympathy with characters presented in
such a way as to appeal to the spectator's sense of truth
and experience of life. This being the case, it is not surprising to find that Galsworthy despises the constructed
plot—stakes, whether of facts or ideas, on which the unfortunate characters are impaled; just as he despises dialogue
when it is used by the dramatist merely as a device to enun-
ciate his own ideas. He says indeed in so many words:
"Take care of character; action and dialogue will take care
of themselves." The drama must be like a tree springing
from a seedling of thought, and taking a shape which will
be gracious in its rounded and balanced proportions.

In view of Galsworthy's sympathy with the humble poor *The Silver*
and his eagerness to find beauty where it is not ordinarily *Box*
looked for, it is not surprising that his first dramatic hero
and heroine should be a drunken member of the unem-
ployed (apparently also unemployable) and a charwoman
of less than ordinary moral fibre. These poor creatures
are set against the power of organized institutions—especially the power of the law—and their struggle ends in
inevitable disaster. Whether it was the result of his short
experience as a briefless barrister, or the even shorter experience he has recounted in his essays as a grand juryman,
or his study of Anatole France, who in a very different
mood has shown the outcast in his vain conflicts with the
majesty of the law—Galsworthy has in many of his writ-
ings—novel, essay or drama—shown a tender-minded regard for those who fail to adapt themselves to the stern
demands of a society based upon mechanical production.
There is very little to be said for Jones as Galsworthy has
depicted him—a mouthing idler, with weak wits and weaker
morals. He can be made to shine only by contrast with

the companion picture of the equally worthless young waster whose faults are condoned because of his respectable and wealthy father. Mrs. Jones is a more moving figure because of a certain submissive helplessness which makes a direct appeal to our sense of pity. The satire on the upper middle-class household by which she is employed is severe without being bitter, and is saved from extravagance by its humanity. They are all poor weak creatures following the line of least resistance, as their passions or prejudices or material circumstances may direct—not one of them has a real will of his own. Yet out of this unpromising material Galsworthy has made a play of deep emotional power. No one is guilty of any particular villainy—merely of a weak yielding to temptation or little acts of meanness, perfectly familiar to ordinary experience. But at the end we are left with an overpowering sense of the inequalities of modern life and of the inadequacy of our social machinery to deal, one need not say sympathetically, but justly, with the miserable specimens of humanity it has produced.

Just a year after *The Silver Box* Galsworthy produced *Joy* what he called "a play on the letter *I*" and entitled *Joy*, from the name of the principal character. It is a study in human egotism—rather a dramatic exercise done in a moment of reaction or depression than a viable play—and its characters have so little vitality that they fail to interest; they have no grip on the imagination, for their struggle is with middle-class conventions and their own petty passions—not with the grim facts of modern life. Galsworthy was well advised in returning to his first field and dealing boldly with one of those bitter industrial struggles in which the interests and passions of men come into acute *Strife* conflict. There is no love interest in *Strife;* the characters are too busy fighting. Galsworthy's sympathy is evidently with the losers, but he does justice to the stern determination and convinced sincerity of the leaders on both sides. David Roberts, a fiery Welshman, is a vivid incarnation of the spirit of revolt, a fanatical agitator who is willing to sacrifice everything for his cause. Set against him is old John Anthony, equally uncompromising, equally convinced of the justice of his own view: Capitalism, involving personal control by the strongest and most capable, is a necessity for the future of English industry, and yielding to the demands of labour means ultimately involving masters and men in common ruin. In the end both are beaten by economic forces—the fear of starvation on the men's side, the fear of financial loss on the part of the directors. Neither side wins a complete victory; the common sense of the moderates prevails to secure the acceptance of the terms proposed by them before the winter-long struggle, with its suffering, loss, and bitter feeling, began. The element of reason in such class conflicts, Galsworthy would have us see, is slight; they are the outcome of men's passions and prejudices, hopes and fears.

In 1907 Galsworthy had published a novel, *The Country House*, dealing with the county society as he saw it, and after *Strife* was produced he wrote a play, *The Eldest Son*, dealing with the same theme and taking over some of the same characters; this play waited three years for production and was not particularly successful on the stage. In the meantime, Galsworthy had returned to his original dramatic field and subject—the misadventures of the humble poor in their encounters with the terrors of the law. *Justice* made a great impression and effected some mitigation of the severities of the English penal system at which it seemed to be especially directed. Undoubtedly the prison scene was and is the most powerful scene of the play, but

Justice

Galsworthy's intentions went deeper than any reform of the details of criminal administration. In answer to an American friend who pointed out to him that the play was not in accordance with conditions in the United States—although as a matter of fact it has been recently revived in New York with conspicuous success—Galsworthy wrote:

Human nature is the same the world over. The machinery, the setting, through which this story of the dispensation of justice is presented may be peculiar to Britain, but the essential features, the usual blind disproportion of the whole business, the departmentalism, the self-preservative attitude of society, and the emotions at work are the same in whatever white man's country you choose to take. The play is a picture of the human herd's attitude toward an offending member—heads down, horns pointed—and of its blind trampling of him out. A picture painted in facts—as all written pictures must be—facts that happen to be English, but which might just as well have been American, or Austrian, or Dutch. If you do not look through them to what lies behind, you have missed the gist and meaning of the play. "Justice" is a machine that, when some one has once given it the starting push, rolls on of itself. . . .

You may not, in America, give vent to your self-preservative herd instinct in similar trial procedure, in solitary confinement, in tickets of leave; but you do in other ways—when once some one has given the starting push. Your institutions may be different from ours, may be more enlightened—I know not; but your human nature is the same. The great majority of you will stand shoulder to shoulder against erring members of your community, just as we do here. . . .

Inevitable and right, you say. So be it! I would merely draw your attention to the disproportionate result which generally ensues.

In this way I have set down the main truth as I see it; cleared my conscience of a bit of vision. If you in America do not think it true because your rules of evidence are not the same, your Judges less formal, your cells more open, and your uniforms a different colour, I am sorry; because those things to me seem mere surface differences. But if, divested of its superficial trappings—the trappings with which an Englishman whose deliberately chosen method is that of actuality must necessarily clothe the story—if, seen naked, seen to the heart, the play still seems to you untrue, that will mean a difference of vision, not between an Englishman and Americans, but between one human being and others; and each will hold to his own, as men ever must, without regret.

The immediate practical details of judicial administration to which Galsworthy drew attention were indeed two: the unfairness of the English divorce law to the poor (since to some extent remedied), and the excessive severity of the convict and ticket of leave system (since mitigated in part in consequence of the impression made by the play at the time of its production on the mind of Winston Churchill, who was then Home Secretary). His more profound purpose was to induce us to contemplate the needless cruelties committed under the impulse of the "herd spirit" to those individuals who from weakness or some personal idiosyncracy do not fit into the standardized and almost mechanical requirements of our social and industrial system. He continued to illustrate this general theme in *The Pigeon,* *The Pigeon* again borrowing from an earlier novel, *The Island Pharisees,* two characters—Ferrand, the French tramp, who is taken over under the same name, and Wellwyn, the sensitive and sympathetic, tender-minded artist, who comes nearer, perhaps, than any other of Galsworthy's creations to presenting us with a humorously exaggerated portrait of the dramatist himself. In the conversations between Wellwyn and Ferrand—chiefly in the latter's vagabond philosophy—we get the most direct expression of Galsworthy's view of what should be done with these misfits in modern life. The magistrate, the professional philanthropist, the clergyman "waste their time trying to make rooks white. Be kind to us if you will, or let us alone, but do not try to change our skins. Leave us to live, or leave us to die when we like in the free air. . . . If I am criminal, dangerous—shut me up! I would not pity myself, nevare. . . . But we in whom something moves—like that flame, Monsieur, that cannot keep still—we others—we are not many—that must have motion in our lives, do not let them make us prisoners, with their theories, because we are not like them—it is life itself they would enclose!"

During the next half-dozen years—including the four-year period of the War—Galsworthy produced no drama of any great significance, with the possible exception of *The Mob*, which was put on at the Gaiety Theatre, Manchester, and the Coronet Theatre, London, in the Spring of 1914, and was revived in New York some ten years later, when the aftermath of the War seemed to make it timely. It refers apparently to the Boer War, though there is no specific mention of any war in particular, and is a study of the herd spirit as applied to political life in a time of national excitement. Its hero sacrifices everything to be steadfast to his ideal, and at the end of the play dies under the knife of one of the mob which has invaded his chambers; the final curtain reveals his statue erected in a sunny square by a nation conscious too late of the nobility of his character. It was a fine conception, but its dramatic development lacks the deft handling and spirited movement characteristic of Galsworthy's best work.

The Mob [margin note]

It was not until *The Skin Game* was put on the London boards in 1920 that Galsworthy's admirers felt that he had recovered his old power. He had picked up the phrase during a recent visit to the United States, and perhaps does not use the term in the American sense in which it is ordinarily accepted, for there is no suggestion of fraud in the

The Skin Game [margin note]

social duel which the Hillcrists and the Hornblowers fight out to the bitter end; but it is a striking and expressive title, and no doubt helped the remarkable success of the play on both sides of the Atlantic. Its theme is the class spirit as illustrated by the struggle between a southern county family and a pushing northern manufacturer fighting for social recognition and the fulfilment of his commercial and political ambitions; in the end he is completely defeated by the aristocrats, but only at the cost of violating every principle of consideration and decency. The old father's pride in his position and his ancestral home is embittered by the thought of what has been paid to preserve them: "When we began this fight, we had clean hands—are they clean now? What's gentility worth if it can't stand fire?"

In *The Skin Game* Galsworthy had a good title and a good subject, and he drove home his point by the skill and tact of his stage handling. This was equally true of *Loyalties*, the theme of which was perhaps suggested to him *Loyalties* by the much-discussed saying of Edith Cavell, "Patriotism is not enough." In Galsworthy's view loyalty to one's own race or nation or family or class or profession or club or regiment, good as it may be in its restricted sphere, is not a sufficient guide for the complex affairs of life. "Keeps faith!" says one of the characters at the end of the play. "We've all done that. It's not enough." Perhaps in this play, as in *The Skin Game*, Galsworthy gave fuller recognition to the importance of the element of action, for the interest in the plot begins with the rise of the curtain and is continued, through many incidents, to the very end, but the intrigue arises naturally from the characters, who are all vividly realized and admirably chosen to illustrate the dramatist's main theme. There was some discussion as to the choice of one of the Jewish race for the leading rôle, but one does not see how otherwise Galsworthy could so well have made his point clear; it is De Levis's racial peculiarities—not unduly emphasized—which prevent him from obtaining fair treatment at the hands of his opponents, whose eyes are blinded by convention and class prejudice. Even the old General, who is the soul of honour, keeps back the telling fact that he discovered that Dancy's coat sleeve was wet immediately after the robbery had been committed. The question of Dancy's guilt or innocence becomes, in fact, a class struggle, in which sympathies and prejudices take the place of reason, and the interests of institutions stand higher than the interests of justice or humanity. As Galsworthy said of one of his earlier dramas, "The play is a picture of the human herd's attitude toward an offending member—heads down, horns pointed." In the set into which De Levis has been foolish enough to push himself, everybody is antagonistic to him, from his aristocratic host down to the butler and the police. It is true that he continually offends against the unwritten code of the set and is personally an unsympathetic character; but it is absurd to treat the play, as some foolish people suggested, as in itself an example of anti-Semitic prejudice. Its tone and purport are, indeed, entirely in the opposite direction; the Jewish population of New York showed their recognition of the fact by attending the performances of *Loyalties* in large numbers and showing cordial appreciation of the dramatist's tact and fairmindedness in dealing with an issue that required very delicate handling in order to avoid just cause of offence.

In this review of Galsworthy's dramatic work, attention has been given to the plays which seem most significant and most likely to hold the stage. He is not always at his best, and sometimes the very difficult conception of dramatic art he has set before himself fails of fulfilment in his hands. He is a very competent dramatic craftsman, and when, as in *Old English*, he puts himself to the task of creating a *Old English* character which will be effective on the stage when interpreted by a veteran actor (Norman McKinnel in London and George Arliss in New York), he can do the trick with consummate skill and tact; the hero of *Old English* is an unscrupulous old buccaneer, with whom, offhand, Galsworthy might be expected to have little sympathy, and the drama has no moral significance; but as a character study it was eminently successful, although as a play it did not satisfy the critics. More often, however, when Galsworthy fails to reach his own high standard of dramatic excellence, it is because of the difficulty of combining his vision of truth—the gist and meaning of the play—with the picture of it painted in facts; for while Galsworthy is essentially a moral philosopher, he is also an artist, and his deliberately chosen method is that of actuality. These "superficial trappings which must necessarily clothe the story" sometimes get in the way and obscure the meaning Galsworthy wishes to convey. The critics, for instance, have failed to discover any clear intention in *Windows*. St. John *Windows* Ervine begins his analysis with the remark: "This play completely baffles me." A. B. Walkley writes:

What precisely is the moral of *Windows* we cannot pretend to say—unless it be the old one that there is, after all, a great deal of human nature in men and women. But Mr. Galsworthy likes to put even the oldest of morals in a new way; he sees everything on its ethical side, but he sees it under a special angle and in a strange light. In the end, by changing the "values," he leaves us a little disconcerted.

The Forest The same confusion resulted when *The Forest* was put on the stage, though the reviewers, with the printed play before them, were able to interpret the theme as "power— men's lust for power and men's abuse of power." In the case of *The Show*, obviously aimed at the cruelty of modern newspaper publicity when it drags into the limelight matters essentially private, the ultimate responsibility was shown to rest upon the morbid curiosity of the public—a weakness of human nature—but the facts presented were of such an unusual kind as to give an air of special pleading to a sound criticism of sensational journalism; a secondary protest against the loose method of accepting evidence in the English inquest, to which attention had been directed by a recent case, as of too restricted interest to give the play the human power of appeal revealed in *Justice.* Such plays as *The Fugitive*, *The Mob*, and *The Show* seem to indicate that Galsworthy is not at his strongest in dealing with special cases of faulty institutions or administration. He is at his best when, as in the plays that have been more fully discussed above, he dives deep down to the springs of human nature, and uses the familiar facts of modern life to suggest their own lesson.

Escape A special interest attaches to *Escape* because Galsworthy before the performance declared that it would be his last play, as he felt inclined to give his whole attention to novel writing. There seems no reason why a dramatist should not share the stage right to a number of "farewells," and one hopes that Galsworthy will change his mind, for this "last" play certainly shows no falling off in power of invention or stagecraft. It is not a great work in point of construction—indeed the author has himself described it as "episodic"—and some of the critics thought it lacking in the "spire of meaning" characteristic of Galsworthy's theory and practice. It deals, however, significantly enough, with the author's favourite theme of the clash between the individual and modern machinery for the administration of justice. A war hero, Captain Matt Denant, falls into conversation in Hyde Park with a girl who is there for professional purposes and who is promptly arrested by a detective set on duty there to put a stop to "accosting." Denant, who was on the point of leaving her, protests that he was neither "accosted" nor molested, and attempts to prevent the arrest. The detective, somewhat truculent in his demeanour, threatens to take Denant too, and an altercation ensues, developing into a physical encounter, in the course of which Denant gives the detective a blow under the chin. The detective falls against the railing and injures his head. Denant finds his heart is no longer beating and sends the girl off with his hat for water. He himself waits by the body and is arrested there by the police, for whom the detective had previously blown his whistle. This completes the prologue of the play, and the remaining action consists of nine episodes. In the first we see Denant picking potatoes on the prison farm at Dartmoor in a fog, having passed a year of the five years' penal servitude to which he has been condemned for manslaughter. He is driven to despair by the monotony and tyranny of prison life, and tells his fellow convict that he is determined to take advantage of the fog to escape; the other convict warns him that no one has ever succeeded in escaping from Dartmoor, but gives him a crust of bread to help him on his way, and as the curtain is falling we see Denant clambering over the farm wall. The next episode shows us the warders searching for Denant in the darkness and almost capturing him—but not quite. He hides for over a day and succeeds in secreting himself under a bed in the neighbouring inn. The young married lady under whose bed he hides knows about his case and after some hesitation lends him a razor, gives him chocolate, a flask of whisky and money, and tells him where he will find her husband's mackintosh, hat and fishing-rod in the hall; he gets clear away to the moor, and is spending the daylight hours fishing in the river when an old gentleman—a retired judge—recognizes him, but after half an hour's conversation with him on prison discipline and the like sends him off with a cigar and good wishes. Denant's next encounter is with a picnic party—the day has cleared up; they are unsympathetic to the escaped convict, and after purloining some bread from them he runs off with their automobile. This increases the heat of the pursuit, and he hides in a gravel pit, where he is trapped by the farmer and his farm labourers and gets away only by the skin of his teeth. The pursuers are on his heels, and he takes refuge with two ladies who are at tea. One is for giving him up, but the strong-minded sporting sister hands him tea, hides him behind a curtain, and tries to put the police off the track. They are soon back, however, and Denant runs to the vestry of the church to claim sanctuary of the young rector. The rector has been in the war and is sympathetic, but his sympathies are divided between his natural humanity and his fear of destroying his influence with his flock; as the rector is being questioned and driven into a position in which he must lie to save Denant, who is hiding in the robe-cupboard, the convict steps out and gives himself up to save the rector's conscience.

Throughout Denant behaves like a sportsman and a gentleman, always willing to sacrifice himself if he is involving his protectors in too great a risk, and the interest of the play, which is keenly sustained, depends not so much on the question of whether he will get away or not as upon the attitude taken toward him by the very different people with whom he comes into contact and the various motives which induce them to help him or to side with his pursuers. The sympathy of the London audience was undoubtedly with the pursued, and some of them applauded vigorously when one or another of Denant's helpers lied promptly and courageously to assist him in getting away. The emotional appeal of the play—and it is by their emotions rather than their intelligence that people lead their lives—makes it clear that in general the common feeling of humanity is far more merciful and far more just than the law. The people who helped Denant to escape were the "nice" people—the people of education and refinement—the people who refused help or joined in the pursuit were the uneducated or narrow-minded who were guided more by convention or prejudice than by humanity and the "sporting spirit." At the first performance a lady in the gallery at the end of the play protested from her seat against "sloppy sentiment about murders," chiefly on the ground, apparently, that her grandfather had been murdered in Ireland, but her protest received no support from the audience or from the critics. Denant is not a murderer in any case, not even an ordinary criminal, and the help given him in his attempt to escape received the enthusiastic approval of the vast majority of the audience. No doubt, if he had been a different sort of convict, people would have behaved differently; but this distinction, which is made by the best representatives of our civilization and is not made, or not sufficiently made, by the law, is exactly the point that Galsworthy wished to bring to the light.

In these plays he has made a distinct addition to the permanent resources of English drama. Institutions pass, and the plays which criticize or satirize them lose all but historical interest; the fundamental weaknesses of human nature change little, and it is here that Galsworthy has found his true field. He has not the originality or the puritanic zeal of Shaw; but he has more balance and greater artistic power. Both have quite unusual dramatic skill, and though no one can anticipate the verdict of posterity, it is hard to see upon what other names the future appreciation of the revival of British drama in this century can rest.

JOHN GALSWORTHY

PLAY LIST

1906 *The Silver Box.*
1907 *Joy.*
1909 *Strife.*
1910 *Justice.*
1911 *The Little Dream.*
1912 *The Pigeon.*
    The Eldest Son, (wr. 1909).
1913 *The Fugitive.*
1914 *The Mob.*
    Hall-Marked.
1915 *A Bit o' Love.*
    The Little Man, (wr. 1913).
1917 *The Foundations.*
1920 *The Skin Game.*
    Defeat.
1921 *The First and the Last.*
    The Sun.
    Punch and Go.
1922 *Loyalties.*
    Windows.
1924 *The Forest.*
    Old English.
1925 *The Show.*
1926 *Escape.*

CHAPTER VI

HARLEY GRANVILLE-BARKER (1877-   )

AMONG the younger contemporaries of Shaw and Galsworthy who brought their talents to the development of the modern theatre, the first place must be given to Granville-Barker. Influenced to some extent by both, more especially by Shaw, he maintained his intellectual independence and created a form of drama which is thoroughly individual, alike in its excellences and its limitations. Born in London of an Italian mother, he took early to the stage and had a careful training with the Ben Greet Company and Mrs. Patrick Campbell. As actor, producer and author, he was associated with the earlier and more significant years of the Stage Society, which was founded in 1898 to give performances on Sunday evenings of plays not likely to find acceptance in the commercial theatres, and which is still an active element in English drama; he assisted in the production of several Shaw plays and one *The* *Marrying* of his own, *The Marrying of Ann Leete*. By 1904 he had *of Ann* *Leete* made himself sufficiently distinguished as a producer to join with a well-known manager, J. E. Vedrenne, in the Royal Court Theatre, which in three seasons gave over seven hundred performances of Shaw plays, introduced Galsworthy to the London stage in *The Silver Box*, and put on what is perhaps Granville-Barker's best play, *The Voysey Inheritance*, as well as a charming version of the Pierrot story, *Prunella*, in which he collaborated with Laurence Housman and himself acted the principal part. After a series of successful productions the management was transferred to the larger and more fashionable Savoy Theatre in the Strand, but this proved too ambitious an enterprise for the intellectual theatre in repertory and it had to be abandoned. Granville-Barker made another effort as manager for Charles Frohman in repertory at the Duke of York's Theatre, but this season also was a commercial failure, though it was distinguished by the production of Galsworthy's *Justice* and of Granville-Barker's *Madras House*, which has since been successfully revived both in New York and London. Convinced that a small theatre was necessary for the successful production of intellectual drama, Granville-Barker declined the invitation of a powerful financial group in New York to accept the management of the New Theatre (now the Century Theatre) on the ground that the auditorium was too large; and subsequent experience of this venture justified his decision. For about ten years before and during the War Granville-Barker was engaged on a series of high-class productions in London and New York, which he managed with brilliant success. Both as a designer of artistic settings and as a trainer and leader of young actors, he proved himself the possessor of extraordinary talents. He was able to bring out the best in his company and to give presentations of plays ranging all through the history of the drama from Euripides to Anatole France, which were more than satisfactory to the mind, the ear, and the eye, and constitute an important chapter in the annals of dramatic production.

It might be thought that this long stage training and intimate acquaintance with dramatic production would have shown Granville-Barker the importance of making

his plays "good theatre," but while experience of the stage
led both Shaw and Galsworthy to pay greater heed to dramatic effectiveness, the more successful Granville-Barker
was in producing the works of other men, the more obstacles he seemed to place in his own way as a dramatic
author. Without Shaw's brilliant wit or Galsworthy's emotional sympathy, he emphasized his natural tendency to
over-intellectualize his dramas until they were beyond the
understanding of an ordinary audience. William Archer,
whom no one would accuse of a lack of intelligence or defi-
cient dramatic insight, has left us in *The Old Drama and
the New* (1923) an amusing account of his inability to
appreciate Granville-Barker's earlier work and his subse-
The quent conversion at the production of *The Voysey Inheri-*
Voysey
Inheritance *tance* in 1905. The passage is worth quotation in full:

> I have known Mr. Barker for several years, and he had done
> me the honour of submitting to me in manuscript three or four
> of his youthful efforts. I saw in them a queer sort of originality,
> but I laboured under the disadvantage of being wholly unable to
> make head or tail of them. At last, tired of writing plays which
> were Hebrew to me, he declared he would write one down to my
> intelligence; and the result was *The Marrying of Ann Leete.*
> He succeeded in a sense; it was written in a language not wholly
> unfamiliar to me; but the characters depicted, and the reasons
> for their sayings and doings, remained utterly enigmatic. Pro-
> duced by the Stage Society, the play was highly praised in many
> quarters. It has been published and may be known to some of
> you. If you like it, your state is the more gracious, and I am
> the more obtuse; but candour compels me to own that, after re-
> peated attempts, I have not yet acquired a taste for it. Being a
> man of the most long-suffering temper, Mr. Barker, more than
> once, asked me whether I would like to read his next play, which
> lay for a year or two in manuscript before it was produced. I
> always answered, "Where is the use? I certainly shouldn't under-
> stand it, and should merely act as a wet blanket to it." Therefore,

when the curtain went up on *The Voysey Inheritance* that November afternoon, I had not the least idea what was in store for me.

Imagine my delight, then, when I found myself from the first interested and absorbed; when I found that I understood almost every word, one or two supersubtleties excepted; and when, at the end, I realized that here was a great play, a play conceived and composed with original mastery, and presenting on its spacious canvas a greater wealth of observation, character and essential drama than was to be found in any other play of our time. The high opinion of Mr. Barker's talent which I there and then conceived was more than confirmed when *Waste* was produced in 1907 and *The Madras House* in 1910. I do not hesitate to say that I consider these three plays the biggest things our modern movement has produced.

Archer's impression of *The Marrying of Ann Leete* is a common experience, and his enthusiasm about *The Voysey Inheritance*, though it leads him in his reaction from his previous state of confusion to some exaggeration of terms, is not without justification: it is a fine play, with a subject originally conceived and clearly worked out through characters, exceptional indeed, but not beyond the bounds of human experience, abounding in vitality and full of interest. *The Madras House* carries further the satire of the tyranny, the hypocrisy, and the boredom of the Happy English Home as it survived in the middle class at the beginning of this century, and of the sterile and meaningless existence to which it condemned its womankind. The picture of the six Miss Huxtables, as like to each other as "one lead pencil and another, as these lie upon one's table after some six weeks' use," is not exaggerated beyond the legitimate limits of satire; such things were, within the memory of the older generation; and the living-in system, with its enforced celibacy, was a worthy subject for Gran

The Madras House

ville-Barker's ironical humour. But the American capitalist in Act III is a sheer impossibility and quite unconvincing, much less life-like than the London merchant who becomes a Mohammedan and goes off to Mesopotamia (where he establishes a harem) in order to escape the intolerable allurements of feminine society in the English metropolis. Act IV peters out in a long conversation which fails to hold the attention of a London or New York audience even when chosen from the intellectuals, and the play does not so much end as lose itself in the sands of inconclusive talk. It is true, as one of the characters suggests, that for the whole thirty-six hours of the action the author has been "perambulating the Woman Question," passing from the dowdy virginity of Denmark Hill to Peckham and Miss Yates. But the perambulation of so large a question is not enough in itself to hold a drama together, and although perhaps redeemed by its many masterly touches of characterization and dialogue, the play as a whole seems ineffective, in spite of the fact that it still holds the stage.

Waste

Waste was refused public performance by the Censor, on account of its incidental reference to an illegal operation in the course of the plot, and had to be put off with a semiprivate production by the Stage Society. It is a powerful drama, dealing with the subject of the relations of private life to public usefulness, which had been brought to the front by the ruin of the political careers of Parnell and Sir Charles Dilke through their appearance in the Divorce Court. The author shows amazing intellectual versatility in the projection of an imaginary political situation and the discussion of the hypothetical political issues upon which the success of the hero depends until his life is broken by the consequences of an evening's folly with a weak woman. Trebell is a fine character and the tragic theme is adequately sustained, but the general effect is intellectual rather than emotional, and while the play leaves the reader with a vast respect for the abilities of the author, it does not stir the depths of one's being as do the great tragedies with which it is not unworthy to be compared.

Granville-Barker has done other things; his paraphrase of Schnitzler's *Anatol* is a model of what such a transference from a foreign stage ought to be. He has written three one-act plays, and a book on the production of intellectual drama entitled *The Exemplary Theatre*. But, in spite of or perhaps because of, these varied activities, his most ardent admirers cannot but feel that he has failed to get out the best that is in him. His last play *The Secret Life* has not yet been put on the stage, and when it was published in 1923, the reasons were only too evident. W. A. Darlington, of the London *Daily Telegraph*, thus describes the experience of an intelligent reader during its perusal:

The Secret Life

A new play from Mr. Harley Granville-Barker's pen is an event. When *The Secret Life* came into my hands I experienced a little thrill of anticipation, and sat down at once and read the play through—and made of it neither head nor tail. This, of course, is a manner of speaking; I understood it well enough to realize that I had been introduced to a group of brilliantly drawn characters—characters who were worth the meticulous care and the depth of imagination that had gone to their fashioning; but I felt, as Mr. William Archer confesses that he still feels when reading *The Marrying of Ann Leete,* that the reasons for the sayings and doings of the characters were utterly enigmatic. I was, however, not without hope that a second reading might shed light in the dark places; and when a fortnight later I sat down to the play again, I found to my joy and relief that this was so. In the light of my previous knowledge of the characters, the whole composition became—I will not say as clear as daylight, but clear enough to restore my confidence in my own ability to understand English. The second reading, with the wider comprehension it has brought me, confirms and deepens the impression made rather vaguely by the first—that here we have a piece of work right above and beyond the scope of most of our leading playwrights, but a piece of work so devoid of the fundamental stage virtue of clarity that I can hardly imagine that it could be successfully produced in the theatre except before an audience of people, who, like me, had read the text through carefully twice before the curtain rose.

Clarity is a fundamental stage virtue, and a play which needs to be read over twice, carefully, before the audience can follow it in the theatre cannot be said to have attained its object. Undoubtedly gifted with high intellectual powers of keen observation of life and the creation of human characters of great interest, Granville-Barker seems likely to have in drama the fate that has befallen George Meredith in fiction—to be highly spoken of but little known by direct contact. It must not be forgotten, however, that in both cases these authors gave a decided intellectual impetus to the forms of literary art to which they devoted their lives.

GRANVILLE-BARKER

PLAY LIST

1902 *The Marrying of Ann Leete.*
1904 *Prunella* (with Laurence Housman).
1905 *The Voysey Inheritance.*
1907 *Waste.*
1910 *The Madras House.*
1911 *Anatol* (Paraphrase from Arthur Schnitzler).
1923 *The Secret Life.*

CHAPTER VII

ST. JOHN HANKIN (1860-1909)

ST. JOHN EMILE CLAVERING HANKIN, born at Southampton and educated at Malvern and Merton College, Oxford, was a successful London journalist, writing for the *Times* and *Punch*, before he became known as a dramatist. His earlier plays were produced at the Court Theatre by Granville-Barker, with whom he shares the anti-sentimental, realistic, satirical tendency of the new movement, due doubtless to the influence of Bernard Shaw. There is a Shavian tang even in the title of his first published volume, *Three Plays with Happy Endings* (1907). The endings are in a sense "happy," that is, the curtain comes down on the best solution possible for the persons most concerned, but the solution is not a happy one in any ideal or conventional sense. All three end in the frustration of marriages that would have been ill-advised and unfortunate, and the frustration is a negative kind of happiness—no doubt preferable to the positive unhappiness which would result in the case of thousands of marriages arranged by the conventional dramatist to bring his comedy to a conventional close.

The Return of the Prodigal   *The Return of the Prodigal* is throughout a satire on English middle-class ideals of social success. The prodigal son returns from his enforced exile in Australia to find his brother on the point of contracting a successful marriage and his father a candidate for the local seat in Parliament. The ne'er-do-well, being naturally more attractive and romantic than his stay-at-home brother, has a fair chance of cutting him out with the charming Stella, and his mere presence in the neighbourhood, if he is not respectably provided for, will be enough to endanger his father's election. He uses these facts to extort a moderate provision—an allowance of £250 a year paid quarterly—and goes off content. This, the author of the play contends, is a happy ending—certainly happy for the prodigal son, and for the father who has produced him, happy in the sense that he gets rid of an intolerable incubus at a reasonably cheap rate.

It is a situation which was used by Lennox Robinson with more richly humorous effect in *The Whiteheaded Boy* (1916). Hankin is, however, so eager to score intellectually at the expense of his conventional squires and business men, their wives and daughters, that he does not allow them to be entirely human. Thus, in *The Return of the Prodigal*, Lady Faringford says: "I don't like this pernicious modern jargon about shopkeepers and gentlefolk being much the same. There's far too much truth in it to be agreeable." As an epigram, this might pass, though it is hardly a likely saying for a woman of Lady Faringford's character and position, but Hankin is not content to leave it at that. In answer to Stella's challenge, "If it's true, why shouldn't we say it?" Lady Faringford is made to continue:

Because we have everything to lose by doing so. We were born into this world with what is called position. Owing to that position we are received everywhere, flattered, made much of. Though we are poor, rich people are eager to invite us to their houses and marry our daughters. So much the better for us. But if we began telling people that position was all moonshine, family an antiquated superstition, and many duchesses far less like ladies than their maids, the world would ultimately discover that what we were saying was perfectly true. Whereupon we should lose the very comfortable niche in the Social system which we at present enjoy, and—who knows?—might actually be reduced in the end to doing something useful for our living like other people.

It is obvious that even if Lady Faringford admitted all this so clearly to herself, she would not put it in this bald fashion to her unsophisticated and rather sentimental daughter. It is not indeed Lady Faringford herself, as the person she is imagined to be, speaking at all; it is the author who is merely using her as an outlet for his vein of social satire.

The **Charity** *that* **Began** *at* **Home** *The Charity that Began at Home* is less happy in conception and less successful in execution. Lady Denison, whose passion for philanthropy is directed by her spiritual adviser, Basil Hylton, the apostle of the Church of Humanity, has carried out his principles of kindness to disagreeable people by inviting to her country house a set of impossibles—Hylton himself in the first place; General Bonsor, an intolerable bore; Mrs. Horrocks, an assertive vulgarian, who claims to be descended from Orosius; Miss Triggs, a stranded German governess; Mr. Firket, a business failure; and Hugh Verreker, who has been forced to resign his commission on account of helping himself out of the regimental mess money. She manages her household on the same plan, engaging servants dismissed for dishonesty, carelessness, or worse. The result is naturally confusion, and the climax is reached when Verreker proposes to and is accepted by her daughter Margery, who, recognizing his weakness, is prepared to marry him in the hope of "preventing him from falling into bad hands." "The only real way of helping people is to love them. And if one loves people of course one should marry them." After a week's engagement Verreker saves the situation by asking to be let off; he still loves Margery, but on every other ground he sees they are quite unfitted for each other. "Surely," Margery pleads, "love is enough." "No. It isn't," Verreker retorts. "Marriage isn't a thing to be romantic about. It *lasts* too long. My dear, it may last forty years. . . . Now what sort of a life should we make of it together if we married, you and I? Why, my dear, we've not an idea or a taste in common. Everything you say makes me laugh, and everything I think would make you blush. It's simply absurd for a girl like you to marry a fellow like me. Let's say so frankly and end it."

Verreker ends, however, by advising Margery to marry the unspeakable Hylton; the dramatist had tried hard to make him human and sincere, but has only succeeded in manufacturing an impossible compound of prig and fool. Of all the impossibles he is the worst—a mere man of straw necessary for the promotion of the central idea of the comedy. Hankin can have known very few philanthropic ladies or their spiritual guides if he supposed they were really so absolutely lacking in common sense and common humanity as they are here represented.

The Cassilis Engagement presents a problem with which Hankin was probably more familiar. What is a mother to do if her only son engages himself to a girl entirely unsuitable in birth, education, and character? Evidently opposition will only unite the young people closer and Mrs. Cassilis takes the one course which promises any hope of effecting a separation; she invites the girl and her awful mother to stay in her house and meet the county society. The girl is bored to death, and in the end so exasperated that she breaks off the match. Mrs. Cassilis has a difficult

The Cassilis Engagement

hand to play, but she plays it with astounding skill and determination. "Marry her! Nonsense, my dear Margaret," she says to her sister as the curtain falls on Act I, but she succeeds in getting her way only by descending to depths of duplicity which are appalling. She is full of affectionate consideration for the intolerable Ethel and her still more intolerable mother, but it is merely a way of luring them into one pitfall after another until her son is completely disgusted and genuinely relieved to be released from his engagement. He marries a girl of his own class and neighbourhood "to the delight of their respective mothers and of the whole county, and unless they break their necks in the hunting field, nothing seems likely to interrupt the even tenor of their happiness." Ethel netted an aged lord and worried him into his grave in six months, "so that she also ended happily."

It is no wonder that "cynical" is the adjective by which Hankin's attitude to life as expressed in his plays is commonly described. Ethel and her mother are sheer adventuresses, and this to some extent excuses the hypocrisy of Mrs. Cassilis, who is as hard as nails underneath her constant display of feline affection for her victims; the son is a complete nincompoop, and does not know, even at the end, how his matrimonial designs have been outwitted by his astute mother; she remains to him simply the sweetest and the best of women. It is a hard and repellent view of human life that is presented to us. In all three plays there is not a single character which might be described as really sympathetic. Those that come nearest to it are the two wastrels—the hero of *The Return of the Prodigal* and Verreker in *The Charity that Began at Home*—and they are both lacking in the elements of common honesty.

Hankin's only other play of any importance, *The Last of the De Mullins*, loses something of this cynical tone, and gains accordingly in solidity and naturalness if not in brilliance.   Janet de Mullin, some nine years before the opening of the play, has borne a child to a young officer with whom she fell in love but apparently could not marry. Driven from home, she assumes a fictitious widowhood and makes a success of a hatshop in London.   Recalled to the parental roof by her father's severe illness, she finds the young officer in the neighbourhood, engaged to marry another girl.   Her father, after the manner of the old general in *Magda*, insists that Janet shall marry him in order to give her child a father, but Janet, first quietly and then passionately, refuses.   Like the other modern heroines in a similar position, she is not ashamed of what she has done:

> Ashamed?   Ashamed of wanting to have a child?   What on earth were women created for, Aunt Harriet, if not to have children?
>
> MRS. CLOUSTON.   To marry and have children.
>
> JANET (*with relentless logic*).   My dear Aunt Harriet, women had children thousands of years before marriage was invented.   I dare say they will go on doing so thousands of years after it has ceased to exist.
>
> MRS. DE MULLIN.   Janet!
>
> JANET.   Well, mother, that's how I feel.   And I believe it's how all wholesome women feel if they would only acknowledge it.   I *wanted* to have a child.   I always did from the time when I got too old to play with dolls.   Not an adopted child or a child of· some one else's, but a baby of my very own.   Of course I wanted to marry.   That's the ordinary way a woman wants to be a mother nowadays, I suppose.   But time went on and nobody came forward, and I saw myself getting old and my chance slipping away.   Then I met

127

—never mind. And I fell in love with him. Or perhaps I only fell in love with love. I don't know. It was so splendid to find some one at last who really cared for me as women should be cared for! Not to talk to because I was clever or to play tennis with because I was strong, but to kiss me and to make love to me! Yes! To make love to me!

DE MULLIN (*solemnly*). Listen to me, my girl. You say that now, and I dare say you believe it. But when you are older, when Johnny is grown up, you will bitterly repent having brought into the world a child who can call no man father.

JANET (*passionately*). Never. Never! That I'm sure of. Whatever happens, even if Johnny should come to hate me for what I did, I shall always be glad to have been his mother. At least I shall have lived. These poor women who go through life listless and dull, who have never felt the joys and the pains a mother feels, how they would envy me if they knew! If they knew! To know that a child is your very own, is a part of you. That you have faced sickness and pain and death itself for it. That it is yours, and nothing can take it from you because no one can understand is wants as you do. To feel its soft breath on your cheek, to soothe it when it is fretful and still it when it cries, that is motherhood and that is glorious!

Hankin's Method

In this passage, one of the last he wrote before his breakdown and suicide, Hankin attained a power of emotional expression that is missing from his earlier work. He was always a competent and conscientious craftsman, and one feels constantly a vigorous and lively intelligence at play behind his craftsmanship. His method of work was outlined by himself as follows: "I select an episode in the life of one of my characters or of a group of characters, when something of importance to their future has to be decided, and I ring up my curtain. Having shown how it was decided and why it was so decided, I ring it down again." His plays give one the impression that they were built on a central idea rather than on a character or situation, but they are well built and made a noteworthy contribution to the development of play-making at a critical point in the history of the modern English drama. His plays have not held the stage, and he has perhaps had less than his due meed of critical appreciation; there is a certain "dryness" about his humour which puts some people off. But he continues to be read, and his intelligence and wit, in combination with his skill in construction and the naturalness of his dialogue (in spite of an occasional indulgence in satirical exaggeration) seem likely to ensure his place in modern dramatic history.

ST. JOHN HANKIN

PLAY LIST

1905 *The Return of the Prodigal.*
1906 *The Charity that Began at Home.*
1907 *The Cassilis Engagement.*
1908 *The Last of the De Mullins.*

CHAPTER VIII

THE IRISH DRAMA AND J. M. SYNGE (1871-1909)

NOTHING could be more Irish than the story of the Irish drama. It began in 1892 with the publication by W. B. Yeats of his lyric drama, *The Countess Cathleen*, and the production in 1894 at the Avenue Theatre, London, of another lyric drama of his, *The Land of Heart's Desire*. Yet in the latter year W. P. Ryan, the first historian of the Irish Literary Revival, could write in absolute good faith, "The real Irish drama is a thing unknown." Yeats, however, was not to be easily discouraged, and in 1898 he and Lady Gregory together laid plans for the foundation of an Irish Literary Theatre. The first step was to invite an English company over to Dublin to give performances of *The Countess Cathleen* and of Edward Martyn's *The Heather Field*. The enterprise was brought off in the Spring of 1899, not without tribulations with the English actors and some hostility in Dublin to *The Countess Cathleen* on religious grounds, but with sufficient success to warrant a repetition of the experiment the following year. In the meantime the promoters had, in an unguarded hour, enlisted the co-operation of George Moore, who had already a considerable literary reputation on the score of half-a-dozen successful novels. Moore was brought over to Ireland to write an Irish drama in collaboration with Yeats on Lady Gregory's estate, and has left an amusing account of their first consultation. Yeats opened the conference with the remark, "The first act of

George
Moore

every good play is horizontal, the second perpendicular."
"And the third, I suppose, circular," was Moore's retort,
and Yeats agreed. Moore apparently thought it best to
seek a way of escape by suggesting that he would prefer
to write his part of the play in French; but this suggestion
also was accepted by Yeats, who added: "Lady Gregory
will translate your text into English. Taidgh O'Donohue
will translate the English text into Irish, and Lady Gregory will translate the Irish text back into English." Moore
is not perhaps the most credible of witnesses, but he pro-
duces a scene in French as proof of the truth of his story;
otherwise, he says, no one would believe "that two such literary lunatics as Yeats and myself existed contemporane-
ously, and in Ireland, too, a country not distinguished for
its love of letters." Moore, in accordance with his scheme,
betook himself to France in search of a suitable atmosphere
for composition, and though he succeeded in convincing
himself that he was the Messiah of the Irish literary movement, his main contribution took the form of the autobiography which astonished and delighted the world under the
title of *Hail and Farewell*.

Yeats completed *Diarmuid and Grania* alone, and it was
produced by English actors at Dublin in 1901; at the same
time a play in Gaelic written by Dr. Douglas Hyde was
produced by members of the Gaelic League. It was during
the rehearsals of the latter play that the idea occurred to
the brothers Fay of forming an amateur Irish dramatic
company for the production of native plays in English.
The upshot was the organization of the Irish National
Theatre Society with W. B. Yeats as president and W. G.
Fay as stage manager. They began in 1902 with George
Russell's *Deirdre* and Yeats's *Cathleen ni Houlihan*, a short
prose play, symbolic and patriotic, which afterwards be-

The brothers Fay

came one of the most acceptable offerings of the Irish Company and is perhaps Yeats's most permanent contribution to Irish dramatic literature.

Yeats was and continued to be untiring in his devotion to the cause, sparing no effort to set the new enterprise on its feet. Lady Gregory was equally tireless in her devotion, and was always ready to produce one of her light and amusing comedies of Irish life at need. But the real stroke of good fortune was the discovery by Yeats in a Parisian attic in 1899 of John Millington Synge, an unknown Irishman who brought to the enterprise the gift of genius. His earliest plays had already been performed by the Irish National Theatre Society in Dublin when Miss Horniman helped the Society to acquire the Abbey Theatre —the old Mechanics Institute on Abbey Street, made over and refitted—and gave it a small annual subsidy which justified the promoters in boasting of it as the first endowed theatre in the English-speaking world. Synge's first play, *In the Shadow of the Glen*, was part of the bill on the opening night, December 27, 1904, and was revived at the celebration of the twenty-first anniversary at the end of 1925 after being performed many times by the Company, not only in Dublin but in the leading cities of Great Britain, Canada, and the United States. It was undoubtedly the development of Synge's genius that changed the Irish drama from an enterprise of merely local or national interest into a contribution to the drama of the world.

In the Shadow of the Glen

In view of Yeats's remarkable lyrical gift, it is not surprising that he should regard it as the principal aim of the undertaking "to get our heroic age into verse" and that in a programme he drew up with Lady Gregory in 1899 he should insist on the need for "beautiful and appropriate language." In the hands of Synge, the Irish drama took

133

a different shape and found a different medium. Yeats himself contributed to the new direction Synge's genius was to follow by persuading him to give up his pursuit of French literature and sending him off to the Aran Isles to renew his acquaintance with the Irish peasant; Synge had previously studied Erse, but had allowed his knowledge of the language to grow rusty. On the Aran Isles, however, Synge made up his mind that the Celtic myths so dear to Yeats were too far away from life; he found inspiration in the fishers, farmers, innkeepers, beggars, tinkers and topers of the islands, the lives they lived and the tales they told of their own lives, not of legendary gods and heroes— as he himself puts it, "anecdotes—not folk tales." It was old Pat Dirane, the story-teller of Inishmaan who told as a personal experience the incidents which constitute the plot of Synge's first play, *In the Shadow of the Glen*, though it is really an old story and Synge exercised characteristic independence in his use of it. The germ of the next play, *Riders to the Sea*, is to be found in a note Synge made as to the finding of the body of a drowned fisherman and the following comment he wrote at that time: "The loss of one man seems a slight catastrophe to all except the immediate relatives. Often when an accident happens a father is lost with his two eldest sons, or in some other way all the active men of a household die together." Again, the use Synge has made of the incident is his own. The story of *The Tinker's Wedding*, which Synge first wrote at the same time that he was working on the two plays just mentioned, though he afterwards rewrote it, he had from the lips of a herd he met at a Wicklow fair. The plot of *The Well of the Saints* has been traced back to a fifteenth-century French *mystère*, but Synge is careful to connect it with a tradition he came across in Aranmor of the old church of

Riders to the Sea

The Tinker's Wedding

Ceathair Aluinn (The Four Beautiful Persons) and a holy well near it that is famous for cures of blindness. *The Playboy of the Western World* also goes back to a story often told him by the oldest inhabitant of Inishmaan about a Connaught man who killed his father with the blow of a spade when he was in a passion and then fled to this island and threw himself on the mercy of the natives, who in spite of the offer of a reward hid him from the police for weeks until they could ship him safely to America. Synge's comment in his book, *The Aran Islands*, is as follows:

The Playboy of the Western World

> This impulse to protect the criminal is universal in the west. It seems partly due to the association between justice and the hated English jurisdiction, but more directly to the primitive feeling of these people, who are never criminals yet always capable of crime, that a man will not do wrong unless he is under the influence of a passion which is as irresponsible as a storm of the sea. If a man has killed his father, and is already sick and broken with remorse, they can see no reason why he should be dragged away and killed by the law.

The use made by Synge of the suggestion was humorous, and it is interesting to note in the same play that the author took over not only general ideas, but scraps of conversation which he turned to account in the dialogue. Old Mourteen of Aranmor, thinking that it was time Synge was getting married, said to him:

> "Listen to what I'm telling you: a man who is not married is no better than an old jackass. He goes into his sister's house, and into his brother's house; he eats a bit in this place and a bit in another place, but he has no home for himself; like an old jackass straying on the rocks."

This is transferred to a speech by Michael Flaherty (*Playboy*, Act III) in a slightly condensed form:

"What's a single man, I ask you, eating a bit in one house and drinking a sup in another, and he with no place of his own, like an old braying jackass strayed upon the rocks?"

The Anglo-Irish idiom Synge says in the preface to *The Playboy* that in this, as in his other plays, "I have used one or two words only that I have not heard among the country people of Ireland, or spoken in my own nursery before I could read the newspapers. A certain number of the phrases I employ I have heard also from herds and fishermen along the coast from Kerry to Mayo, or from beggar-women and ballad-singers near Dublin; and I am glad to acknowledge how much I owe to the folk imagination of these fine people." The Anglo-Irish idiom was not discovered, much less invented by Synge—Dr. Douglas Hyde and Lady Gregory had used it before him in their renderings of old Irish literature—and in its main peculiarities it is a genuine folk speech in which Gaelic locutions are substituted for current English, and some older English words and usages, gone out of fashion in modern English, are retained; as Yeats puts it, it is "the beautiful English which has grown up in Irish-speaking districts, and takes its vocabulary from the time of Malory and of the translators of the Bible, but its idiom and its vivid metaphor from Irish." Yeats showed a generous enthusiasm when his desire for "beautiful and appropriate language" was fulfilled by Synge, though not in the way Yeats had expected or intended. Yeats agrees that "perhaps no Irish countryman had ever that exact rhythm in his voice," and insists on Synge's genuine originality in the use of the newly discovered literary medium: "He made his own selection of word and phrase, choosing what would express his own personality; above all, he had word and phrase dance to a very strange rhythm"—a rhythm, it may be added, that others since Synge have striven to reproduce, but never with the same effect of mysterious beauty and natural music.

Synge felt, no doubt rightly, that his use of this idiom was something more than a trick of speech. He says that "in countries where the imagination of the people, and the language they use, is rich and living, it is possible for a writer to be rich and copious in his words, and at the same time to give the reality, which is the root of all poetry, in a comprehensive and natural form." It seems to him that modern literature is divided between the artificial styles of Mallarmé and Huysmans on the one hand, and on the other the drabness of Ibsen and Zola, "dealing with the reality of life in joyless and pallid words." Two thin seemed to him essential to the modern drama—"reality and "joy." It was the combination of these two things that he sought. "In a good play every speech should be as fully flavoured as a nut or apple, and such speeches cannot be written by anyone who works among people who have shut their lips on poetry." Only by the combination of poetry with reality can the drama give "the nourishment, not very easy to define, on which our imaginations live." Only in its infancy or decay is the drama didactic; "the drama, like the symphony, does not teach or prove anything."

St. John Ervine remarks that whatever influence was exercised over the minds of young Irish dramatists was exercised not by George Moore or Yeats or "A. E." but by Synge; and he thinks it was a destructive force, "since it was the influence of a sick and bitter man." Sick indeed Synge was during the period in which his plays were written, but his unfailing humour contradicts the accusation of bitterness. He was not haunted, as so many of the Celts and Latins are, by the fear of death; it was the fear of old age which is the constant terror of his characters. It is

this fear that possesses the mind of Nora, the heroine of
The Shadow of the Glen; it is the torment of Mary and
Martin Doul in *The Well of the Saints;* it is this fear
which drives Deirdre and Naisi to death. There is no evidence that Synge failed to face life courageously and cheer-
fully; the evidence of his plays and of those who knew him

A master
of irony

well is all the other way. He was a master of irony, and
he was a pagan; there was a pagan side in the Aran Islanders that appealed to him, and he had little sympathy with
their Christian beliefs, which he doubtless regarded as
mere superstitions. The Catholic clergy are presented by
him in his plays with a touch of humorous contempt,
whether it is the wandering Friar of *The Well of the
Saints* or the priest who is so unceremoniously dealt with in
The Tinker's Wedding, or Father Reilly of *The Playboy,*
backed up by the Lord Bishop of Connaught, "the Holy
Father and the Cardinals of Rome." A Protestant by
birth and education, Synge during his residence in France
had acquired a detachment from the ordinary religious beliefs, which was as far as possible removed from the primitive faith of the Aran Islanders or the bigotry of some of
the larger Irish centres. Yeats gives us a curious instance
of this detachment from current religious and political
prejudices in Synge's response to a suggestion from the
Abbey Theatre Company that he should write a play on
the Rebellion of '98. "After a fortnight he brought them
a scenario which read like a chapter out of Rabelais. Two
women, a Protestant and a Catholic, take refuge in a cave,
and there quarrel about religion, abusing the Pope or
Queen Elizabeth and Henry VIII, but in low voices; for
the one fears to be ravished by the soldiers, the other by
the rebels. At last one woman goes out because she would
sooner accept any fate than such wicked company." Synge

lived at Dublin a life apart from everything except the Abbey Theatre, "as it were in a ship at sea," and Yeats says that during their long and intimate acquaintance in Dublin Synge never spoke of politics or said anything that implied any sort of nationalist conviction. This curious detachment of the self-contained artist explains some of the difficulties that arose between him and his fellow countrymen when his plays were first produced on the Dublin stage. During the first performances of his first play, *In the Shadow of the Glen*, considerable resentment was shown at the author's choice of a truant Irish wife as a heroine. As Professor Morgan put it, Synge "had dared to lay hands on the morality of the Irish peasant woman whom nationalist Ireland preserved as sacrosanct in a case of rose-tinted glass." In fact, Synge had deliberately changed the ending of the original story, in which the old husband, having feigned death in order to entrap the wife he suspects of infidelity, gets up to give her and her lover a thrashing, and the resentment of the audience, unless it was, as Professor Nicoll suggests, merely political, indicates a lack of appreciation of the change of view and emphasis shown, not merely by the different ending of the play, but by Synge's whole conception of Nora's character. Nora is not so much a faithless wife as a magnificent creature aspiring for some colour and outlet in life beyond the shadows of the mist-shrouded glen in which she is immured. She is one of the most sympathetic examples of the rebellious woman of the modern drama, and Synge, who has endowed her with a fine sense of poetry and romance, was probably quite oblivious of the storm his impersonation of the longing for something beyond was likely to arouse. Nor is there indeed any just cause for offence. The incident—it is little more—is treated humorously from beginning to end, and what is distinctive of Nora is not her lack of loyalty to her old curmudgeon of a husband but her courage and elevation of spirit. In her final speech she reveals in a single sentence that sense of poetry and of realities which was characteristic of Synge's own mind: "I'm thinking it's myself will be wheezing that time with lying down under the Heavens when the night is cold; but you've a fine bit of talk, stranger, and it's with yourself I'll go." The manner of her exit is as significant as that of the more famous Nora of Ibsen,—the dramatist whom Synge disliked.

It was no doubt considerations of prudence that withheld from performance *The Tinker's Wedding* with its rollicking humour, mainly at the expense of the Catholic clergy and the sacrament of marriage; but *The Playboy* at its first performance, not only in Dublin but in New York and Philadelphia, met with strenuous disapproval, the offence being not so much the condonation of murder, but the mention by Pegeen of the word "shift" and the implication that a respectable Irish publican's daughter would not object to being left alone in the house at night with a man to whom she was not married. The demonstrations had the effect of advertising the play and bringing Synge's work more prominently before the public. It has, on this account, attained a fame which it probably deserves on account of its larger canvas and greater variety, though in absolute mastery of artistic form and detail it hardly comes up to the gemlike perfection of Synge's first two plays. Synge never surpassed the concentrated humour of *The Shadow of the Glen* or the intense pathos of *Riders to the Sea*, culminating in the characteristic restraint of the last sentence:

"Michael has a clean burial in the far north, by the grace of the Almighty God. Bartley will have a fine coffin out of the white boards, and a deep grave surely. What more can we want than that? No man at all can be living for ever, and we must be satisfied."

There is perhaps a wider and deeper appeal in some of the speeches of Deirdre, but this last play of Synge's had not the advantage of his final revision, and as a whole *Deirdre of the Sorrows* has not, either in language or characterization, the power over his material which distinguishes his earlier work.

Deirdre of the Sorrows

At the time of his death Synge was meditating a Dublin slum drama which would have taken him into a field brilliantly occupied more than a dozen years later by Sean O'Casey. What his success might have been when separated from the Irish peasantry who appealed so strongly to his affectionate admiration, it is hard to say. When Yeats found him in Paris, he had nothing to show, after prolonged study of Continental literature, "but one or two poems and impressionistic essays, full of that kind of morbidity that has its roots in too much brooding over methods of expression and ways of looking at life, which come, not out of life, but out of literature, images reflected from mirror to mirror." Yeats's call to the Aran Isles and later to the Abbey Theatre gave Synge a new subject and a fresh interest, half-a-dozen years of glorious creation, the love of one of the most charming of the Irish players—and death from cancer before he was forty. It was a fate one of his own heroes might have chosen, if the end could have been foreseen as clearly as Deirdre sees the inevitable doom to which she conducts her lover and herself: "It's a pitiful thing . . . yet a thing will be a joy and a triumph to the ends of life and time."

J. M. SYNGE

PLAY LIST

1903 *In the Shadow of the Glen.*
1904 *Riders to the Sea.*
1905 *The Well of the Saints.*
1907 *The Playboy of the Western World.*
1908 *The Tinker's Wedding,* (pub. 1907).
1910 *Deirdre of the Sorrows.*

CHAPTER IX

ST. JOHN GREER ERVINE (1883-   )

THERE is general agreement that after the death of Synge the Irish drama fell into decay. Andrew A. Malone, writing in *The Nineteenth Century and After* (April, 1926), says the Abbey Theatre made its reputation during the first ten years and "very little of consequence has been done since. . . . At present the supply of Irish plays would seem to have almost ceased, and the Abbey Theatre is given over to revivals of Goldsmith, Ibsen, and Shaw." He suggests, it is true, that a new era of brilliance may be about to dawn with the advent of Sean O'Casey, and excuses the dearth of the preceding decade by the turmoil through which Ireland passed from the great Dublin strike of 1913 to the civil warfare of 1923. Ernest Boyd, revising in 1922 his admirable history of *Ireland's Literary Renaissance*, expresses the same opinion: "Ireland finds herself in literature and politics back in the era of Davis and Mangan." "A. E." (George Russell) lamented that Irish dramatists, instead of holding the mirror up to nature, reflected only decadence. St. John Ervine in 1923 thought the collapse of the Irish Dramatic Renaissance was complete, and quoted the lines of Yeats:

> Romantic Ireland's dead and gone,
> It's with O'Leary in the grave.

Ervine himself laid aside the Irish subjects with which he had begun his dramatic career, and after managing the

Abbey Theatre in 1916, fighting in the Great War, and visiting the United States, settled down in London as a dramatic critic. There have been attempts to question his claim to be an Irish playwright at all, though he says himself, "I am as Irish in my origins and emotions as any man," adding that for more than three hundred years his forefathers on both sides were born and bred and buried in County Down. Ervine's disqualification in the eyes of his nationalist antagonists was, of course, that he came of Ulster Protestant stock, and began his career as dramatic critic of the *Daily Citizen* in Belfast, where he was born and educated. "I came," he says, "from a family which mitigated its Presbyterian piety with a wicked love for the theatre. . . . I was not permitted to play any game on Sunday or to read secular books or to go out of doors, except to church and for restrained walks, but I was allowed to choose which of the stories in the Bible I would read. I always chose the story of Samson pulling the Temple down about the ears of the Philistines." Wider experience enabled Ervine to detach himself considerably from his Philistine environment, and when he was manager of the Abbey Theatre during the rebellion of 1916, according to his own account he spent hours on his knees praying hard that it would be blown to pieces either by the British or by the Sinn Feiners.

With the compensation we would get from the British government (whoever destroyed it) we could then build a bigger and handsomer theatre. But Heaven did not heed me. A gunboat knocked down most of the buildings round it, but did not break even a pane of glass in the Abbey. When I went down for the first time after the Rebellion to see the theatre, I found ruins everywhere, except in the Abbey. There it stood, unshattered, although nearly the whole of the houses on the other side of the street were level with the pavement; and when I saw how poor was the gunnery of the Navy, and how ineffectual the fire of the Sinn Feiners, I swore deeply and loudly that I had no respect either for the one or the other.

Ervine succeeded in scoring off Protestantism in both Ulster and England by making the leading character of his one-act play, *The Magnanimous Lover*, go from his North Irish village to Liverpool and add North of England smugness to his native bigotry; he used also as a dramatic motive the refusal of a girl to be made respectable by marriage to a former lover for whom she had no longer any respect—a situation already made use of by St. John Hankin in *The Last of the De Mullins*, and to be used again by Stanley Houghton in *Hindle Wakes*. At the time he wrote it Ervine thought *The Magnanimous Lover* was a wonderful play, but later he had doubts about it, and was inclined to share the view of the critics that his dramatic career really began with *Mixed Marriage*, which was put on the stage before *The Magnanimous Lover*, though written after it. This time we see the tragic consequences of religious bigotry in Ulster as illustrated by the refusal of a stern Presbyterian father to allow his son to marry a Catholic girl; the issues are complicated—as happens often enough in Belfast—by an industrial dispute, and in the riot that follows, the girl is killed by a volley from the soldiers sent out to quell the disturbance; the father whose action has helped to intensify sectarian bitterness says at the end of the play, "A was riht. A know A was riht," but his gentle wife, who knows better, comforts him with the compassionate words, "Aw, my poor man, my poor man." The tragedy is powerfully constructed with sympathetic characters clearly drawn; in spite of his stubbornness and highhandedness, the old father is felt to be not so much to

The Magnanimous Lover

Mixed Marriage

blame as the unbending dogmatism in which he has been brought up.

Jane Clegg   In his next play, *Jane Clegg*, Ervine turned from the grim tragedy of Ulster factions to the sordid realities of lower-middle-class life in England. It is a singularly unattractive household presented for our acquaintance—such, no doubt as could be found by the score in any large manufacturing town. The husband is an "absolute rotter" who steals his employer's money in order to run away with a girl he has got into trouble; he is a persistent and reckless liar whose clumsy fabrications fall to pieces almost as soon as he has uttered them. He has been spoiled by his foolish, querulous old mother, who now spoils his two noisy, squabbling young children as she has spoiled him, and nags at her daughter-in-law as she has formerly nagged at her late husband. A wretched "bookie" to whom the husband owes money and a colourless clerk from the employer's office complete the list of characters. The wife is the only one who shows any deviation from absolute commonplace; she has a quiet reserved strength—and a small legacy—which enable her, when her husband is driven to admit the truth, to pay up his defalcations and gambling debts and send him off to Canada with his "fancy woman." She is left saddled with the old grandmother and the two young children, but she gets rid of a most undesirable husband at an expenditure of £165, and it is cheap at the price. The treatment is steadily photographic—the uncompromising application of the "slice of life" theory; there could hardly be a more complete example of Synge's biting phrase—"dealing with the reality of life in joyless and pallid words." Thus, when the clerk Morrison comes to Clegg's house to recover the stolen money, the following conversation takes place:

MORRISON.	It's a nice night, isn't it?
CLEGG.	Yes, I thought we were going to have some rain, but it's kept fine.
MORRISON.	Yes, we don't want any more rain just yet, do we?
MRS. CLEGG.	There's been a lot of rain lately. I expect it's good for some people, farmers and people like that. I must say I don't like it. I always get the rheumatism that bad.
MORRISON.	They do say that a man that's had his leg cut off can always tell when it's going to rain.
MRS. CLEGG.	Indeed!
MORRISON.	Yes. He gets a funny feeling in the stump—sort of pins and needles.
CLEGG.	That's funny, that is. You'd wonder why that was.
MRS. CLEGG.	I expect it 'as a meaning, if we on'y knoo it. There's nothink without a meanin'. I've always said that, an' I believe it.
JANE CLEGG.	Hadn't we better settle Mr. Morrison's business, Henry? I expect he is anxious to get away.
MORRISON.	Oh, I'm in no hurry, Mrs. Clegg! . . .

Many other examples might be quoted of dialogue which has no significance beyond that of emphasizing the dreary, drab monotony of Jane Clegg's whole existence. There is not, as there is in the similar empty phrases of banal conversation in *The Madras House*, a comic effect which relieves the sense of utter boredom, for in *Jane Clegg* there is not a spark of humour from beginning to end. It is odd that Ervine should speak of Synge's plays as noteworthy for "a queer kind of bitter beauty and a joyless sort of characterization—essentially the work of a sick man." There is no beauty and no joy in *Jane Clegg*—merely the faithful presentation of commonplace ugliness. Even Jane Clegg herself, though she shines by contrast with her wretched surroundings, is raised above them only by somewhat superior intelligence and character. Her plaint is that of every aspiring woman of the lower middle class: "I never see anything or go anywhere. I have to cook and wash and nurse and mend and teach"—and her husband repays her by unfaithfulness. Perhaps this was precisely what Ervine wished to make us see—that there are thousands of superior women in uncongenial surroundings, unappreciated and deceived by worthless husbands, incapable for economic reasons of escaping from a position that is odious to them, for it is only the lucky chance of the legacy that permits Jane Clegg to show her husband the door; she had previously passed through a similar experience with him, but then, being without money, she was helpless. Certain it is that the play made a great impression, both in London and New York, and had a long and successful run; the critics, including Ervine himself, were greatly pleased by its deft craftsmanship.

John Ferguson

Ervine thought his next play, *John Ferguson,* though perhaps inferior in construction to *Jane Clegg,* was deeper in feeling. He said to an American interviewer at the time of his visit to New York in 1920: "I am interested first and foremost in human beings, and I try to see them as they are and to find out why they do things. A man like John Ferguson, who contends with things bigger than himself, but who has a faith, knows why he has it and sticks to it in spite of everything, is a man worth studying." The play is assuredly a much more moving one than *Jane Clegg.* It contains some melodramatic elements, but John Ferguson is a finely conceived example of that stern religious faith to which an Ulster man can cling in spite of the bitterest trials. Deprived of his farm, his daughter dishonoured, his son on the way to the gallows for avenging his sister's shame, John Ferguson does not abandon his trust in the God of his fathers, and the play ends with his acceptance of divine judgment as a punishment for some unknown transgression; as the last curtain falls, we see him sitting with his wife at family worship, with his Bible on his knees.

John Ferguson seems to mark the height of Ervine's dramatic achievement. One doubts whether anything he wrote for the stage is as good as his novels, *Mrs. Martin's Man* and *Changing Winds*. He has done good service as a lively —even pugnacious—dramatic critic, and has written other plays in addition to those mentioned above. Of these the most serious is *The Ship*, a somewhat melodramatic treatment of the romance of the shipbuilding business, which is the chief industry of Belfast. *Mary, Mary, Quite Contrary* is a farce, and the critics were divided as to whether it was really funny or not; one of them describes it as "a singularly unfunny play." *The Lady of Belmont* is an ambitious attempt to write a sequel to *The Merchant of Venice*. Shylock has become a Christian (for business purposes only); Bassanio is carrying on an intrigue with Jessica; Gratiano has taken to drink, and the play ends with Shylock and Portia placidly discussing together the future of the Jewish race. Shylock says: "We are a proud and narrow race, and our proud and narrow minds have ruined us. I have the power to govern men. Here in my breast I feel the power to govern men. My heart stirs when I think of generous government and of kindly races striving, each with each, for greater love and beauty and finer men and women. But I'm condemned, because I am a Jew, to be a usurer and spend my mind on little furtive schemes for making money." Portia retorts: "You have no roots. Your race is shallow in its growth. . . . You were a nomad race in Israel, shifting like your own sand; and you're still a nomad race, rootless, unstable, blown by self-interest round the world, with no place that's your own. There is no hope for Jews, Shylock, till they have learned to share the lot of all of us, to live and, if there be need, to die for some poor soil they call their native land."

If modern realism could do no better than this, most readers would prefer Elizabethan romantic comedy. Ervine has still, one hopes, many years of dramatic activity before him, and may do better things than anything he has yet done, but so far it seems likely that his reputation as a dramatist will stand or fall with *Jane Clegg* and *John Ferguson*. The former is an excellent example of twentieth-century realism, pushed to its utmost limit of depression; the latter is a play of strong characterization and great emotional appeal, which carry the spectator safely over one or two points of weakness in its construction.

ST. JOHN ERVINE

PLAY LIST

1911 *Mixed Marriage.*
1912 *The Magnanimous Lover,* (wr. 1909).
1913 *Jane Clegg.*
1915 *John Ferguson.*
1921 *The Wonderful Visit* (with H. G. Wells).
     The Ship.
1923 *Mary, Mary, Quite Contrary.*
1924 *The Lady of Belmont* (pub.).

CHAPTER X

STANLEY HOUGHTON (1881-1913) AND OTHER REALISTS

I T IS a significant fact that *Jane Clegg*, generally regarded as St. John Ervine's best play, was first produced at the Gaiety Theatre in Manchester under the direction of Miss A. E. F. Horniman, whose financial help in putting Shaw's *Arms and the Man* on the London stage and in establishing the Abbey Theatre in Dublin has been already noted. It was with her money and under her direction that the first repertory theatre in Great Britain was founded in 1907. The efforts in London of J. T. Grein in connection with the Independent Theatre of 1891 and of Granville-Barker in connection with the Stage Society, at the Court Theatre with J. E. Vedrenne, and at the Duke of York's Theatre with Charles Frohman, have also been mentioned, but all these efforts came to an end without the establishment of any permanent repertory theatre in the English metropolis. Miss Horniman, along with the fortune she inherited from her father, a successful London tea merchant, well known for his educational philanthropies, had inherited also considerable business capacity, and had added to these qualifications a keen interest in the new movement in drama, and some knowledge of theatrical management—at any rate to the extent of learning how quickly money could be lost in giving the public, not what it wanted, but what it ought to have. All in all, she was an ideal person to play the part of fairy godmother

Miss Horniman

to the modern English drama, which was still in need of help and encouragement.

There were many reasons for leaving the London field, already promisingly occupied by Granville-Barker and his associates, to turn to the provinces, and for choosing Manchester as the scene of the experiment. Manchester is the centre of a crowded and homogeneous population, self-reliant and strongly conscious of its own virtues and capacities, and the city had shown its concern for the musical, artistic, and intellectual life of the community by the successful organization of its concert society, art gallery, and university; there was already, in and about Manchester, a considerable body of amateur actors and playwrights, interested in the new drama; and the dramatic criticisms of the *Manchester Guardian* were held in high esteem all over the country.

In the next few years Miss Horniman's Manchester Company became the most effective of the organizations for bringing to the front new playwrights and new actors. **The Repertory Age** It had a large share in sustaining what E. Graham Sutton calls the Repertory Age of British Drama, which extended from 1900 to 1914—a period "still remembered affectionately by some of us (though cut off by the remorseless cleavage of a time when only the commercial drama could flourish) as an age in which theatres gave wider scope to the young playwright than he has since enjoyed. Then they did curtain-raisers; they did curtain-droppers (if that be the right name for them); they even did triple bills. And they did all these things as they did full-length plays (including tragedies!), with frequent changes of programme; wherein the young playwright seized his chance, rejoicing. . . . The one-act, one-week play gave tyros their opportunity—first to find out what they could do, and then to consider whether they felt like doing something bigger."

The Horniman Company produced plays of many kinds by various hands, but one type in particular came to be almost as notable in its way as the Manchester School in politics. It was not a new type, but, like that school, it reflected the interests and characteristics of the Lancashire manufacturing community for which most of the plays were written. *Jane Clegg* is an excellent example of the type, though it is by no means the earliest, even on the English stage; it deals with ordinary people, presents no direct lesson, is the product of careful craftsmanship treating intelligently and naturally phases of life familiar to the audiences for whom it was intended. The Théâtre Libre founded by Antoine at Paris in 1887, the pioneer of all the modern independent movements, had begun with a natural reaction from the characteristic weaknesses of the theatre of the previous era—the romantic tradition, intellectual emptiness, Philistine morals, stereotyped construction, artificial dialogue, and conventional acting. The new tendencies were roughly summed up in the term "realism" or "naturalism," and were immediately adopted on the German stage under the leadership of Gerhart Hauptmann. For reasons which have already been outlined in the first chapter of this volume, the onward movement in England was somewhat retarded, and, under the stress of British independence, took a different direction from the general line of Continental development. The compromises between the old drama and the new attempted by Jones and Pinero were no doubt necessary, but they took time, and when Shaw at last brought in the new movement with his rush tactics, he gave it the impression of his own strong personality; he regarded the stage as a platform for social propaganda. Granville-Barker and St. John Hankin, who were influenced by him, retained something of the same tendency; Galsworthy, with his strong moral and social interests, made a "spire of meaning" the apex of his dramatic structure. It was not until the English dramatic revival of the twentieth century was well on its way that the type of realistic play that had been common in Continental drama before the end of the nineteenth century came to be generally written by the younger English playwrights. Propaganda was dropped; the drama was not shaped to inculcate new ideas, but the new ideas already stirring in the minds of the younger generation were used as dramatic motives, and in some cases presented sympathetically, though not obtrusively; the main purpose was to reproduce the life of the immediate present as it really was, to develop situations and characters not unfamiliar to experience, and to use in the dialogue the idiom of everyday life, so handled as to gain and hold the attention of the audience, but not stiffened by stage convention or twisted out of recognition by literary artifice.

Of this type of play the most gifted exponent was Stanley Houghton, a Lancashire man whose business career had made him familiar with the life he portrayed, and whose natural gift for drama, which, up to the organization of the Horniman Company had sought an outlet in various amateur enterprises, found in the Manchester theatre the opportunity for a short but brilliant career. Beginning with a one-act play for the Horniman Company in 1908, within four years he took the London stage by storm, and was almost immediately struck down by disease, when he was little more than thirty years of age. His early death left us one masterpiece, *Hindle Wakes*, which within a year of its production had been acted two thousand times in

Hindle Wakes

155

Manchester, London, New York and Chicago, and remains as a vivid and faithful picture, full of humour and human nature, of the life of the Lancashire workpeople and their employers, done in their characteristic idiom and revealing their striking virtues, downrightness of thought, speech and manner, and piquant turns of phrase. Hindle, it should perhaps be explained, is any Lancashire manufacturing town (there is actually one near Manchester called Hindley) and the Wakes are the annual festival which sends the whole working population for a holiday, usually to one of the beaches on the neighbouring western seacoast. William Archer, in his last book, *The Old Drama and the New*, gives well-merited praise to the skill with which the exposition is accomplished in the opening scene:

> If Miss Horniman's enlightened public spirit had brought into being nothing but this one scene, it would not have been thrown away. The thing is absolutely real, not an unnatural word is spoken, and the sequence of incidents involves no departure from the normal and probable course of life. Yet you cannot but feel in the atmosphere of the dingy Lancashire sitting-room that strain of suspense, that throb of emotion, which was, is, and ever shall be the central secret of the drama,—that which differentiates it from all other arts and lends it such irresistible magic. A better piece of drama than this opening scene was never written. . . . It gives us a complex satisfaction, the pleasure arising from a scene of intense and yet of absolutely truthful and natural emotion, and the pleasure arising from the recognition that the artist is making the best possible use of his medium, developing its highest potentialities.

The situation presented is one taken from familiar experience. During the Wakes, the son of a successful Hindle manufacturer has picked up at a seaside resort an attractive and lively girl with whom he is already acquainted as one of his father's employees, and after dancing with her has taken her off in his automobile to spend the week-end with him in a hotel at another watering place. It is an adventure into which both parties have gone with their eyes open; there is no hint of compulsion or seduction, no promise of marriage, the young man being already engaged to a daughter of a neighbouring manufacturer. It is just a "lark," but the carefully laid plans for secrecy break down and the escapade comes to the immediate knowledge of the girl's parents. Although workingpeople, they are friends of the young man's father, whose energy and enterprise have raised him to be the owner of the mill in which Fanny Hawthorn's father is still a handworker. The older men are still on terms of familiarity, addressing each other by their Christian names—a situation which was not unusual in the earlier stages of the Lancashire cotton industry. When Fanny's parents demand that Alan Jeffcote shall do the right thing by Fanny by marrying her, his parents agree, his father insisting on it under pain of disinheritance. Alan is reluctant, incalcitrant, but is reduced to submission when his fiancée also takes the view that Fanny has the prior claim—all in accordance with the ideas of the time and the community to which these good people belong. But, to everybody's surprise, Fanny refuses to accept the arrangements for her rehabilitation according to Victorian standards. After remaining stubbornly silent during the conference between the two families, she suddenly breaks out with the remark: "I was just wondering where I come in. . . . You'll hire the parson and get the licence and make all the arrangements on your own without consulting me, and I shall have nothing to do save turn up meek as a lamb at the church or registry office or whatever it is." Her parents, are, of course, dumbfounded at this exhibition of feminine perversity, and the Jeffcotes, while not displeased, are very much taken aback. Alan, who sees both the girls—and he likes both of them—slipping out of his hands along with his father's money and position, grasps at the opportunity to assert himself; he is sure a quarter of an hour's talk with him alone will bring Fanny to her senses. It is the same situation, though handled quite differently, as Galsworthy presented in *The Eldest Son*, which was written in 1909, but did not reach the stage until 1912—the same year that *Hindle Wakes* was put on at the Aldwych Theatre (June 16), by Miss Horniman's Repertory Company. Freda, the lady's maid of the Galsworthy play, makes her renunciation almost passively through the mouth of her father. Fanny, on the other hand, flings to the wind the banner of woman's independence in a sharp dialogue which lasts only a few minutes—not even the quarter of an hour allotted to Alan for the exercise of his persuasive eloquence. He hears some wholesome truths:

FANNY. Don't you kid yourself, my lad! It isn't because I'm afraid of spoiling *your* life that I'm refusing you, but because I'm afraid of spoiling *mine!* That didn't occur to you.

There were other things that didn't occur to Alan. He says dispiritedly to Fanny: "You didn't ever really love me?" The answer is prompt and clear:

FANNY. Love you? Good heavens, of course not! Why on earth should I love you? You were just someone to have a bit of fun with. You were an amusement—a lark.
ALAN (*shocked*). Fanny! Is that all you cared for me?
FANNY. How much more did you care for me?
ALAN. But it's not the same. I'm a man.
FANNY. You're a man and I was your little fancy. Well, I'm a woman, and you were my little fancy. You wouldn't

prevent a woman enjoying herself as well as a man, if
she takes it into her head?

ALAN.   But do you mean to say that you didn't care any more
for me than a fellow cares for any girl he happens to
pick up?

FANNY.   Yes. Are you shocked?

ALAN.   It's a bit thick; it is, really!

FANNY.   You're a beauty to talk!

ALAN.   It sounds so jolly immoral. I never thought of a girl
looking on a chap just like that! I made sure you
wanted to marry me if you got the chance.

FANNY.   No fear! You're not good enough for me. The chap
Fanny Hawthorn weds has got to be made of different
stuff from you, my lad. My husband, if ever I have one,
will be a man, not a fellow who'll throw over his girl
at his father's bidding. You're not man enough for me.
You're a nice lad, and I'm fond of you. But I couldn't
ever marry you. We've had a right good time together,
I'll never forget that. It has been a right good time,
and no mistake! We've enjoyed ourselves proper! But
all good times have to come to an end, and ours is over
now. Come along, now, and bid me farewell.

Fanny, with her downrightness, is perhaps the most attractive of the tribe of Ibsen's Nora, from whom she obviously descends. When she is reproached by her mother for
not letting Alan make her into an honest woman, she retorts: "How can he do that?"

MRS. HAWTHORN.   By wedding you, of course.

FANNY.   You called him a blackguard this morning.

MRS. HAWTHORN.   So he is a blackguard.

FANNY.   I don't see how marrying a blackguard is going
to turn me into an honest woman!

MRS. HAWTHORN.   If he marries you he won't be a blackguard any
longer.

FANNY.   Then it looks as if I'm asked to wed him to
turn him into an honest man!

The advance on the position taken by Ibsen in *A Doll's House* and *Ghosts* is as notable as the general resemblance, but during the intervening period there had been much discussion of woman's right to equality with man, and at the time the play was produced it was the burning question of English politics. In making Fanny the spokeswoman of the advanced guard, Houghton had the consciousness not only of her native Lancashire independence of spirit, but of the security of her financial position. When Alan, accepting her refusal, shows a final spark of generosity by offering to see that she is provided for, she smiles her disdainful rejection. "It's right good of you, Alan, but I shan't starve. I'm not without a trade at my fingertips, thou knows. I'm a Lancashire lass, and so long as there's weaving sheds in Lancashire I shall earn enough brass to keep me going. I wouldn't live again at home after this, not anyhow! I'm going to be on my own in future."

In her stout defiance of the social, religious, and moral restrictions recognized by the community in which she has to live, Fanny was a good deal in advance of her time, but her vigorous independence and courage appeal so strongly to our admiration that we are ready to forgive her creator for putting on the clock a little, if only for the artistic use he has made of a character pushed perhaps a little beyond the probabilities. The swing, the savour, the unfailing humour of the play are a delight, even if one reads it and so loses the supreme pleasure of the tang of the Lancashire accent, produced truthfully and without exaggeration by Miss Horniman's players. The play was the success of the season in London on its first production; New York was at first rather puzzled by it—first of all by the title. The *Sun* described the play as shocking the public; the *Herald* thought it *risqué*. "It will never qualify at the Children's Theatre," meditated another sapient critic, and *Current Opinion* classified Fanny as "the dangerous new woman." Well, well, what a lot of water has run under the New York bridges since the theatrical season of 1912-13. Chicago, be it said to its credit, welcomed Fanny without reservations.

ELIZABETH BAKER

A somewhat earlier play than *Hindle Wakes* was *Chains* **Chains** by Elizabeth Baker, less brilliant but perhaps closer to type in its adherence to the humdrum truth of life. Herself a London clerk until she became a private secretary, an amateur in the sense that she wrote plays in her leisure hours for her own pleasure, Elizabeth Baker (Mrs. J. E. Allaway) was familiar with the life of the lower middle class both in the office and in the small suburban homes in which so many of the clerical workers take refuge from the high rents and noise of the city. Just such a household is revealed to us in the first act of *Chains*—a young married couple thoroughly estimable, industrious, thrifty, respectable to the last bone of their bodies and the last thread of their clothes, with some slight pretensions to interest in art, music, and literature of a lower-middle-class sort; the young husband potters in a wretched back yard which he calls his garden; the young wife does the washing (to the ruin of her hands) and takes in a lodger to eke out their scant income. It is the lodger who makes the trouble— not by making love to the guileless and irreproachable Lily, who is the model of all a Victorian wife should be—but by throwing up his job and deciding to go to Australia. This makes the young husband restless, and, piqued by a reduction in his salary, he determines to go, too, as he has enough laid by to provide for his wife until he is able to send for her. His wife, however, backed up by her family, regards his proposed emigration as desertion and at the last minute stops it by letting him know—most delicately and tactfully—that the small, sure income will soon have to provide for three instead of two. The chains of circumstance are too well riveted; he gives up his projected voyage and puts on again the badges of his servitude, the cuffs and silk hat he must wear to go to the office. This is the whole action, save a small side issue: the lodger's pluck in throwing up a safe job for an uncertain venture fires the wife's sister to renounce her marriage with a well-to-do widower, to whom she has engaged herself in order to escape from the office—a not unusual expedient in England, although perhaps on the other side of the Atlantic the more usual practice is to take to the office as an escape from an uncongenial marriage; but Maggie sees that once married she is bound by English law and social custom to endless mediocrity, while from the office she can some day cut and run if she has the courage; she can go out to Canada as a servant! The characters illustrate precisely what Gissing described as the life of the ignobly decent; they have no vices—at any rate none of those interesting from a dramatic point of view; they are simply dull, some of them absolutely inane in their colourless virtue. They read cheap papers, and sing silly songs on weekdays, and on Sunday chant vapid hymns:

> Count your blessings, count them one by one
> Count your blessings, see what God has done.
> Count your blessings, count them one by one,
> And it will surprise you what the Lord has done.

It is with this sacred lyric, as the curtain falls, that Lily welcomes the advent of her first child and her second lodger.

It sounds as if the play must be insufferably dull, and yet such is the delicate art of the dramatist and her fine insight for telling detail that it is just the opposite. William Archer in *Playmaking* says of it:

> If anyone had told the late Francisque Sarcey, or the late Clement Scott, that a play could be made out of this slender material, which should hold an audience absorbed through four acts, and stir them to real enthusiasm, these eminent critics would have thought him a madman. Yet Miss Baker has achieved this feat, by the simple process of supplementing competent observation with a fair share of dramatic instinct.

Chains was first acted at the Court Theatre, London, in 1909, and has been often revived by repertory companies. Miss Baker's next important play, *The Price of Thomas Scott,* found its natural home in Miss Horniman's Theatre at Manchester. Thomas Scott is a fanatical puritan with a failing business in a decaying suburb, and the play centres upon a conflict between his principles and his interests. An earlier dramatist might have represented him as a hypocrite as well as a puritan, but Miss Baker's art is too fine and deep to be content with such a superficial judgment. Scott has a rooted objection to what he regards as the vice of dancing, and he has a chance of selling his deteriorating property to a company which will convert his business premises into a dance hall. At first he is inclined to acquiesce, because the money will enable him to provide for his wife and educate his young son; but in the end his principles are too strong for him and he refuses. His daughter Annie has wished to attend a dance organized by the local reform party and had been at first forbidden to go by her father, but in the turmoil of mind caused by consideration of the business deal about the

The Price of Thomas Scott

dance hall he withdraws his objection. She declines to take advantage of a permission which she knows her father has not freely given, and answers criticism of his intolerance with the plea: "I think it is brave whenever a man hurts himself for a cause—even if it does seem a silly cause." Again, in spite of the pettiness of the issues, the dramatist succeeds in making Thomas Scott something of a heroic figure and not entirely unsympathetic, but even her art cannot make the intellectual and spiritual atmosphere in which he lives other than depressing; the air lacks vitality and Scott's fanaticism broods over it like a thundercloud on a sultry summer's day.

Miss Robinson

In *Miss Robinson*, a post-War play, Miss Baker has introduced a considerable element of action and intrigue so that it seems almost melodramatic by comparison with her earlier work. Miss Robinson, a private secretary, becomes engaged to the son of her employer, a successful and well-to-do member of Parliament, and her lower-middle-class relatives, though observed with unfailing accuracy and skill, are used rather for comic effect in their somewhat grotesque efforts to adapt themselves to superior surroundings. In spite of the play's wider interests and resources, it does not seem so much of a piece as the earlier studies of humble life, and it is artistically less effective.

GITHA SOWERBY

Rutherford and Son

The name of Githa K. Sowerby (Mrs. John Kendall) is perhaps less known than the title of her best play, *Rutherford and Son*, a powerful middle-class play which made a great impression on both sides of the Atlantic, partly, no doubt, owing to the excellent acting of Norman McKinnel in the leading part. John Rutherford is one of those captains of industry who has put his whole life and energy into his business. He comes home worn out by his exertions and orders his daughter to unlace his boots; he rules the family with the same iron hand that he directs the glass factory. The women of the household fear him, and, with nerves all on edge, take it out of each other by constant nagging. Mary, the son's wife, who has come to this stern Tyneside family from a softer south and is still regarded as an outsider, says to her husband: "It's like a prison! There's not a scrap of love in the whole house. Your father . . . never questioned, never answered back—like God! and the rest of you just living round him—neither children nor men and women—hating each other." Her husband, young John, says family life's like that more or less, and they have to put up with it till his invention gives him "the whip hand of the Guv'nor." But old Rutherford, using his authority as master, worms the secret of the new process out of John's helper, the workman Martin, who has been with the firm for twenty-five years and has for it the same superstitious devotion as Rutherford himself. The secret won, Rutherford discharges Martin on account of a clandestine love affair with his daughter Janet and turns Janet out of the house, not, however, before she has at long last had the courage to speak her mind to her father, whom she strongly resembles, except that her passionate energy has gone into her love of Martin, not into the business. This last talk between her and her father is the climax of the play. Janet defends her right to love and be loved: "I was thirty-six. Gone sour. Nobody'd ever come after me, not even when I was young—you took care o' that. Half of my life was gone, well-nigh all of it that mattered . . . What have I had of it, afore I go back to the dark? What have I had of it? Tell me that." Her father tells her he has tried to make a lady of her. "What more did you want, in God's name?"

JANET. Oh, what more! The women down there know what I wanted—with their bairns wrapped in their shawls and their men to come home at night time. I've envied them—envied them their pain, their poorness—the very times they hadn't bread. Theirs isn't the dead empty house, the blank o' the moors; they've got something to fight, something to be feared of. They've got life, those women we send cans o' soup to out o' pity when their bairns are born. Me a lady! with work for a man in my hands, passion for a man in my heart! I'm common—common. . . . You think you've made us different by keeping us from the people here. We're just the same as they are! Ask the men that work for you—ask their wives that curtsey to us in the road. Do you think they don't know the difference? We're just the same as they are— common, every one of us. It's in our blood, in our hands and faces; and when we marry, we marry common.

RUTHERFORD. Marry! Common or not, nobody's married you that I can see.

JANET. Leave that—don't you say it!

RUTHERFORD. It's the truth, more shame to 'ee.

JANET (*passionately*). Martin loves me honest. Don't you come near! Don't you touch that! . . . You think I'm sorry you've found out—You think you've done for me when you use shameful words on me and turn me out o' your house. You've let me out o' gaol. Whatever happens to me now, I shan't go on living as I lived here. Whatever Martin's done, he's taken me from you. You've ruined my life, you with your getting on. I've loved in wretchedness, all the joy I ever had made wicked by the fear o' you. . . . (*Wildly*) Who are you? Who are you? A man—a man that's taken power to himself, power to gather people to him and use them as he wills— a man that'd take the blood of life itself, and put it into the Works—into Rutherford's. And what ha' you got by it—what? You've got Dick, that you've bullied till he's a fool—John, that's waiting for the time when he can sell what you've done— and you've got me—me to take your boots off at night—to well-nigh wish you dead when I had to touch you. . . . Now! . . . Now you know!

After this scene of concentrated passion—the conflict of two iron wills—ending Act II, it would seem impossible to sustain the interest of Act III, but there is no let down. John, finding his secret has been stolen, retaliates by emptying his father's cashbox and running away from his wife and baby. It is the mild-mannered Mary, stung to action by the needs of her child, who in the end brings old Rutherford to terms. To the father-in-law who has hardly spoken to her during the three months she has lived in his house, she proposes a bargain:

MARY. A bargain is where one person has something to sell that another wants to buy. There's no love in it—only money—money that pays for life. I've got something to sell that you want to buy.

RUTHERFORD. What's that?

MARY. My son. (*Their eyes meet in a long steady look. She goes on deliberately.*) You've lost everything you have in the world. John's gone—and Richard —and Janet. They won't come back. You're alone now and getting old with no one to come after you. When you die, Rutherford's will be sold—somebody'll buy it and give it a new name perhaps, and no one will even remember that you made it. That'll be the end of all your work. Just—nothing. You've thought of that. I've seen you thinking of it as I've sat by and watched you. And now it's come. . . . Will you listen?

RUTHERFORD. Ay.

She sits down at the other end of the table facing him.

MARY. It's for my boy. I want—a chance of life for him—his place in the world. John can't give him that, because he's made so. If I went to London and worked my hardest I'd get twenty-five shillings a week. We've failed. From you I can get what I want for my boy. I want—all the good common things: a good house, good food, warmth. He's a delicate little thing now, but he'll grow strong like other children. I want to undo the wrong we've done him, John and I—if I can. Later on there'll be his schooling—I could never save enough for that. You can give me all this—you've got the power. . . . That's the bargain. Give me what I ask, and in return I'll give you—him. On one condition. I'm to stay on here. I won't trouble you—you needn't speak to me or see me unless you want to. For ten years he's to be absolutely mine, to do what I like with. You mustn't interfere— you mustn't tell him to do things or frighten him. He's mine for ten years more.

RUTHERFORD. And after that?

MARY. He'll be yours.

RUTHERFORD. To train up. For Rutherford's? You'd trust your son to me?

MARY. Yes.

RUTHERFORD. After all? After Dick, that I have bullied till he's a fool? John that's wished me dead?

MARY. In ten years you will be an old man; you won't be able to make people afraid of you any more.

RUTHERFORD. Ah! Because o' that? And because I have the power?

MARY.   Yes. And there'll be money for his clothes—and
               you'll leave the Works to him when you die.

Rutherford ironically congratulates her on having "a
fair notion of business for a woman," but he softens as he
thinks of his own early plans for his own children, and his
old courage returns as he thinks of himself at his death
handing on to his grandson the business of Rutherford and
Son which he himself had inherited from his grandfather.
He is warming to his theme when Mary interrupts him
with a gesture and a "Hush!"

RUTHERFORD.   What is it? (*They both listen.*) The little lad.
               He's waking. *Mary runs out. The room is very
               silent as Rutherford sits sunk in his chair, think-
               ing.*

Miss Sowerby wrote other plays, both before and after
the War, but nothing which comes up to the concentrated
force of *Rutherford and Son,* nor is this a reproach to her.
Her one masterpiece is by far the best play of this realist
group; while terribly grim, alike in its moorland landscape
and the immediate surroundings of the Rutherford family, it does not give the feeling of hopeless depression
aroused by some of the other plays. Rutherford, Janet,
and Mary are real people without being commonplace, and
in the conflict of their wills and passions there is an emotional interest which the vain and fitful struggles of the
mere flies caught in the spider web of industrialism cannot
evoke in us. Her technique is no less masterly than that
of her contemporaries dealing with the merely weak and
obscure, and there is no straining of probability in order to
bring off a theatrical effect. Close-knit, the tissue of the
play unfolds itself inevitably and arrives at an inevitable
conclusion—unforeseen, but felt to be right and necessary after it has been unfolded.

ARNOLD BENNETT (1867-   )

Of the English realists in narrative Arnold Bennett is easily first. No one knows the English middle class better (especially of his own midland towns), no one has observed them with more loving fidelity or portrayed them with more skilful sympathy. In the long list of his novels it is easy to pick out half-a-dozen masterpieces; among his many plays it is hard to find one that stands securely, even in the second rank.

Before Bennett took the drama seriously, he said in that amusingly frank autobiography, *The Truth about an Author*, that it was a great deal easier to write a play than a novel, the number of words being so much smaller, and in those days he wrote plays to make money; but after he had become an artist and had done a dozen plays into which he put his best efforts (and most of them were comparative failures) his view was rather different. In an article on the English drama published in the *New York Times* of October 18, 1925, he writes:

People say solemnly that the theatre would be better if authors of standing outside the theatre did not turn to the theatre merely as a means of money-making. They don't. The rewards of the successful play are grossly exaggerated in the public mind. No novelist of established prestige and good circulation, in search of money, would leave writing novels for a time in order to write plays—unless he was an ass.

With novels there are no risks for authors of established prestige. Some success is absolutely certain and the bulk of the reward comes punctually on the day of publication. Year in and year out, there is, for such authors, far more money, far less humiliation, infinitely less risk, in novels than in plays. If they do turn to the stage, it is because they aie driven thereto by a powerful instinct, even to their financial disadvantage.

If we take Bennett at his own serious valuation, what has he contributed to modern drama? A London critic describes his last effort, *The Bright Island*, as "the worst play written by a celebrated man for a long time past," and there are half-a-dozen others over which the kindly hand of oblivion has already passed. Even a clever topical comedy such as *The Title*, written in the spate of after-War honours, is recalled with difficulty. *The Great Adventure* was an excellent farce-comedy, but the story *Buried Alive*, on which it was founded, will outlast its fame. *Milestones* (done in collaboration with Edward Knoblock) is more noteworthy for its deft handling of a real idea—not altogether new—the inability of each successive age to accept the new ideas and manners of the next generation. We were shown first a mid-Victorian middle-class family in the full bloom of confident enterprise, with their quaint customs, dresses, furniture, and household arrangements—still deliciously familiar to the older members of the audience. Then a generation passes, bringing us to the last quarter of the nineteenth century; and finally we see the present, with the alterations in opinion and habit effected by the lapse of time, the older characters, who in their youth had been almost revolutionary, now steadily conservative and lamenting the decadence of the younger generation. All this was very skilfully woven together with just enough plot to connect the characters from one generation to another, and a carefully chosen Victorian sentimental song brought down the final curtain with the reminder that throughout all changes human emotion keeps on unchanged, and the passions, struggles, and failures of our forefathers have a tender interest for us, in spite of the curious dresses they wore, their extraordinary pictures and furniture, and their still stranger points of view as to

Milestones

What the
Public
Wants
morals and manners.   There was an idea, too, in *What the
Public Wants*, and the burlesque of the private office of a
newspaper magnate was amusing; but it is noteworthy that
the midland scenes and the midland people had much more
vitality than the London part of the play, which came to
a most ineffective conclusion.   How is it that Bennett's
men and women, so full of vigorous human nature in his
novels, become so often mere puppets when they mount
the stage?   His narrative work is uneven, still more so
his popular philosophics, but never does he sink quite so
low as when he has (according to his later view, at a great
financial sacrifice) endeavoured with the assistance of capable actors to create figures that will take on the semblance
of flesh and blood and incidents which will have at least a
momentary appearance of probability.   From *What the
Public Wants* and *Milestones* there has been a steady de-
preciation in his dramatic work until it has ceased to count
as a factor in the present, and one must go back to pre-
War days for a recollection of the time when it seemed as
if he might really do something for the commercial theatre.

ALLAN MONKHOUSE (1858-   )

Allan Noble Monkhouse, justly honoured as the
dramatic critic of the *Manchester Guardian*, whose regular
readers never fail to linger over any article with the
significant initials at the foot of it, was closely connected
with the repertory theatre movement, not only in Manchester but in Liverpool and Birmingham.   He was a
favourite with Miss Horniman, who put on his *Reaping the
Whirlwind* at the beginning of her Manchester experiment
and followed it with *The Choice*—these were one-act plays
—and *Mary Broome*.   Somewhat given to over-smart

literary dialogue in his earliest work and never quite freeing himself from this limitation, Monkhouse in *Mary Broome* succeeded in giving a new turn to realistic comedy by combining with it an element of fantasy, which he presented in a spirit of irony. In *Mary Broome* he takes the situation of the middle-class father who by the threat of withdrawing supplies compels his son to offer marriage to a lower-class girl—in this case the housemaid—whom he has got into trouble—and the girl accepts. Leonard Timbrell is a conscienceless artist after the manner of Shaw's Louis Dubedat, with the added disqualifications that he never earns anything and that he is constantly indulging his talent for saying the smart and unexpected thing. His marriage to Mary Broome makes no difference in his habits, and the spice of the play lies in the contrast between his clever epigrams and the matter-of-fact speeches of his simple-minded wife on the one hand, the pompous conventionalities of his father on the other. A rather jarring note is introduced in the third act by the death of Mary's baby while Leonard is away on a fishing party, from which he refuses to return for the funeral; and Mary announces her determination to go off to Canada with the milkman with whom she was "walking out" when Leonard was making love to her, before her marriage. Leonard's family are, of course, scandalized when Leonard accepts her decision with his usual airy irresponsibility. His father storms at Mary in the best Victorian manner, but Mary pays no attention to his harangues, as she is afraid of missing her train. At last he turns to his son and asks him angrily: "Do you mean to tell me you're going to submit to this?"

LEONARD.   I don't see that a scrap with George Truefit

	would help much. I've lost Mary. That's plain.
TIMBRELL.	Well, well. I've no more to say.
LEONARD.	It has been an extraordinarily interesting episode. The most stimulating thing that has ever happened to me. I must thank you for that, Mary.
MRS. TIMBRELL	(*turning suddenly on Leonard*). Doesn't it hurt you? Can you get outside it like that?
LEONARD.	Oh! Yes. It hurts me splendidly.
TIMBRELL.	Your conduct is despicable, sir. The man who allows his wife to leave him is not a man.
LEONARD	(*snappishly*). Oh! Don't talk rubbish. Your wife left you long ago. She never came to you. You've never had a wife.
TIMBRELL.	I don't understand you. I don't want to understand you. I pray that I may never understand you.
LEONARD.	Of course you don't want to understand. That's just it. I think sometimes that people like you are just as intelligent as we are, but you're timid, you daren't let your thoughts stray, you have secrets from yourselves. Well, mother, I shall have to look to you now that Mary's gone.
MRS. TIMBRELL.	I can do nothing for you. You've ceased to be a child.
LEONARD.	To him—to my father—yes. Not to you.
MRS. TIMBRELL.	Yes. You know too much. You can only pretend to be my child.
LEONARD.	I'm to be alone, then. Mary, I shall be quite alone.
MARY.	I dare say you'll pick up somebody.
LEONARD.	You've no sentiment at all.
MARY.	I must go. Good-bye, ma'am.

It is very clever and amusing, but we are conscious that the characters are all on paper, the mouthpieces for Monkhouse's wit, not people who have any life in his imagination. At times they drop into the colloquial speech of real life;

they even arouse momentary emotion; but for the most part their language is as much a stage convention as the epigrams of Sheridan or Oscar Wilde, and the occasional protrusion of realistic dialogue only disturbs the current of our intellectual enjoyment. It is the same with *The Education of Mr. Surrage*, which was put on the following year (1912) at the Liverpool Repertory Theatre. This play is a reversal of the father and children situation of *The Madras House;* the children are anxious that their father should share—at his own expense, of course—their "liberal developments," and with his consent they invite some advanced young people as his guests to assist in his education. Mr. Surrage shows that he is quite able to look after himself and to deal with his young instructors according to their deserts.

Of Monkhouse's post-War plays the most brilliant— though perhaps the most extravagant in fantasy—is his one-act piece, *The Great Cham's Diamond*. More serious is *The Conquering Hero*, which deals with the issue of whether in war it is the artist's duty to go and get himself killed for the sake of his country. Chris. Rokeby, a young novelist, as yet unpublished, thinks it is not, but he is the son of a Colonel, his sister Margaret is married to a Captain, and all the family pressure is brought to bear on him to enlist. At first he resists:

CHRIS. I stand for something, too.
MARGARET. What good is it now? Who wants your novel? or your pretty little stories? He's writing a play.
CHRIS. They are not pretty.
MARGARET. What does it matter? What does the world want? What does England want?
CHRIS. Yes! when the pipe bursts you send for the plumber; and the plumber's the most important person in the world. What's the good of being amusing or charm-

175

	ing, or wise, or virtuous? Are you a plumber? Why aren't you a plumber?
MARGARET.	You can't understand a man like Frank.
CHRIS.	I think I do. He's not just a machine of destruction to me—no, nor of saving us from destruction. Yes, and the plumber may be a charming man, but all you want is that he should plumb. So do I, for the moment.
HELEN.	This is the moment.
CHRIS.	Don't you see—don't you see—the point is that some of us have to keep the eternal going.
HELEN.	Why you?
CHRIS.	Because I'm an artist. It's my work—my duty, if you like. It isn't only Frank we want; it's the idea of Frank. Now, I can give you that.
MARGARET.	This is rubbish. You are exasperating, Chris. You are out of place. You're not serious enough now.
HELEN.	The world has left you behind.
CHRIS.	The world doesn't exist without me—I speak for the lot of us—wars are not worth fighting but for me.

But in the end he goes, and passes through the experiences described in C. E. Montague's *Disenchantment*. He is not killed, and when he returns home, the village would meet him with a brass band, but his family can hardly believe that he has not let them down.

First Blood

Monkhouse's last play, *First Blood*, (published in 1924, acted in 1926) has been compared with Galsworthy's *Strife*, but has more in common with Houghton's *Hindle Wakes*, and suffers in comparison with either. The fantastic element which is characteristic of the author clashes with the realistic setting and the tragic close. In the stage of development of the cotton industry portrayed by Stanley Houghton, social contacts between employer and employed such as he has made use of for the purposes of his plot were not impossible or even improbable, but Monkhouse is not content, by the device of an automobile accident, to bring Lionel Stott, son of the head of Stott's Limited, to tea in the house of one of his operatives in Act I; in Act II, he brings the shop steward, Tom Eden, to tea in the house of Lady Stott, with her husband carrying the tea tray, and Phyllis Livsey, an operative with whom Eden is in love, helping to serve tea as the parlour maid in the Stott household. Sir Samuel Stott is one of the author's heavy fathers, stuffed with poses and platitudes; Lionel is a young intellectual with a gift for smart phrases: even Tom Eden adorns his conversation with such oratorical flourishes as: "The present movement is calml calculated, inevitable, inexorable." Phyllis suggests to Lionel that she has come to the house as parlour maid "after" him: "P'raps I want to marry you"; and when he, as an experiment, puts his arm round her, she calmly lays her head on his breast. As a result of the experiment Lionel tells Tom not to think of Phyllis as a wife: "She's only fit to be a mistress"; but in the end, when the strikers attack the Stott mansion, Phyllis, after acknowledging her love for Tom, dies from a shot aimed at Lionel, which she purposely intercepts, and a subsequent shot kills Lionel. This melodramatic ending jars with the fantastic attitudes and dialogue of the first three acts and makes the whole play ineffective. The exaggerated characters and hypothetical situations can be enjoyed only on the plane of polite comedy.

Monkhouse's ironical fantasy has not the humour or the human nature of Barrie's, so that his people rarely seem to come quite alive; but his plays are excellent reading, and as the speeches have enough wit to carry themselves without any great demands on the actors, they have been much in request for amateur performances and repertory companies on both sides of the Atlantic.

PLAY LISTS

STANLEY HOUGHTON

1908 *The Dear Departed.*
1909 *Independent Means.*
     Marriage in the Making.
1910 *The Younger Generation.*
1912 *Hindle Wakes.*
1913 *The Perfect Cure.*

ELIZABETH BAKER

1909 *Chains.*
1913 *The Price of Thomas Scott.*
1918 *Miss Robinson.*

GITHA SOWERBY

1912 *Rutherford and Son.*
1914 *A Man and Some Women.*
1917 *Sheila.*
1924 *The Stepmother.*

ARNOLD BENNETT

1908 *Cupid and Commonsense.*
1909 *What the Public Wants.*
1912 *Milestones* (with Edward Knoblock).
     The Honeymoon.
1913 *The Great Adventure.*
1918 *The Title.*
1919 *Judith.*
     Sacred and Profane Love.
1922 *The Love Match.*
     Body and Soul.
1923 *Don Juan de Marana.*
1925 *The Bright Island.*

ALLAN MONKHOUSE

ALLAN MONKHOUSE

1911 *Mary Broome.*
1912 *The Education of Mr. Surrage.*
1918 *The Great Cham's Diamond.*
1924 *The Conquering Hero.*
1926 *First Blood,* (pub. 1924).

CHAPTER XI

JOHN MASEFIELD (1874-   ) AND OTHER POET-DRAMATISTS

M ASEFIELD is a man of letters of remarkable versatility; primarily a lyric poet, he has a genuine gift for narrative (both in prose and in verse); he has written one of the best books on Shakespeare, one of the best descriptions of the War (*Gallipoli*), and his dramatic work shows extraordinary variety.   He began in 1907 with *The Campden Wonder*, a tragedy of domestic realism,

The Campden Wonder

which was put on the stage of the Court Theatre under the Vedrenne-Barker management, and was later furnished by the author with a sequel which is called *Mrs. Harrison;* but in neither was there anything to distinguish the play from the other realistic studies, tragic or comic, which were in fashion at the time.   In *The Tragedy of Nan*,

Nan

which followed, he attempted (and with striking success) a more imaginative treatment, though the characters are still taken from the humblest walks of life and the happenings do not stray from ordinary experience.   The medium is still prose (largely dialect) and room is made for a more romantic setting by putting back the action a century or so from the present.   Probably Masefield's friendship with Synge (of whom he has written in terms of high admiration and affection, both in prose and verse) suggested a more poetical way of dealing with ordinary experience.   The heroine is an orphan living on a Severn farm with an uncongenial aunt, who uses the blight thrown over Nan's life by the hanging of her father for sheep-stealing to induce her lover, Dick Gurvil, to throw her over, and engage himself to the aunt's daughter, Janet. In her loneliness and despair, Nan finds consolation in the poetic, half-distracted murmurings of the old Gaffer about the Severn harvest tide, as it rushes up its narrow bed, sweeping all before it. The tide exercises a strange fascination on her mind; at first she thinks of herself in its grip with shuddering horror: "A strange fish in the nets tomorrow. A dumb thing knocking agen the bridges. Something white—something white in the water. They'd pull me out. Men would. They'd touch my body. I couldn't. I couldn't." But news comes that the innocence of her father has been established by the confession of another man, and the Government officer sends her fifty pounds as compensation for the wrong done. It seems a bitter irony, which is only made more bitter when Dick Gurvil, who was really put off more by Nan's poverty than by the supposed stain on her father, comes back to her with the proposal that he should marry her and throw over Janet. To test him, she bids him give the money to Janet's mother as a peace offering, and when he hesitates she sees him for the selfish, sensual, treacherous fellow he is. She determines to spare other women from his wiles and stabs him dead. As the other members of the family open the door in answer to his outcry, the sound of the tide is heard rushing up the Severn, and Nan goes out to meet it with the words: "The tide is coming up the river. . . . A strange fish in the nets tomorrow."

Some have seen in all this only a sordid story of crime, but the critics generally recognize it, not only as the best thing Masefield has done in drama, but as a leading modern example of domestic tragedy, worthy for its artistic restraint and imaginative power to be compared to Synge's *Riders to the Sea*. It contains elements of crude realism which give offence to the tender-minded—such as the scene in which Nan forces Janet to eat the poisonous mutton pie—but this was essential to Masefield's conception of his method—Synge's method of the combination of reality and poetry. In a note prefaced to a later edition of the play, Masefield justifies himself in these words:

> Tragedy at its best is a vision of the heart of life. The heart of life can only be laid bare in the agony of dreadful acts. The vision of agony or spiritual contest, pushed beyond the limits of dying personality, is exalting and cleansing. It is only by such vision that a multitude can be brought to the passionate knowledge of things exalting and eternal.

Pompey the Great

The success of *Nan* on the stage was striking enough to have encouraged Masefield to proceed further on the same line, but he turned aside from it to classical tragedy in *Pompey the Great*, which was produced by the London Stage Society in 1910 and again, in a revised form, by the Manchester University Dramatic Society in 1915, but has not been admitted to the commercial theatre. The two versions differ materially, and the author's revision may be held to imply that some changes were needed. But neither version is really effective for stage representation. Possibly Masefield had in mind to do for Pompey what Bernard Shaw had done for Julius Cæsar in *Cæsar and Cleopatra*—to interpret him as a man of modern ideas, not without human failings, but defeated in his life purposes by the stupidity of those he had to deal with. Pompey is represented as a faithful servant of the Senate, who opposes Cæsar only because he believes Cæsar is actuated by motives of personal ambition. He determines to outwit Cæsar by withdrawing to Macedonia and refusing to fight, but just when Cæsar is reduced to desperation by inability to feed and pay his troops, the disloyalty of Pompey's generals forces him into an engagement by order of the Senate. Pompey obeys the order, but he sees that it is the end of the Rome that he had dreamt of and striven for, whether he wins or loses. He says to his generals, who are thinking only of their own party and personal interests: "You have your will, now. This is the end. And at the end, think what it is that you destroy. Rome is nothing to you—only the reward of greed, and hate, and pride. The city where justice was born—a little while ago she was a market-town, governed by farmers. Now she rules Europe. And in herself no change. Cramped still. Fettered. The same laws, the same rulers—like iron on her heart. And forty years of civil war. All my life. A blind, turbulent heaving towards freedom."

Masefield has succeeded in conveying the elevation of Pompey's aims and character, not as Shaw showed that of Cæsar by flashes of insight, wit and wisdom, but by a continuous high-mindedness, revealed by the noble expression of great thoughts. It is well done, but it does not, as the theatre people say, "get over." One misses the movement, the quick change of mood and situation, the rapid alternation of humour and tragedy which make *Cæsar and Cleopatra* a first-rate acting play. *Pompey the Great* is closet drama; only in the scene on the Lesbian merchantman, enlivened by the seaman's chanties, does Masefield seem at home, dealing at ease with his material.

Yet he persisted in the thankless task of forcing on the public a genre they did not appreciate. His next play, *Philip the King*, showing the effect on the mind of Philip of Spain of the reports of the defeat of the Armada, was in rhymed couplets; and the next, *The Faithful*, was a tragedy with many lyrical passages, dealing with a Japanese revenge story; both are merely "interesting experiments in long-lost and antiquated forms."

Even less happy was the choice of the trial and crucifixion of Jesus as a subject for two tragedies, one, *Good Friday,* in rhymed couplets, where the action is conveyed through reports to Pilate, and the other, *The Trial of Jesus,* beginning with the agony of the Garden of Gethsemane and ending with the Crucifixion. On account of the inclusion of Jesus in the list of characters in the latter play, its public performance was forbidden by the Censor, but it was acted in 1925 in the small theatre erected by the poet in his own grounds at Boar's Hill, near Oxford, and again in 1926 at the Royal Academy of Dramatic Art in London. The critics speak of the performances as impressive, with a reservation about the choruses as "more of an interruption than an emotional relief."

Of more interest, because allowing greater freedom of treatment, was Masefield's tragedy dealing with another *A King's* Biblical subject, *A King's Daughter,* dramatizing the story *Daughter* of Jezebel after the manner of Euripides and with a good deal of the Greek tragedian's independence of spirit. Even in one's schooldays—the good old days when boys were compelled to read the Old Testament for their future welfare—one could not help admiring the proud defiance with which Ahab's queen attired herself to stand at her palace window and hurl down at the murderous usurper the final taunt, "Had Zimri peace who slew his master?" From this passage Masefield has taken his cue, and he presents Jezebel to us, not as a foul idolater, but as the representative of a foreign but superior civilization trying in vain to make head against the barbarism and intolerance of the Israelites; Ahab, of course, cuts a poor figure, but

Jezebel is a woman of insight and courage; she sends her
maids away to safety before she paints and decks herself
to meet her murderer, "like a Syrian woman and a queen."
Provided with lyrical passages which are recited between
the acts by a chorus of two young girls—and are in themselves poems of distinguished beauty—the tragedy is
evidently not intended for the ordinary theatre, but it
was put on for the opening of the new Playhouse at Oxford
on May 25, 1923, an occasion of all the more interest
because the Vice-Chancellor of the University had shown
some reluctance to allow the new theatre to open at all—
and his licence was necessary. The players, with one
exception—the lady who took the part of Jezebel—were
members of the amateur company organized by Mr. and
Mrs. Masefield for their private theatre at Boar's Hill.

It was for this theatre that Masefield translated Racine's
Esther and adapted *Bernice*—a laudable endeavour to
encourage the appreciation of French classical drama in
its most refined form, but nevertheless a sidetrack; and
Masefield's return to the contemporary theatre was welcomed by many convinced admirers of his creative power.
What he gave them was hardly what most of them
expected. *Melloney Holtspur* adopts the device of using
characters from the other world, revived by Barrie, Pinero
and others after the War, when there was a recrudescence
of popular belief in spiritualistic phenomena. The house
of Holtspur has its ghosts, chief among them the sister
of Lady Mento, Melloney, who was deceived by a visiting
artist, Lonny Copshrews. In the opening scene of the play
we see Bunny, the son of Lady Mento, making love to
Lenda, the daughter of the betrayer, who passionately
returns his attachment. Then in the same room the ghosts
of Melloney Holtspur and Lonny Copshrews re-enact their

*Melloney
Holtspur*

love scene of old up to the arrival of Lonny's wife, Mrs. Copshrews, now his widow, whose appearance still in the flesh, among the ghosts, has been criticized as one of the weak points in the play. Lenda learns from Lady Mento the story of her father's treachery which puts a fateful bar against her marriage to Lady Mento's son. Her father's ghost finds his worst punishment in the realization that his ancient sin will prevent the fulfilment of his daughter's happiness. But a new turn is given to the story by the change of heart of the injured Melloney, who lays aside the thirst for revenge characteristic of her Elizabethan predecessors, and interferes, as Professor Nicoll puts it, "leaning, like Rossetti's blessed damozel, out of the bars of her spirit world," to unite the two young people, whose love has conquered her hate; so love blesses the dead as well as the living and gives the distracted spirits peace. At this point, Professor Nicoll says, "we cease to believe in the reality of the picture," although he gives unstinted praise to the play's beauty of thought and expression, and the technical skill with which the author has woven together not only two periods of time but two planes of existence. The objection to the intermingling of dead and living characters on the stage seems to be sound, unless the poet's imagination can create an atmosphere of illusion permitting a momentary suspension of disbelief on the part of the spectator. Ghosts that walk and talk among people still enjoying the light of day are not within the limits of ordinary experience, and the poet must cast his spell over the audience to make them dramatically credible. Lessing, in his *Dramaturgie*, contrasting the ghost of Voltaire's *Ninus* with that of Shakespeare's *Hamlet*, laid down the limits of credibility in such matters, and though intelligent people were perhaps more credulous as to communication with the dead in the first quarter of the twentieth century than they were in the last quarter of the eighteenth, Lessing's principles still hold good.

Masefield is a philosopher as well as a poet, and none of his experiments in drama fail of noble enrichment in detail; but in their general form and tendency, they are reactionary, and, so far as the future development of the drama is concerned, futile. It seems a pity that so gifted an artist, who has given us one good play, should so often spend his energies in ventures which are indeed interesting to the student of the drama, even as unsuccessful experiments, but have little or no significance for the theatre as it exists today, either as a place of popular amusement or as an opportunity to interpret and illumine modern life. But he is quite convinced in his own mind that he is on the right track. He said in the summer of 1926: "So long as there remain two enthusiasts and a plank there will still be a poetical stage."

JOHN DRINKWATER (1882-   )

Like Masefield, John Drinkwater is primarily a poet. He was associated with Rupert Brooke in the confident and successful effort to create a new poetic age which began in 1912 with the publication of *Georgian Poetry* and was almost brought to an end after the publication of *New Numbers* in 1914. In the latter enterprise, which would have been published quarterly if the outbreak of the War had not killed it after its first issue, Drinkwater was one of the four authors concerned, the other three being Wilfrid Wilson Gibson, Lascelles Abercrombie, and Rupert Brooke; and after Rupert Brooke's death Drinkwater enshrined his friend's memory in one of his *Prose Papers* (1917). The group had much in common in purposes and ideas, and came as near as is perhaps possible in England to forming a school—the new "Georgians."

It is not without significance that of the five plays preceding *Abraham Lincoln*, one, produced and printed *Rebellion* privately in 1914, was entitled *Rebellion*. Its hero, Narros, gives voice to the protest against Victorian limitations and restrictions; to Drinkwater, as to his fellow-poet and dramatist, Lascelles Abercrombie, "prudence, prudence is the deadly sin." So Narros, not seeing that he will be ultimately victorious, recalls, in the hour of his temporary defeat, the Georgian desire for a full and unfettered life, unhampered by petty commercial consideration and dead conventions:

> When I was grown
> To man's full vehemence, there was fixed in me
> A will to know the sap of life, a will
> To live ungoverned by the prudent hands
> That are instruction. I watched this King and all of you
> Spending the marrowy bounty of your days
> In lean and patchy argument, as who
> Should bear this right or that, who carry in
> And who go laden forth, what gain should be
> Marked for this trading, what forfeiture for that,
> How should the tithes be reckoned, should those ships
> Be chartered so, divided so the spoils
> Of each man's labour. And I sickened then
> For a state should foster in a man the will
> For life not netted in these prudences;
> I saw life simple, and you peopled it
> With idiot ghosts that would not let me rest
> Till I too mouthed it, and denied myself.

Of the other four early dramas, published in 1917 as *Four Poetic Plays*, as has been pointed out by Professor

Morgan, *The Storm* has much in common with the poems and plays of humble life done by Drinkwater's older comrade, Wilfrid Wilson Gibson. The scene is a shepherd's cottage in the mountains, to which comes a tourist who sees in the wind and snow only a magnificent exhibition of the powers of nature for him to enjoy and battle against successfully. But to the shepherd's wife the storm spells tragedy and "it is not good to praise it." To her it seems "drenched in treachery and sin"—an outburst of the powers of evil. And the end justifies her foreboding, for her husband's life is lost in it. *The Storm*

$X = O$: *A Night of the Trojan War* (1917) is a War play, going for its inspiration to the greatest of anti-war dramatists, Euripides. In the first scene two Greeks, Pronax and Salvius, are sitting in camp at night outside Troy, and Pronax, not at all liking the job, goes out to slay one of his adversaries on the walls of the city; these walls are shown in the next scene, with Ilus leaving Capys to pick off some Greek straggler. Pronax, having accomplished his mission, returns to find Salvius dead; Ilus returning finds the body of Capys, slain by Pronax. Two young lives have been extinguished—cancelled out. Where is the gain? "$X = O$." And these young men had neither hate nor envy in their hearts. It is theirs "merely to die," and with them dies not only youth but beauty. "Beauty is broken." $X = O$

Both the above plays were first acted at the Birmingham Repertory Theatre, and it was here, too, that *Abraham Lincoln* had its original production under the direction of the author on October 12, 1918. Drinkwater was uncommonly fortunate in his choice, for as the War was nearing its successful close, there was a strong feeling of gratitude in Great Britain for the help of the American *Abraham Lincoln* soldiers, some of whom had marched through the cheering throngs of London on their way to the front, and a new and lively interest in the United States was aroused. Lincoln was one of the few heroes familiar to the British public—was there not a statue to him by an American artist outside the House of Commons?—and Lord Charnwood in his excellent biography had given the reading public some appreciation of the elevation of Lincoln's character and of the difficult issues he had to deal with; incidentally, the biography had also provided the dramatist with the necessary facts, in a striking and convenient form. Drinkwater was fortunate in the hour and also in the man, but it must not be forgotten that before him half-a-dozen American dramatists had done their best to put Lincoln effectively on the stage and had failed. With all allowances for the opportuneness of the moment, which made Drinkwater's tragedy a popular success on both sides of the Atlantic, it must be acknowledged that *Abraham Lincoln* is not only a craftsmanlike job but a moving play, rising to the height of its great argument. Lincoln's spirit of "malice toward none, charity for all" spreads angelic wings over the scene, but it is not so much as Drinkwater's earlier work a drama of ideas; it is a drama of character. The two Chroniclers, who serve in the play the same purposes as Shakespeare's Chorus in *Henry V*, make this clear in the Prologue:

> Kinsmen, you shall behold
> Our stage, in mimic action, mould
> A man's character.
> This is the wonder always, everywhere—
> Not that vast mutability which is event,
> The pits and pinnacles of change,
> But man's desire and valiance that range
> All circumstance, and come to port unspent.

The event is a mere agency: "the bearing of man facing it is all."

> So kinsmen, we present
> This for no loud event
> That is but fugitive,
> But that you may behold
> Our mimic action mould
> The spirit of man immortally to live.

Lincoln was great because he was "the lord of his event," and it is not his political struggles, much less the conflicts on the battle field—merely things of chance remembrance at a fireside,

> But the ardours that they bear,
> The proud and invincible motions of character—
> These—these abide.

So, after an introductory scene presenting to us Lincoln in his modest home at Springfield, accepting the presidential nomination, the Chroniclers indicate that a year has gone by and invite us to contemplate

> A heart, undaunted to possess
> Itself among the glooms of fate
> In vision and in loneliness.

We see Lincoln struggling with his Cabinet, worried by pacifists and profiteers, signing the Emancipation Proclamation, and visiting Grant on the eve of Lee's surrender. Then the two Chroniclers foreshadow Lincoln's death under the similitude of the fall of the rose:

> And out of the night it came,
> A wind, and the rose fell,
> Shattered its heart of flame,
> And how shall June tell
> The glory that went with May,

> How shall the full year keep
> The beauty that ere its day
> Was blasted into sleep?
>
> Roses, oh, heart of man:
> Courage, that in the prime
> Looked on truth, and began
> Conspiracies with time
> To flower upon the pain
> Of dark and envious earth. . . .
> A wind blows, and the brain
> Is the dust that was its birth.

Finally come the short assassination scene and the reminder that "events go by":

> But, as we spoke, presiding everywhere
> Upon event was one man's character
> And that endures; it is the token sent
> Always to man for man's own government.

In many familiar touches the dramatist has helped us to remember the kind of man Lincoln was—homely, human, dominated in small things by his wife, in great matters controlled by no one, sympathizing with the simple-hearted, and not afraid to put an end sternly to the self-seeking of the ambitious and pretentious. Lincoln's great aim is clearly set forth in his own words, "My paramount object in this struggle is to save the Union." But along with this, we are made conscious of his hatred of slavery. In the first scene, he says to the delegation which brings the news of his nomination:

While we will not force abolition, we will give slavery no approval, and we will not allow it to extend its boundaries by one yard. The determination is in my blood. When I was a boy I made a trip to New Orleans, and there I saw them chained, beaten, kicked as a man would be ashamed to kick a thieving dog. And

I saw a young girl driven up and down the room that the bidders might satisfy themselves. And I said then, "If ever I get a chance to hit that thing, I'll hit it hard."

The final scene makes use of a sentence or two from the Gettysburg speech. But through it all we are aware of Lincoln as a man, bearing in loneliness a terrific responsibility in order to "make as one the names again of liberty and law." His talks with the old negro and with the soldier condemned to death are perhaps the scenes which best illustrate his rich humanity, but this is the centre of Lincoln's character as Drinkwater conceived it, and we are never allowed to forget it. We see the man as he was—humorous, shrewd, kindly, gentle, hating force, but accepting the war "in the name of humanity, and just and merciful dealing, and the hope of love and charity on earth."

Behind all this is the thought, brought out especially in the poem of the rose quoted above, of the evanescence of all things human. At the height of his power and wisdom, just when his spirit of charity and forbearance was most needed, Lincoln is snuffed out by the revolver of a cowardly assassin.

> Disaster strikes with the blind sweep of chance,
> And this our mimic action was a theme,
> Kinsmen, as life is, clouded as a dream.

In an earlier scene the dramatist has recalled as one of Lincoln's favourite passages from Shakespeare the lines from *The Tempest:*

> We are such stuff
> As dreams are made on, and our little life
> Is rounded with a sleep.

In the Prologue above cited Drinkwater had named Cromwell as the one man fit to be put by the side of Lincoln

Oliver Cromwell

as "lord of his event" and it was not surprising that after the success of *Abraham Lincoln, Oliver Cromwell* should quickly follow (written 1920, published 1921, acted 1922). The events of Cromwell's life do not arrange themselves so readily for dramatic presentation as those of Lincoln, and the play enjoyed only a *succès d'estime.* An even harder

Robert E. Lee

fate befell *Robert E. Lee* (1923) which was rejected at Richmond, Va., as giving "a false idea of the principles for which Southern people suffered and died" and "not worthy of the great name it bears."

In the preface to his collected plays Drinkwater, after replying to the critics who accused him of historical inaccuracies and insufficiencies, set forth his method as essentially that of a dramatist, not of a biographer; he endeavours to give a truthful and consistent picture of the man as bringing out certain principles and ideas the poet-dramatist wishes to illustrate; and he is at liberty to omit matters irrelevant to that theme. Lincoln, Cromwell, and Lee are all examples in Drinkwater's view of the qualities and aims of leadership:

> There was the man who, certain of his aims, had to face all the cunning and malice of unscrupulous intrigue in order to preserve what he conceived to be the only sure foundations of society as he knew it. This was leadership determined to preserve a great establishment. There was then the man who was convinced that society as he knew it was being destroyed by corruption and tyranny, and who was determined with a religious zeal to sweep away the old order and found a new one. Then again, there was the leader who felt, with absolute purity of heart, that loyalty to his own tradition was the first, and altogether becoming, duty of man. Here, then, were the three aspects of my problem, or perhaps one should say three of the aspects: the leader inspired by a great moral idea to the vindication of a system, the leader inspired by a great moral idea to the overthrow of a system, and the leader for whom a system became a great moral idea in itself.

It is not difficult to see why, for dramatic purposes, Lincoln was a much better subject than Cromwell or Lee— he is more human, more various, with a character and a cause that come home more directly to the hearts of the English-speaking peoples; and his sudden taking off gave a tragic ending which is lacking in the other two instances of leadership, notably in the case of Lee, who lived for many years after his defeat a comparatively obscure life as President of a Southern College; his complete abnegation so far as politics were concerned and his devotion to the educational interests of his people were nobly generous, but they could hardly be made effective on the stage. *Abraham Lincoln* remains Drinkwater's one masterpiece, and in the opinion of competent critics it is a masterpiece that will endure.

Perhaps a word should be said about *Mary Stuart*, which was of about the same period as *Cromwell* and was even less successful. The critics were more divided about it than the public. Professor Nicoll thinks it Drinkwater's subtlest drama, embodying the idea that "there are some women who have hearts so wide, who have ideals so high, that they cannot find any one man great enough to satisfy their soul's love. . . . Darnley and Bothwell and Rizzio are merely portions of that larger whole for which she craves. She desires strength and beauty and passion: perhaps she finds one of these qualities in one of her lovers, another in another, but never has she discovered all in one man. She is not fickle and faithless; it is simply that her ideal is too high for human attainments."

Mary Stuart

Admitting this as a possible frame for the portrait of Mary, E. Graham Sutton contends that the figure Drinkwater has drawn is too small for it; Mary should appeal to our admiration and sympathy by some greatness within herself, and she has not even true passion—"only a green-sick, posturing pursuit of the *idea* of love."

Drinkwater was apparently more encouraged by one success than dismayed by three failures, for the newspapers credit him with the intention of dealing dramatically with the character of Byron and also with that of Burns—neither of them, one would think, as promising as those he has tried already for the chronicle play centred about an idea. He is to be commended for his persistence in following a line of development which seems rarely to have the good fortune of winning public approval; and indeed for the lover of English drama one such success as *Abraham Lincoln* is consolation enough for many reverses, especially when the unsuccessful experiments involve such points of interest in characterization and philosophy as *Mary Stuart*, *Oliver Cromwell*, and *Robert E. Lee*.

JAMES ELROY FLECKER (1884-1915)

Like Drinkwater, so far as the stage is concerned Flecker is the author of one successful play, and in his case the success is of rather dubious significance, but his personality is interesting and there is no doubt as to his being a true poet. A precocious boy, he got into the sixth form at Uppingham at an unusually early age, and at seventeen won an open classical scholarship to Trinity College, Oxford. At Oxford he made many friends, and Sir Walter Raleigh, then Professor of English Literature, told him he was the coming poet of his time. From Oxford he went to Cambridge to prepare for the consular service, and was in due time appointed to a position in the East, where he spent the last few years of his short life. His residence in the East gave him not only subjects for poetry and drama, but profoundly affected his view of life. At Cambridge he came very near agnosticism, and wrote: "Whatever you do, don't call me Evangelical. I am neither Evangelical nor High Church, nor Methodist, nor Roman Catholic, nor Rechabite, nor Perezzite, nor Baptist, nor Sectarianist, but purely, simply, and plainly, a Christian." Further developments in his religious beliefs are thus indicated by J. C. Squire:

Flecker went through the normal stresses and changes of the intellectual and ardent undergraduate. But what happened afterwards? He went to the East, with a great sense of the glamour of the East. He found the colour and the brightness, the sun, the moon, the vermilion, the green, and the sapphire of his dreams; but he found also an indolence, a cruelty, and a crookedness that disgusted him. The spectacle of Mohammedanism made him react towards Christianity: he saw Europe and the religious tradition of Europe in a new light; his theological reasonings reached, simultaneously, a new stage; and, at the end, if he did not die in the Roman Catholic faith, he was certainly on the verge of it.

The cruelty as well as the colour of the East are mirrored in Flecker's oriental drama, *Hassan*, and this accounts to *Hassan* some extent for the diverse opinions of the critics. Flecker himself was convinced that it was a masterpiece, in spite of his failure to get it put on the stage during his lifetime. He wrote:

Hassan is being read by ————. I await with resignation the inevitable disappointment. It is a masterpiece, but I shall never live to see it come into its own. . . . The only way to get an actor-manager to read a play is to stand over him with a revolver. Remember this is *such* an important thing.

Hassan played would make me independent for life in all probability. . . . I'm feeling very wretched. I have got so much to say to the world, and no one will let me say it. It was the only thing I had left me, and it has failed.

It was not put on till eight years after the poet's death, and though it ran all through the season of 1923-24, it had a very mixed reception from the critics. Some hailed Flecker as one of "the inheritors of unfulfilled renown," a second Shakespeare nipped in the budding; but the harrowing torture scenes at the end of the play met with general condemnation, while there was universal praise for the ballets of Fokine and the music of Delius. Undoubtedly the gorgeous oriental setting had a great deal to do with the prolonged and enormous popular success. The more considered criticisms of the play as published are some of them mainly favourable, some almost completely hostile. Professor Morgan thinks the play a notable effort, showing great imaginative reach, but he makes important reservations. E. Graham Sutton writes: "*Hassan* is a lovely thing, loveliness gathered at the moment of ecstasy, like flowers the gatherer has watched bloom, but preserved imperishable." He regards *Chu Chin Chow*, which delighted London audiences for season after season, as the *reductio ad absurdum* of the spectacular mode and a sure sign of dramatic decadence, as indeed do all the serious critics. *Hassan* marks the swinging back of the pendulum by the recognition of the necessity for wedding spectacle to poetry:

Hassan was spectacle subdued to its proper use—or very nearly so. There were still one or two excrescent "effects," some a little precious, such as those interminable waits in a darkened theatre which are so liable to result in lemonade being spilt down the devotee's neck: some a little crude—one could have wished that the fountain had run blood to the mind's eye only; or if that were impossible, that some preparation more resembling blood could have been shed (who would have thought the old Greek to have had so much Grenadine in him?).

Professor Nicoll, as becomes his academic position, was more serious, but also more severe:

> Hassan, published in 1922, was performed in 1923, with gorgeous scenery and the plentiful introduction of ballet and music. In some ways it deserves praise as a piece of literature, there being unquestionably an atmosphere of poetry throughout the whole; but as a drama it is negligible. Fundamentally it is but a Chu Chin Chow made more glorious. The Eastern setting may charm, but the characters are crudely drawn and the situations are forced. Perhaps a certain romantic intensity envelops the figures of Rafi, King of the Beggars, and the slave-girl, Pervaneh, but these cannot raise the whole to the levels of high art. The ridiculous buffoonery of Hassan, the unmitigated savagery of Haroun, the idealistic rapture of the poet Ishak, and the love-passion of the two forlorn figures whose tortured screams are heard in the last act make the poem a mere patchwork of heterogeneous elements without harmony and without form. Hassan, save for its poetic elements, (not by any means always dramatic), must be placed alongside and hardly above other Eastern fantasia, of which Edward Knoblock's Kismet (1912) was the best known and most popular. The spectacular play still makes periodic efforts to rise to that position it occupied in the early nineteenth century, as is witnessed by the recently produced Decameron Nights, but it will always remain a trivial form of dramatic effort.

Flecker wrote one other play, Don Juan, which was declined by manager after manager and drove the author himself to despair when he tried to remodel it. "I can't do anything with that impossible Don Juan," he used to say. Bernard Shaw praised one scene in it as "a stroke of genius" and wrote to Flecker:

> With tact and experience you ought to go far, for you certainly have the trump cards. Only do for Heaven's sake remember that there are plenty of geniuses about, and that the real difficulty is to find writers who are sober, honest, and industrious, and have been for many years in their last situation.

Don Juan

Poor Flecker never had the chance to acquire experience and he showed no sign of tact for the stage. *Don Juan,* like *Hassan,* came short of success in the attempt to make "a coherent whole out of a mass of incongruous materials and a jumble of antagonistic styles." With horrors a plenty, the play falls off into melodrama and even into burlesque. But like *Hassan,* it has many good things in it. H. C. Minshin singles out as dramatically effective the scene commended by Bernard Shaw. The mistress whom Juan had callously forsaken appears at his door as a shabby and weather-beaten street-singer. Moved at last with compunction, and aghast at the change from her former brilliance, he proposes a renewal of their old relationship, only to find that her spirit is broken as well as her body, and that she obviously has no heart for the adventure. "She is not mad?" he asks his hanger-on, who has loved Tisbea all along. "No," is the reply, "she has become sane: she dreams of love no longer: she does not think that she is a princess in an old story and you a fairy prince. She knows that she is a fisher-girl and that you are a gentleman. You have not hurt her mind: you have destroyed her soul."

LORD DUNSANY (1878-   )

Edward John Moreton Drax Plunkett, Lord Dunsany, though his dramas are not in verse, clearly belongs to the poetic group. Educated at Eton and the English Military School of Sandhurst, he entered the army and saw active service during the South African war. On his return he interested himself in the Irish literary movement, and his first play was produced at the Abbey Theatre in 1909. It was doubtless to W. B. Yeats that he owed his conception of the drama as a way of escape from life, and Yeats gave him also valuable hints for the composition of the one-act plays with which Dunsany won his first success. "Surprise . . . is what is necessary, Surprise, and then more Surprise, and that is all." Dunsany proceeded to better the instruction of his master, and has written a score or more plays which are well known on the stage throughout the English-speaking world. After one more play at the Abbey Theatre, *The Gods of the Mountain* found him in 1911 in possession of the stage at the London Haymarket. A year or two later Stuart Walker of the Portmanteau Theatre introduced his work to the United States, where several of his plays have had their first production and where his popularity has been increased by personal visits, during which he submitted with his usual grace to the sufferings endured by the lionized lecturer.

The Gods of the Mountain

He has stated his aims and methods so clearly and succinctly that it seems best to let him speak for himself:

> Something must be wrong with an age whose drama deserts romance. Romance is so inseparable from life that all we need to obtain romantic drama is for the dramatist to find any age and any country where life is not too thickly veiled and cloaked with puzzles and conventions, in fact to find a people that is not in the agonies of self-consciousness. For myself, I think that it is simpler to imagine such a people, as it saves the trouble of reading to find a romantic age, or the trouble of making a journey to lands where there is no press.

The above is from Dunsany's *Romance and the Modern Stage,* which is reprinted in the revised edition of Bierstadt's *Dunsany the Dramatist* (1919). From the same volume come the following passages from a letter written by the dramatist in answer to an inquiry from Mrs. Emma Garnett Boyd as to the significance of some of his plays:

I will say first that in my plays I tell very simple stories—so simple that sometimes people of this complex age, being brought up in intricacies, even fail to understand them. Second, no man ever wrote a simple story yet, because he is bound to colour it with his own experience. Take my *Gods of the Mountain*. Some beggars, being hard up, pretend to be gods. Then they get all that they want. But Destiny, Nemesis, the Gods punish them by turning them into the very idols they desire to be.

I am not trying to teach anybody anything. I merely set out to make a work of art out of a simple theme, and God knows we want works of art in this age of corrugated iron. How many people hold the error that Shakespeare was of the schoolroom! Whereas he was of the playground, as all artists are.

Dunsany has a power of invention which enables him to respond easily to the Yeats prescription of "Surprise and more Surprise." He inherited the Celtic glamour by right of birth, and often adds to his plays of oriental fantasy a touch of Western irony. The combination is extraordinarily effective, and earnest seekers (especially in the United States) have discovered in his plays meanings which the author modestly accepts as "all unconscious, though inevitable." "That is the kind of way that man does get hit by destiny." This was apparently with special reference to *The Gods of the Mountain*, but it would no *The Glittering Gate* doubt hold good for his first play, *The Glittering Gate*. Two burglars decide to break into Paradise, and after much trouble succeed in passing through the glittering gate to find—Nothing. Rupert Brooke about the same time used the same idea—no doubt, independently—in one of his earlier poems—but he meant it. Lord Dunsany, presumably, used it "without deliberate intention"—merely for the sake of surprise.

It would be easy to read a similar ironical interpretation into *The Gods of the Mountain*, but the reader will do it on his own responsibility. The true gods are seven images of jade squatting in the mountain far off from the city, where seven beggars take it upon themselves to impersonate the gods for what they can gain by it. The gods come to the city and in their wrath turn the beggars into stone, whereupon the beggars are accepted as divine by all the citizens, even by those who were previously inclined to scepticism.

A Night at an Inn is perhaps a better illustration of Dunsany's powers of illusion—for those who are ready to be illuded. Three desperate English adventurers have stolen the huge ruby which is the one eye of an Eastern idol; they are pursued to England by the priests of the fane, who are lured into a lonely spot and there slain, one by one, so that the thieves think themselves at last secure. They are just rejoicing in their success when the Idol himself gropes his way in, and in the face of the terror-stricken adventurers, picks the ruby up and walks off with the sure step of a man who can see. The passage in which the doom of the thieves is described is a good example of Dunsany's power to evoke an atmosphere of horror by suggestion rather than by realistic description: *A Night at an Inn*

THE TOFF.	O great heavens!
ALBERT	(*in a childish, plaintive voice*). What is it, Toffy?
BILL.	Albert, it is that obscene idol (*in a whisper*) come from India.
ALBERT.	It is gone.
BILL.	It has taken its eye.
SNIGGERS.	We are saved.
A VOICE	*off* (*with outlandish accent*). Meestaire William Jones, Able Seaman.
	The Toff has never spoken, never moved. He only gazes stupidly in horror.
BILL.	Albert, Albert, what is this? (*He rises and walks*

out. One moan is heard. Sniggers goes to the window. He falls back sickly.)

ALBERT   *(in a whisper).* What has happened?

SNIGGERS.   I have seen it. I have seen it. Oh! I have seen it! *(He returns to the table).*

THE TOFF   *(laying his hand very gently on Sniggers' arm, speaking softly and winningly).* What was it, Sniggers?

SNIGGERS.   I have seen it.

ALBERT.   What?

SNIGGERS.   Oh!

VOICE.   Meestaire Jacob Smith, Able Seaman.

ALBERT.   Must I go, Toffy? Toffy, must I go?

SNIGGERS   *(clutching him).* Don't move.

ALBERT   *(going).* Toffy, Toffy.

VOICE.   Meestaire Jacob Smith, Able Seaman.

SNIGGERS.   I can't go, Toffy, I can't go. I can't do it. *(He goes.)*

VOICE.   Meestaire Arnold Everett Scott-Fortescue, late Esquire, Able Seaman.

THE TOFF.   I did not foresee it.

If

If is a dream play, possibly intended as a reply to Barrie's *Dear Brutus,* the obvious lesson of which is that a second chance in life would find us exactly the same persons as we were without it. According to Dunsany, who sees romance in life, there must be more room for chance. He imagines one John Beale, a commonplace Londoner who turns back the wheel of life and catches a train which he once missed. From that point on, his life is entirely different. He finds himself carried by the stream of opportunity from one thing to another until he becomes a petty despot in the interior of Persia, surrounded by savage luxury and wielding powers of life and death. An insurrection leads to his deposition, but before he can have further adventures he wakes up—in his suburban home on the outskirts of London. Perhaps because *If* was a play of modern life and was invested by the dream device with a certain air of plausibility, it was the most successful of Dunsany's dramas and enjoyed a long London run. O. Henry used the idea of the difference made in life by taking one or another turning in *Roads of Destiny*, but in his story it is less effectively worked out.

The above examples suggest only a part of Dunsany's extraordinary versatility in devising a thrilling plot and investing it with an atmosphere which, for a few moments at any rate, makes it almost credible. This is not a romantic age, but we are nearly all willing to return to the fairy-tale stage of our childhood, if the tale is well enough told. Dunsany has apparently an inexhaustible store of romantic adventures, and he has unusual skill in putting them into dramatic form. It is almost inevitable that this form should be the one-act play—even if there should be at some point a momentary dropping of the curtain. Clayton Hamilton is no doubt right in his definition of this *genre* as distinct from the full length play "not by the time required for its presentation, nor by the number of its pauses," but by the production of a "single dramatic effect with the greatest economy of means that is consistent with the utmost emphasis."

The one-act play

In English drama, in which the one-act play was formerly not so much neglected as despised, being intended to enable late-diners and late-comers generally to get to the theatre half an hour after the programme began without missing anything, Dunsany shares with Barrie the credit of having lifted the one-acter, which requires a peculiar and comparatively rare skill, to the level of an acknowledged form of art.

PLAY LISTS

John Masefield

1907 *The Campden Wonder.*
1909 *The Tragedy of Nan.*
1910 *The Tragedy of Pompey the Great.*
1914 *Philip the King.*
1915 *The Faithful.*
1916 *Good Friday.* (*Fortnightly Review,* Dec. 1915).
    The Locked Chest.
    The Sweeps of "98".
1917 *Anne Pedersdotter* (trans. from Hans Wiers-Jenssen).
1922 *Esther* (trans. from Racine).
    Bernice (adapted and partially trans. from Racine).
    Melloney Holtspur.
1925 *A King's Daughter.*

John Drinkwater

1911 *Cophetua.*
1914 *Rebellion.*
1915 *The Storm.*
1916 *The God of Quiet.*
1917 *X=O.*
1918. *Abraham Lincoln.*
1922 *Mary Stuart.*
    Oliver Cromwell.
1923. *Robert E. Lee.*

James Elroy Flecker

1923 *Hassan.*
1925 *Don Juan* (pub.).

Lord Dunsany

1909 *The Glittering Gate.*
1911 *King Argimenes and the Unknown Warrior.*
    The Gods of the Mountain.
1912 *The Golden Doom.*
1913 *The Lost Silk Hat.*

1914 *The Tents of the Arabs.*
1916 *A Night at an Inn.*
The Queen's Enemies.
1918 *The Prince of Stamboul.*
Fame and the Poet.
1919 *The Laughter of the Gods.*
The Murderers.
1920 *The Compromise of the King of the Golden Isles.*
A Good Bargain.
If Shakespeare Lived Today.
1921 *Cheezo.*
If.
1922 *The Flight of the Queen.*

CHAPTER XII

AFTER-WAR PLAYWRIGHTS

Effects of the War

THE War, bringing economic and social disaster in its train, in England as elsewhere, had devastating effects upon the serious drama. The intellectual class upon which the serious drama depended for support suffered in their pockets as well as in their persons; financially, they shared neither in the increased wages of the working class nor in the profits of the war-manufacturer and trader. Of the seven repertory theatres successfully established at Birmingham, Dublin, Bristol, Glasgow, Huddersfield, Liverpool and Manchester, only the two first-mentioned survived. The commercial theatres found it a patriotic duty as well as a profitable enterprise to provide for the frivolous tastes of the flappers and the men on leave who brought them or were brought by them to the play; Albert de Courville, a leading London manager, estimated that the theatre crowds consisted of "ninety per cent soldiers or people engaged on national requirements accompanied by soldiers"—*i. e.*, young munition girls and the like. He added: "Men on leave are cramming as much amusement as possible into the short period of their vacation." Obviously it was no time for the presentation on the stage of social or psychological problems or for the consideration of the interests of dramatic art. The unusual profits made led to theatrical speculation such as had never been known before. Huntly Carter in *The New Spirit in the European Theatre 1914-24* says of the London situation:

208

Theatrical gambling and profiteering took place on an unprecedented scale. They were the outcome partly of the development of wartime amalgamation, and partly of a phase of theatrical prosperity due to the conclusion of the War. Every year during the War had seen the formation of big theatrical financial combines composed of directors and managers interested in commercial, industrial and theatrical enterprises more for profit than for the elevation of the theatre and drama. Thus, the English theatre had become largely a soulless machine joined to the Stock Exchange, which used current social events simply because it could not work without them.

A London journalist writes in 1917 that with the exception of *Damaged Goods*—Brieux's disease play put on to keep the young soldiers off the sick list—"there is not one play of distinction now being acted on the London stage. There is no Shakespeare, no Shaw, no Galsworthy, no Barrie. The stage is in the thrall of revues, farces, and light comedies, not one worthy of more than passing notice." The 1918-19 season was no better: Huntly Carter summarises the productions as "crook plays, romantic melodramas, bedroom and pyjama farces, undressed revues, and costly spectacles." The London *Times* during Armistice week noted that there were thirty-four theatres open, "all offering indifferent entertainment, with the exception of the Court Theatre with a play by Shakespeare."

The leaders of the new dramatic movement were either immersed in war work or dramatically inactive. Bernard Shaw had disappeared under a cloud of political unpopularity, and his *Playlets of the War*, composed during this period, attracted little attention. Galsworthy was working in a French hospital. The younger men were at the front, and those of them who escaped serious injury, came back to the distracted and disheartened England of the after-War years.

The established playwrights, as they recovered from the effects of the War, regained possession of the stage either in London or New York or in both. Galsworthy "came back" with *The Skin Game* in 1920 and repeated this success with *Loyalties* in 1922. Bernard Shaw, as has been noted, returned to the London stage by way of New York, and his *Saint Joan* is perhaps the surest of the English after-War plays to win a permanent place in dramatic literature. Others of the older dramatists resumed their former activity, some with diminished power, some with added depth. Of the latter, the most notable was Somerset Maugham, who before the War enjoyed a considerable reputation as a writer of novels and light comedies, and after the War set a new standard for the English comedy *The Circle* of manners in *The Circle* (1922). For years, to use Graham Sutton's phrase, Maugham had been sitting "without undue fidgeting in the house of Sardoodledom," and it was something of a surprise to his admirers that he should suddenly rise to a new level of power and significance. *The Circle* is a well-made play, but it is something more. The characters belong to that section of English upper-class society so often shown on the stage as possessing neither morals nor brains, except for the apt expression of shallow epigrams obligingly invented for them by the author. One wonders sometimes how the persons in such plays can talk so cleverly and show such a lamentable lack of sense. In *The Circle* there is cleverness enough and to spare in the dialogue, but one does get passages of real thought and real feeling. The two young people who dare all for love in spite of the disastrous experience and open warnings of their elders who have tried the same rash experiment are

drawn sympathetically but not romantically, and the issue
of the adventure is left open to question. The misery which
followed on the elopement of Lord Porteous and Lady
Kitty is set forth with grim humour, but Porteous concludes the play with the reflection: "If we made rather a
hash of things perhaps it was because we were rather trivial
people. You can do anything in this world if you are
prepared to take the consequences, and consequences
depend on character." The more conventional ending of
the young wife's clinging at the last moment to the security
of her own home and accepting a dutiful submission to her
unloved husband lay ready to the dramatist's hand, but he
preferred the more original and effective solution of letting
the young people repeat the mistake of their elders—as
young people mostly do, unterrified by the elders' warnings. The effectiveness of the decision is increased by the
failure of the ingenious stratagem of generosity devised
by the deserted husband of the previous generation for
the advantage of the unloved husband of the present;
perhaps in the last scene Porteous changes too suddenly
from mere irascibility to common sense and good feeling,
while Champion-Cheny, who has hitherto shown signs of
intelligence, unexpectedly develops an almost imbecile self-
conceit; but the situation is amusing enough to bear the
strain, and Maugham was prudent enough to end on a
note of comedy rather than on the moral tone of condemnation for the escaping lovers or the romantic one of condonation of their offence.

A. A. MILNE (1882-   )

Alan Alexander Milne, educated at Westminster School
and Trinity College, Cambridge, took to journalism in

London when he was twenty-one and had been assistant editor of *Punch* for eight years when the War broke out and he joined the Royal Warwickshire Regiment. In the Introduction to his *First Plays*, he explains that but for the War they would hardly have been written. "Playwriting is a luxury to a journalist, as insidious as golf and much more expensive in time and money." As a journalist, he was sure of his market, but with a play "there is no certainty of anything save disillusionment." When he became a (temporary) professional soldier, however, the case was different: there was no reason why he should not amuse himself in his spare time by writing plays, just as other subalterns played bridge and golf; he had no serious thought of making money or winning fame, though he **Wurzel-** cherished secret hopes. *Wurzel-Flummery* was the im-
Flummery mediate result, and though it had to be cut down from three acts to two, and from two to one, it gained a place on the stage at the height of war excitement, probably because it was a war play only in the sense of being as light as possible in tone and completely free from any reference to war issues. It is a fanciful absurdity, resting upon the offer of legacies of fifty thousand pounds each to two ambitious members of parliament on condition that they take the name of Wurzel-Flummery; and Milne was doubtless right in concluding, after the operation, that the one-act version was the best. There is not enough in the invention to carry through three acts.

Belinda, the next play produced, is a similar trifle, although it has just enough plot and characterization to enable Irene Vanbrugh to win for it a popular success. A more ambitious effort, which was written earlier though it came some years later to the stage, was *The Lucky One*, contrasting the fortunes of two brothers—one brilliant and

charming, the other dull and unsuccessful; the latter
blunders into prison from sheer stupidity, but manages by
an appeal to pity to win the girl on whom they have both
set their hearts; the unsuccessful lover is, however, consoled by an important diplomatic appointment and the
ending of the play left the audience rather at a loss as to
the dramatist's estimate of the relative values of his own
characters.

In the Introduction to *First Plays* Milne acknowledged
his "great debt" to J. M. Barrie, and this indebtedness is
even more marked in the *Second Plays*. *Make Believe* is a
children's play, and Milne frankly owns that "the difficulty
in writing a children's play is that Barrie was born too
soon." The Barrie note is equally clear in *Mr. Pim
Passes By*, which obtained a great popular success, partly
due to its clever combination of Barrie's sentiment with a
gentler satire which is Milne's own. Irene Vanbrugh was
this time a charming widow remarried to George Marden,
a Buckinghamshire County Magistrate and magnate. She
has accepted rather easily the assurance of the newspapers
that her first husband, Jacob Telworthy, an Australian
convict, is dead, and she accepts in the play, with even
greater ease, the assumption, in the first place that he is
still alive, in the second that he died after her re-marriage,
simply on the chance remark of a Mr. Pim (whom she has
never seen before) that he met on the boat coming from
Australia a swindler named Telworthy whom he had previously known in Sydney. Marden accepts it, too, and
says to his wife: "Our union has been unhallowed by the
Church. Unhallowed even by the Law. Legally, we have
been living in—living in—well, the point is how does the
Law stand? I imagine that Telworthy could get a—a
divorce." He goes further: "I believe the proper method

*Mr. Pim
Passes By*

213

is a nullity suit, declaring our marriage null and -er- void. It would, so to speak, wipe out these years of -er- irregular union." It is, of course, obvious that no one, not even a Buckinghamshire J. P., would talk in this strain, and the audience does not take the situation seriously; they know there must be a way out and Mr. Pim in Act III comes forward to say that his Australian criminal was not Telworthy but Polwistle; the name of Telworthy stayed in his mind unconsciously from having been mentioned to him just before as that of Mrs. Marden's first husband. There is a subplot of young lovers and a good deal of sentiment, pretty talk—it would almost be worth while to count the number of "darlings" in the dialogue—and innocent embracings—just the right mixture to catch the taste of the particular public for which it was intended.

The Romantic Age

In *The Romantic Age* Milne went even further in the direction of sentiment for the public, and much too far for the critics, who pointed out that in the year 1920 girls like Melisande did not exist and nobody behaved like that nowadays. Milne admitted that no particular girl exists who talks and behaves like this, but he asserted that "there is a type of girl who, in her heart, secretly, *thinks* like this." This was a domain into which the critics could not follow, but there was general satisfaction when in his next play Milne left fairyland and kept firm touch with reality. *The*

The Truth About Blayds

Truth About Blayds makes no further demand upon the credulity of the audience than the assumption that in the Victorian era it would be possible for a minor poet to pass off the posthumous works of a young friend of his, who was a genius, as his own, and that by publishing these poems at judicious intervals he could win reputation, royalties, and the adulation that comes to a man who is the popular poet of his generation. Blayds takes in everybody, including George Meredith and Thomas Carlyle, and reveals his secret only on his deathbed; he is a magnificent *poseur* and tyrannizes over his family to his heart's content. His daughters and son-in-law worship at the shrine and are exploited by him or join in exploiting the other worshippers, but the deathbed confession puts them into a position of great embarrassment until they work themselves round to the point of disregarding it as an old man's hallucination. The original assumption is a considerable one, but once accepted, it develops itself naturally and reasonably in Milne's skilful hands. The characters are well drawn, especially that of Blayds himself, who is so managed as not to be altogether unsympathetic. There is a good deal of wit and some gently satirical humour of character and situation; best of all, there is real feeling. There was general agreement that Milne had done something worth while, and might be expected to do even better in the future.

To those who entertained these expectations *The Dover Road* was a disappointment. It presents to us the frankly fantastic hypothesis that an eccentric man of wealth living near the Dover Road spends his time and money in intercepting and entrapping runaway wives and husbands on their way to the Continent and convincing them that an irregular venture is no more likely to be permanently successful than the first regular venture into matrimony which has turned out a failure. We are asked further to believe that on this occasion he has caught within one week a wife running away from her husband and this same husband running away from his wife, each unconscious of the other's escapade. There is some amusing dialogue, but never the slightest pretence of probability; characters and situation are, from first to last, obviously impossible.

The Dover Road

Success   The critics fell heavily upon *Success* on the score of probability and not without reason. The successful politician who on account of a dream resigns a minor portfolio to run away from his wife with the love of his youth, and withdraws his resignation to remain with his family as Chancellor of the Exchequer is too fantastic a conception for Milne's skilful dialogue and pretty sentiment to carry off.

Ariadne   With *Ariadne, or Business First* (1925) the hopes of the critics and the public faded. The comedy deals in a somewhat patronizing fashion with provincial society and its excessive devotion to business. Ariadne is annoyed by her husband's suggestion that for business reasons she should be nice to one of his clients whom she does not like, and she is nice to him to the extent of arranging to meet him in London, leaving for her husband a letter of explanation that has the air of an elopement. He and his friends are discussing this possibility when Ariadne returns, the client having missed his train to attend to a matter of business. No one in the play displays a glint of common sense after this highly artificial situation has been arrived at, and the resulting misunderstandings are funny only to those who have gone to the theatre with a desperate desire for amusement, even at the sacrifice of all resemblance to actual life.

C. K. MUNRO (1889-   )

C. K. Munro comes from Belfast, but so far the subjects of his dramas have been English or international, and the plays have been performed in London by the Stage Society. *At Mrs. Beam's*   He first won attention by a satirical comedy, *At Mrs. Beam's*, (given in New York by the Theatre Guild, 1926), a study of a London boarding house with the usual group of middle-class eccentrics, brought to fresh life by a touch of originality. Of these the most elaborately drawn is Miss Shoe, "very pretty twenty-five years ago," who drowns everything and everybody in an overwhelming flood of loquacity. She makes up her mind that two newcomers to the boarding house, obviously of the adventurer type, are the "French Bluebeard" and his next victim, an attractive girl, who is destined, in Miss Shoe's opinion, to disappear in the big trunk they bring with them. Miss Shoe learns that the pair are not married and this leads to their immediate dismissal by Mrs. Beam, a typical London landlady:

> The fact that matters to me is that you're living in my house with a woman that isn't your wife, and I can't have it. . . . The reason is that I've got my living to earn, and if you stay in my house, my living will be gone. . . . This isn't a prison or a monkey-house, though I sometimes think it looks like it, some of the people that come—I'm not referring to the present company, of course—and I can't force people to come in here. And with you living here with a girl, they wouldn't come. I've got to live off them, not to judge them, and if they don't like harems, I'm not here to blame their funny taste. And I tell you they wouldn't come, and what's more, they'll go away if you stay, and the servants too. You're a luxury, Mr. Dermott, that's a bit too expensive, if I may say so. So I'm afraid I shall have to ask you to leave tomorrow, along with your young lady. You're not the first bad card I've dealt with. You're very nice people, some of you, but you're no good to me.

Dermott agrees to go, but after dinner he holds the boarders enthralled by a passionate explanation of his relations to Laura while the latter is engaged in going through every bedroom and clearing money and jewellery into the big trunk. When she has got off in the taxi, Dermott runs after her and disappears.

**The
Rumour**

The next two plays, *The Rumour* and *Progress*, are satires on international politics. In the first, a young British diplomat in a small state, which is being exploited by his fellow countrymen, spreads a rumour that the neighbouring less progressive state of Loria is about to make a war of aggression to recover a slice of territory taken from it fifty years before. Labour has been imported from the more backward state, as it is cheaper, and the daughter of a British workman, having fallen in love with one of the Lorian young men, attends one of their meetings. She is killed by a stray bullet that comes through the window—presumably from the opposite party—and the incident is magnified by the British press into a murderous assault upon her by the Lorians, the result being a war in which both little states lose, and the final treaties are arranged to the advantage of the British and French exploiters. Munro is careful to explain that the names "England" and "France" have been used to typify any great modern states. "No special reference is intended: America, Germany, any nation wealthy enough to finance enterprise in smaller states, would have done as well."

Progress

The same proviso attaches to *Progress*, in which Great Britain makes an alliance with Germany against France in order to obtain the island of Kokoland, and, being obliged to divide Kokoland with Germany in consequence, later makes an alliance with France against Germany; in the upshot, Great Britain wins the war, but is obliged to hand over all Kokoland to France as compensation for her services. The Kokos are informed that from this time on they are Frenchmen and Catholics—not British and Protestant any more; they are now exploited by the British and French jointly; to achieve this result both nations have

suffered enormous losses, and they can get nothing out of
Germany. The German delegate says:

Forty-two per cent of the manhood of our nation has been destroyed or maimed. Of wealth we have none, it has all gone. Of
industries, none. Our fields are unploughed, our cattle are all
dead; disease is rife amongst us, for we have no medical appliances
and few medicaments. We are at this moment a nation of unem-
ployed, a whole complete nation without employment or the means
to employ ourselves and earn our way in the world. You can
take us and make us your vassals, you can add our territories to
your empires, and rule over us, but you will find no profit, for we
possess little but disease, and with difficulty, for we still possess
our souls. You can take our bodies and make slaves of us; you
can import us into your dominions to work for you—if your
people desire that, but I do not think they do—but our bodies are
now all that you can have. If you do not take them, you can take
nothing, for we possess nothing else.

There are many speeches—too many and too long. Even
in *At Mrs. Beam's* the author had to admit that it was
desirable to make cuts for production, and there the flow
of words has its justification, or at any rate mitigation, in
its comic effect. The political and diplomatic speeches are
as tiresome in the plays as they are in real life, without the
excuse of dealing with actual facts or supposed facts.
Munro does them well and brings out very cleverly the
banality, and even the hypocrisy of political and diplomatic
oratory, but it does not seem necessary to bore people in
a theatre to such an appalling extent for the sake of
bringing home to them the unveracity of these exercises
in political eloquence. Most of them are sufficiently convinced already or can easily convince themselves by hearing
the actual orations or reading them in the newspapers.

Storm returns to a less ambitious subject—the philan- *Storm*
dering that goes on at hydropathic hotels between the hus-

bands of the married guests and the unmarried ladies. This struggle between the wives and the spinsters is "The Battle of Tinderley Down" which has been going on for over a century and never comes to a decisive issue. Miss Gee, with her Human Relationship Society to combat the terrible notion that the only thing a man and a woman can do together is to make love, is an amusing figure, but neither the characters nor the theme have enough in them to carry the play through the interminable conversations.

Munro has ambitions and ideas about the drama, and it may be that he will yet succeed in carrying them out effectively. He defines the reasonable tests of a good play thus: first, is the action presented recognizable in terms of human action; second, if recognizable, is it natural, does it ring true when so translated; and third, if so, is the whole action *significant*—does it produce a definite and complete impression? Poetic drama is human action in modified form; fantastic drama makes no claim to naturalness or probability. He is not attempting either of these, but aims at making the spectator instinctively feel, through the reactions the persons of the plays display to their environment, that here are living human beings like himself. In this effort Munro has measurably succeeded and he has won the respectful attention of the critics; but they cry out upon him for prolixity. St. John Ervine in the course of an elaborate analysis of Munro's last play, *The Mountain, or the Story of Captain Yevan* (1926), writes as follows:

The Mountain

Something must be done about Mr. Munro. His passion for using six words where one would do does not diminish; it grows; and if we are not careful he will presently be using twelve where one would be enough. This play occupied nearly four hours in performance, and would have occupied more than four hours if it had not been "cut." I do not complain of length, but I do complain of unnecessary length. There are whole scenes in *The Mountain* which are either useless or irrelevant. Two of them, at the beginning of the second act, were cut in performance, but the whole of the third scene of the same act and of the first scene of the fourth act are of no value to the play, which would be improved by their excision. I take it that Mr. Munro is not writing plays merely for the entertainment of those who have sufficient leisure to be able to spend four hours on a Monday afternoon in a theatre, and that he is anxious to have them performed before the general public. Need he so wilfully raise obstacles to prevent their performance before that public? I use the word "wilfully" because it is evident from a close study of *The Mountain* that Mr. Munro is working on a theory to which he holds with the utmost tenacity. The great length of his play is not due to the inexperience of a young dramatist; it is deliberately devised by a dramatist who has now had six plays performed, and may be presumed to know what he is doing. The de-humanising of the characters in this piece is purposely done; the effect of monotony is intentionally achieved; the use of dull and unvaried dialogue is deliberate; the repetitions, the cinematograph technique, the indistinguishable people, all these things are done by Mr. Munro because he has a theory to expound, and is determined to expound it in defiance of the facts. Something must be done about it. Mr. Munro's mind must somehow be delivered from the bondage of mechanics into which it has fallen.

NOEL COWARD (1899-

Noel Coward is the most brilliant of the younger dramatists, and he is still so young that much may be expected of him, if he does not wear himself out prematurely. He made his first appearance on the stage at the age of 11, and at 21 had a play produced and published; at 25 he was still acting in his own play, *The Vortex*, which was "the *dernier cri* in the theatrical mode," both in London and New York. Its success was startling in its suddenness, and no doubt the main situation and the vicious frivolity of the whole atmosphere of the play was a contributing element in arousing public curiosity. The author denies that he has ever had the second-rate ambition to be "daring" or "shocking," and his record of production previous to *The Vortex* bears out his denial. His first play, *I'll Leave it to You*, produced at the New Theatre, London, in 1920, is the lightest of light comedies, absolutely devoid of offence—a sympathetic but amusing sketch of a family of well-to-do young people driven by the death of their father and the encouragement of a returning American uncle to exert themselves to earn their own livelihood. *The Young Idea*, which followed at the Savoy in 1923, has some lively satire of English county society, but its main idea is the reconciliation of a divorced couple through the ingenious efforts of their children; it is true that the second wife helps on the plot by running away with her lover, but this is a quite subordinate interest. *The Rat Trap*, printed in 1924 without being produced, presents the familiar theme of a young couple torn asunder by the contending literary aspirations of husband and wife, but the play ends in a reconciliation when the wife reveals to her husband that she is going to have a child. There is nothing of modern sophistication in the wife's final cry to her husband: "Oh God! Why aren't we ordinary normal people without these beastly analytical minds? I'd willingly give up every particle of brain, intellect and talent if only I could recapture the old longing for you—I hate being able to pry about and criticize—I want not to know anything—just to love you, but I can't—I can't, and now—now I feel so alone—and so dreadfully frightened."

So far no accusation could lie against the author of choosing "unpleasant" subjects or "decadent" types. *The*

I'll Leave it to You

The Young Idea

The Rat Trap

Vortex was different; on his defence, the author says the   *The Vortex* minor characters "drink cocktails, employ superlatives, and sometimes turn on the gramaphone. Apart from these mild amusements their degeneracy is not marked." The real situation is more truthfully represented by the dramatist's stage direction at the beginning of Act II: "There must be a feeling of hectic amusement and noise, and the air black with cigarette smoke and superlatives." It was probably this scene that produced the scandalous impression which contributed to some extent to the success of the play and afterwards raised an outcry of protest, although the attack was directed rather to the central situation—the mother's loss of her lover to the girl who is engaged to her son. The younger woman has few scruples, for the engagement is "only a sort of try out, you know— just to tread water for a bit," and the lover she recaptures has been her lover before. The boy she throws over is a drug-taker and a neurotic—far from a sympathetic character, but there are no sympathetic characters in the play. One does not see, however, how the author could otherwise arrive at the powerful situation he develops in Act III, in which the son reproaches his mother for ruining not only his life but his character by her neglect and selfish frivolity:

NICKY.   You've given me *nothing* all my life—nothing that counts.

FLORENCE.   Now you're pitying yourself.

NICKY.   Yes, with every reason.

FLORENCE.   You're neurotic and ridiculous—just because Bunty broke off your engagement, you come and say wicked, cruel things to me—

NICKY.   You forget what I've seen tonight, mother.

FLORENCE.   I don't care what you've seen.

NICKY.   I've seen you make a vulgar, disgusting scene in your own house, and on top of that humiliate yourself before a boy half your age. The misery of losing Bunty faded away when that happened—everything is comparative after all.

FLORENCE. I didn't humiliate myself.

NICKY. You ran after him up the stairs because your vanity wouldn't let you lose him—it isn't that you love him —that would be easier—you never love anyone, you only love them loving you—all your so-called passion and temperament is false—your whole existence has degenerated into an endless empty craving for admiration and flattery—and then you say you've done no harm to anybody. Father used to be a clever man, with a strong will and a capacity for enjoying everything—I can remember him like that, and now he's nothing—a complete nonentity because his spirit's crushed. How could it be otherwise? You've let him down consistently for years—and God knows I'm nothing for him to look forward to—but I might have been if it hadn't been for you.

There may be little hope of fulfilment in the promises of reform made by mother and son to each other at the final curtain, but this makes little difference as to the effect of the play on the audience. There is certainly no encouragement to or condonation of vice: the tone of the play is severe; there are few more scathing exposures of the utter vapidity of the life of the idle set which devotes its whole time and energy to frivolity. The dialogue is amusing, but largely because of its emptiness and vulgarity; it is sometimes smart, but seldom epigrammatic. Often it is brutally rude, almost to the point of barbarism. None of the critics of the "unpleasant" atmosphere of the play ventured to question the fact that this kind of life and this kind of people exist, and no one contends that they are not legitimate objects of dramatic satire. That they represent only the froth—or the dregs—of a comparatively small class may be granted, but mankind has always been more interested in the misdoings of the fast and fashionable than in the uneventful labours of modest virtue.

James Agate, perhaps the keenest of the London critics, agrees that *The Vortex* had "lots of morals, sufficient in any case to make you feel that the writer had dabbled in low things out of the highest motives," but with *Fallen Angels* "the case for the author as scourger of modern manners seemed pretty thin." "Do I believe in Mr. Coward's fallen angels? Yes. Would they get drunk and deceive their husbands? Yes. Do I care if they do? No. Can *anything* they do interest me? No." *Fallen Angels*

Agate's point—and it seems to be well taken—is not that the characters are naughty or unpleasant, but that they are devoid of interest because they are without real feeling and therefore excite no real feeling in the audience. One of Agate's earlier volumes on *The Contemporary Theatre* was honoured by an Introduction from Noel Coward, who protested that he "would sooner be blamed by Mr. Agate than praised by almost anyone else." In this volume's notice of *The Vortex* there were agreeable phrases such as "wit of the best theatrical kind," "a very fine piece of work," "the imprint of truth," "craftsmanship beyond reproach"; but in 1925 the critic, further irritated by the young dramatist's later plays, relieved his mind as follows:

Mr. Noel Coward at the moment has four plays running in the town, and all of them as barren of emotion as a money-lender is of generosity. *The Vortex* has a certain quality of hectic excitement which may make the galled Society jade wince, but will not wring the withers of the man in the street. Comparatively few of us, after all, possess mothers who go off with their son's sweetheart's discarded lover. It is not to be imagined that if Mr. Noel

Coward's Queen Gertrude and her precious son, Hamlet, were drowned in a bucket of disinfectant—a consummation devoutly to be wished—it is not thinkable that in the course of three hundred performances one single tear would be dropped. Charles Lamb declared that if one of Congreve's or Wycherley's personages were placed in a modern play, his virtuous indignation "shall rise against the profligate wretch as warmly as the Catos of the pit could desire." Why does not our virtuous indignation rise against these two profligate madams in *Fallen Angels,* seeing that they are placed in a modern play where we are supposed to judge of the right and the wrong? The reason is because neither creature has, or ever could have, an emotion, their sentimental peripatetics being dictated solely by appetite. We are certain that our wives, mothers, sisters, and daughters are not made in this mould, and we are as much amused and as little touched as if the spectacle were that of a Hottentot *ménage.*

As to *Fallen Angels,* Coward protested that it "aimed no higher than to be an amusing evening's entertainment," and this excuse might also apply to the play that followed —*Hay Fever*—a clever study of the family life of a once popular actress, now the mother of two grown-up children and retired from the stage, but still "trailing clouds of glory" from her former triumphs. This play pleased the critics but did not attract the public. The next play, *Easy Virtue,* by its very title was a challenge to conventional morality, and the Manchester City Council, apparently lacking the courage to prohibit the performance, took the half-measure of forbidding the announcement of the title —a sad falling-off for the community which produced Stanley Houghton and Allan Monkhouse. *Easy Virtue* accordingly appeared in Manchester as "a play by Noel Coward," and as it had already won a *succès de scandale* on both sides of the Atlantic, no harm was done to anybody and the City Fathers saved their faces.

Easy Virtue was acted first in New York and then in

Easy Virtue

London with Jane Cowl in the principal part. It is a satire on what Galsworthy called the "crassness" of county society. The young son brings home as his wife a lady of unknown antecedents he has picked up at the Cannes Casino. Larita is a magnificent creature who speaks English "with the faintest possible foreign accent" and all that she reveals to the family as to her past is that her first husband divorced her after she ran away from him on account of his brutality. Between Act I and Act II we are given to understand that Larita—a mature woman of cosmopolitan experience whose favourite fiction is Marcel Proust—has for three months endured life in the country house with its impossible inmates—Mrs. Whittaker, entrenched in every prejudice of her class; her elder daughter Marion, who has taken refuge from repressed sex-impulses in religious devotion; the hoydenish Hilda, whose first enthusiasm for Larita turns to hate when the young man in whom Hilda is interested attempts a flirtation with the older woman. It is Hilda who precipitates the explosion in Act II by the production of a newspaper cutting about a scandalous divorce suit in which Larita was mixed up and her photograph appeared in the papers with a list of her supposed lovers. It is the situation of *L'Aventurière* and *The Second Mrs. Tanqueray* reversed, the sympathy being thrown against the bourgeois society which turns its thumbs down in condemnation of the adventuress at bay. The real weakness in Larita's situation is that her young husband has ceased to love her and has transferred his affections to the sweetheart of his boyhood, Sarah Hurst, a boyish athlete of practical common sense who will be content with a life of perpetual tennis and small talk. It is not easily conceived how John Whittaker, young and foolish as he is, could imagine that Larita would fit into the kind of life his parents live, and it is still more difficult to imagine that Larita could ever think she would. Her explanation is that in "a panic of restlessness and dissatisfaction with everything" she fell in love with John and married him in the expectation that his passion for her would be succeeded by "real love and affection." She realizes that the marriage was a mistake from her point of view—John is "charming and weak and inadequate, and he's brought me down to the dust." She makes a sensational exit and leaves the field clear for Sarah Hurst, but not without an attempt to make her point of view clear to the family:

> Your treatment of all this shows a regrettable lack of discrimination. You seem to be floundering under the delusion that I'm a professional *cocotte.* You're quite, quite wrong—I've never had an affair with a man I wasn't fond of. The only time I ever sold myself was in the eyes of God to my first husband—my mother arranged it. I was really too young to know what I was doing. You approve of that sort of bargaining, don't you?—it's within the law.

Larita's talk about "values" and "inhibitions" and "physical purity" is all in the modern style, but there is rather too much of it; she talks smartly, but her intelligence and charm have to be taken for granted—or conveyed by the actress who plays the part. She serves as an admirable foil for the complacent virtue and intellectual emptiness of the Whittaker family, and the clash between the two points of view in Act II is excellent theatre, but after that the excitement dies down, mainly because one does not really care what happens to Larita. She has cut her way out of the net in which she had involved herself, and it is hard to believe that her affection for young Whittaker was really more lasting than the love affairs that had gone before.

In *The Queen was in the Parlour*, the last London play of 1926, the author did not take his art or his audience seriously. In his curtain speech at the first performance, he said that it was not a great play, being mainly intended as a suitable medium for the talents of the leading actress, Madge Titheradge. He did not say that his generosity had extended to providing Lady Tree with the part of the Grand Duchess Emilie of Zalgar and Ada King with that of an old English governess, both of them practically superfluous to the action. Called by its author a "romance," the drama is a cast-back to the type of which *The Prisoner of Zenda* is a familiar recollection to older English and American playgoers, and one of the characters provokes a laugh by the remark that "Father and Rupert of Hentzau were at school together." But of course the conventions of Victorian romance have to be adjusted to the standards of the newer naughtiness. Princess Nadja, the heroine, has a scarlet past, and we first see her after a very lively party in her Parisian flat with her young lover Sabien, to whom she is just going to be married. An assassination calls her to the throne of Kraja, and though she is desperately in love with Sabien, she deserts him to obey the call of patriotic duty. He follows her, saves her life from an assassin's bullet, (assassinations are not uncommon in Kraja), and pleads for a last night with her before her marriage to Prince Keri, the political consort who is to re-establish her damaged reputation with her people. Though she likes Keri, she is still in love with Sabien, and consents; but as a revolutionary mob attacks the palace that night, Sabien is unable to escape from her room, and saves the situation by shooting himself. Prince

Keri and the Queen have in the meantime succeeded in calming the mob and presumably marry later in the day, to live happily ever after. On paper, this does not sound either natural or probable, but the play is "good theatre," with thrilling situations sandwiched into smart dialogue of the sophisticated Noel Coward style. The sentiment of the older type of romance has gone by the board, and the substitution for it of sheer physical passion does not make the dramatist's task any easier. The revival and the modification of a type so long discarded are of interest, but the play adds nothing to the author's previous achievements and rather discourages the expectations formed of his future performances.

Satire of County Society

Apart from occasional indulgences in mere entertainments, Noel Coward has consistently pursued his satire of county society—its limitations and prejudices, its conventions and ideals. It is a disappearing society, for the old county families are being crushed out by taxation and high prices and in modern industrial England they have no longer the responsibilities which once made their position one of real power. The place of the older landowners has been largely taken by the new rich, who adopt the amusements of their predecessors without assuming their duties, for which they substitute the excitements and excesses of city life. The members of this transition class are very much in the public eye, and it can hardly be said that their manners are not worth powder and shot. Noel Coward has won the ear of the public by his apt reproduction of the catchwords and conventional attitudes of the class, and has given a vivid impression of the inanity and occasional viciousness—above all the utter boredom—of their round of games and flirtations. He has yet to show that he can deal with subjects of deeper emotional significance and wider social import. *This Was a Man,* which was prohibited *This Was a Man* by the London censor and put on the New York stage in the fall of 1926, is a trifling play of casual adulteries—a little better made than *Fallen Angels* but presenting the same set of worthless women and fatuous men—and the recurrence of the same theme and similar characters does make one impatient that the author is content to fritter away his talent on such nonentities. But he has on his side youth, a practical knowledge of the theatre, and a natural gift for dialogue and situation; there seems good reason to hope that maturity will bring to him a grasp of larger issues and the ability to create characters of some depth and power instead of the fashionable butterflies and county stupidities to whom he has hitherto devoted his talents.

SEAN O'CASEY (1884-

Sean O'Casey is the greatest discovery since the War, not merely of the Abbey Theatre but of the European drama. He has not only brought upon the stage a new kind of life—the life of the Dublin slums—but he has used that life in such a way as to create a new form of art. His realism is so close to the facts that it has been called photographic, and yet it is instinct with romance and pathos; it is tragic in intent, and yet, for three-fourths of the dialogue, the audience is stirred to uncontrollable laughter; the sense of overwhelming tragedy may be in the background, ready in a moment to come out in grimmest reality, but until the climax is reached, it seldom obliterates for more than a moment or two the pervading atmosphere of grotesque humour.

No ordinary dramatist, educated and trained in the usual way, would have thought of attempting what O'Casey has accomplished: the difficulty of transferring the tone of a play from comedy to tragedy and back again to comedy is too appalling for the regular dramatist to contemplate: it is against all the rules. O'Casey does it many times in the course of a play and sometimes in the same scene. No contrasted tragic and comic effects are too difficult for him to bring into juxtaposition: at the end of *The Plough and the Stars* the English Tommies drink the tea made by Nora in her insanity and sing a popular song with the body of the woman they have killed still lying on the stage; in *Juno and the Paycock* the mother's lament over her slain son is immediately followed by the drunken maunderings of the boy's father.

The Dublin tenements Brought up in the tenements of Dublin and himself a member of the Citizen Army, O'Casey must have known by experience the sharp contrasts presented by the desperate ventures to which some of the rebels went forth and the sordid homes to which they returned—or failed to return. In the clash between the splendour of their political ideals and the squalour of their material surroundings he saw a dramatic irony as moving to tears and laughter as a Greek protagonist's struggles against fate or a romantic hero's overwhelming by circumstance and some inner flaw. He could not have dealt with the humours and tragedies of these obscure victims of modern civilization unless he had known and loved them; and he could not have turned their quaint speech and petty interests to artistic purpose if he had not had the gift of genius—the natural power to reveal them in their essential humanity so that we recognize their failings and aspirations as those which move the hearts of men in all times and places. His knowledge of these people is profound and sympathetic; he knows them because he was one of them, as he has himself related to a correspondent of the London *Observer*, published on November 22, 1925:

I knocked at a door in the hall of a high tenement house in Dublin.

A man in his shirt-sleeves answered. The man was Sean O'Casey, whose play, *Juno and the Paycock,* is now at the Royalty Theatre, London.

As he finished dressing in the darkness of the room where he lives, works, and sleeps, cooking for himself as he did when a bricksetter's labourer, two years ago, he talked in his soft Dublin tongue, using the speech of a writer and the accent of a workman. "Born in a tenement house, I write about people in tenement houses," he told me. "If the London production is a success, I'll leave 'em for ever."

Mr. O'Casey is forty-one, is frank, unaffected, likeable, and (so he says) lazy. A slim, hatchet-faced man, with pointed nose and chin, and brown, twinkling weak eyes, so weak, I believe, that he has to hold his manuscript six inches or so from his nose to read what he has written. He works at all hours when the mood and the idea are there. "I make no divisions of day and night," he said. He writes in copybooks, leaving the play loose and flexible, and then types it out twice, altering, altering. "It would not be true, perhaps, to say that the first draft bears no resemblance to the finished play, but they are very different."

I spoke to him of technique. "I abominate it," he said. "They tell me *The Shadow of a Gunman* (his first accepted play) breaks all the rules. If characters live and the play holds the audience, that's enough."

Mr. O'Casey has had a hard life. He told me his father died when he was three, and that his mother brought the family up. "We had dry bread and a drink of tea in the morning, and that again at night if we were lucky." For nine years he half-starved. At fourteen he taught himself to read; at fifteen he worked for a newsagent from 4 a. m. to 7 p. m. for 9s. a week. After that he navvied and laboured for fifteen years. His last job, oddly enough, was on a building near the Abbey Theatre, which he has visited for the past ten years and into which he drops nearly every evening.

He has views on education. "Education is a terrible drawback to a dramatist—I mean the sort of primary and secondary education we get in Ireland. You can see from the way my plays are written I never went to school." He said that quite seriously. "The first book I bought was Shakespeare. I spent nearly all my money on books."

I mentioned the criticism that has been made that his plays are a series of photographs, that he writes only of what he knows, of his own experiences. "What in the name of Heaven should a man write about?" he asked. "What did Euripides and Aristophanes write about? My next play will be *The Red Lily*—about a prostitute. I wonder if that will suit them? I worked with Captain Boyle, a character in *Juno,* for five years. I didn't even alter his name. No, I don't think he ever saw the play."

On the subject of acting he said he had acted a little in an amateur way. "But I go to all the rehearsals in the Abbey, and I sometimes act the characters for them there."

The Shadow of a Gunman

To the greater public O'Casey is known by the three plays—*The Shadow of a Gunman,* first produced at the Abbey Theatre on April 12, 1923; *Juno and the Paycock,* produced about a year later; and *The Plough and the Stars,* produced in February, 1926. All three have the tenements for background, and all three deal with the disturbances in and about Dublin since the beginning of the European War—the last with the outbreak of the rebellion in 1916, the middle one with the situation under the Free State in 1922, and the earliest with the struggle between the insurgent guerillas and the Black and Tans—the Auxiliaries employed by the British Government to suppress them in May, 1920. In this, the first of O'Casey's plays to be acted, we see in a tenement room a figure perhaps suggested by the author's own pursuit of literature under difficulties—Donal Davoren, a poet whose efforts at

234

composition are constantly checked and interrupted by visits from tenement neighbours. Davoren gets rid of his fellow lodger, Seumas Shields, and the lodger's friend Maguire, a soldier in the Irish Republican Army, who calls to leave a bag, supposed to contain pedlar's wares belonging to Shields. He has more difficulty in getting rid of the landlord, (who wants to turn him out because of a report that Davoren is "a gunman on the run"), of some ignorant neighbours who want him to enlist the protection of the Irish Republican Army in their own petty quarrels, and of Minnie Powell, who admires him as a rebel and a poet. The last visits appeal to his vanity, though he is not really a gunman at all, and the act closes with his acknowledgment to himself that he is attracted to Minnie, and "what harm can there be in being the shadow of a gunman?" In the next act, the scene being the same tenement room, at night, his meditations are interrupted by the sound of a raid on the house by the British Auxiliaries, and Seumas and he, in their hasty search of the room that they may destroy any incriminating papers, find that the bag left by Maguire (who has been killed earlier in the day, in an attempt to ambush the British soldiery) contains bombs. Seumas and Davoren are still engaged in terrified recriminations when Minnie rushes in, and finding the bombs on the table, takes off the bag to her room, saying, "Maybe they won't search it; if they do aself, they won't harm a girl. Goodbye . . . Donal." When the Auxiliary soldier comes in, Seumas and Donal disavow any connection with politics, and the Black and Tan goes off as soon as he hears that his comrades have discovered a bottle of whisky on a lower floor. Seumas and Donal, in a state of abject terror, listen to the Auxiliaries searching the house, and the following dialogue takes place:

SEUMAS. If they come across the bombs, I hope to God Minnie'll say nothing!

DAVOREN. We're a pair of pitiable cowards to let poor Minnie suffer when we know that we and not she are to blame.

SEUMAS. What else can we do, man? Do you want us to be done in? If you're anxious to be riddled, I'm not. Besides, they won't harm her, she's only a girl, an' so long as she keeps her mouth shut it'll be all right.

DAVOREN. I wish I could be sure of that.

But they sit still in their own room, even when they hear Minnie Powell arrested and shouting, "Up the Republic!" The sound of shots is heard and the two men seek shelter by cowering down in the room, although a minute before Seumas has been boasting how his firm bearing got rid of the Black and Tan. A neighbour comes in to tell them that the Auxiliaries have been ambushed in the street and in the firing Minnie Powell has been killed. Davoren brings the play to an end with the lamentation: "It's terrible to think that little Minnie is dead, but it's still more terrible to think that Davoren and Shields are alive! Oh, Donal Davoren, shame is your portion now till the silver cord is loosened and the golden bowl be broken. Oh, Donal Davoren, Donal Davoren, poet and poltroon, poltroon and poet!"

It will be seen that, shorn of the humours of the tenement, the action of the tragedy is simple and direct. That of the next play, *Juno and the Paycock*, is more complicated and more enriched with humour, extending to three (practically four) acts as against the two of the earlier play. Instead of the single room of *The Shadow of a Gunman* we have the two tenement rooms—bedroom and bed-sitting room—occupied by "Captain" Boyle, his wife, son and daughter. Boyle is a character drawn from the life, by O'Casey's own acknowledgement, but he is none

Juno and the Paycock

the less one of the author's greatest creations. He is called "Captain" on the strength of a single voyage he has made as a seaman in an old collier from Dublin to Liverpool, but is more generally known as "the Paycock," because his walk is a slow, consequential strut; he is a confirmed toper and idler, with a great gift of the gab. His constant companion is the equally drunken and idle Joxer, who sponges on him, flatters him, steals from him on occasion, and ridicules him behind his back. Mrs. Boyle has been named Juno by her husband because she "was born an' christened in June. I met her in June; we were married in June an' Johnny was born in June." Juno's life has had little other relation either to the summer month or to the goddess; in favourable circumstances she would have become a handsome, active and clever woman, but her face has been worn down into "a look of listless monotony and harassed anxiety blending with an expression of mechanical resistance." Her daughter Mary, a good-looking girl of twenty-two, is torn by the struggle between her squalid and ignorant environment and the desire for better things she has acquired from reading. Johnny, her younger brother, is a delicate boy who has been wounded in the hip by a bullet during the rebellion of Easter Week, 1916, and has had his arm torn off by a bomb during the fight in O'Connell Street between the forces of the Free State and the Die-Hard Republicans. He is nervous and irritable, and his nervous irritation is increased to hysteria when Mary reads from the newspaper an account of the slaughter of one of his former Die-Hard comrades, Robbie Tancred, who had been the leader of an ambush in which a Free State soldier was killed; it is not until later in the play that we learn that Johnny has given information which has led to his comrade's discovery and death. In the first Act we are mainly concerned with the vagaries of the Paycock and Joxer, the Paycock's shifts to avoid work and Joxer's stratagems to enjoy the hospitality of the Boyle household without encountering the wrath of Juno. Two characters come in from outside the tenement—Jerry Devine, a trade union organizer and Mary's discarded suitor, and his successor in Mary's affections, the dandified Charlie Bentham, school teacher and law student, who brings the news of a legacy to Captain Boyle under the will of a relative, which Bentham himself has drawn up.

In the next Act the Boyle family is in the full tide of prosperity. The legacy has not been paid—only a few days have elapsed—but on the strength of it the Boyles have borrowed all round the neighbourhood. The furniture of the bed-sittingroom is more plentiful and more vulgar— a glaringly upholstered armchair and lounge, cheap pictures and photos everywhere. Every available spot is ornamented with huge vases filled with artificial flowers; crossed festoons of coloured paper chains stretch from end to end of the ceiling. The Paycock bullies Joxer and domineers over his family; the neighbours are called in to assist in their rejoicings—which are suddenly interrupted by the funeral of young Tancred. One of the neighbours tries to console the bereaved mother with the assurance, "He died a noble death, an' we'll bury him like a king." Mrs. Tancred's reply is characteristic of O'Casey both in its simple pathos and in its deeper significance:

An' I'll go on livin' like a pauper. Ah, what's the pains I suffered bringin' him into the world to carry him to his cradle, to the pains I'm sufferin' now carryin' him out o' the world to bring him to his grave! . . . Me home is gone, now; he was me only child, an' to think that he was lyin' for a whole night stretched out on the side of a lonely country lane, with his head, his darlin' head, that I of'en kissed an' fondled, half hidden in the wather of a runnin' brook. An' I'm told he was the leadher of the ambush where me nex' door neighbour, Mrs. Mannin', lost her Free State soldier son. An' now here's the two of us oul' women, standin' one on each side of a scales o' sorra, balanced be the bodies of our two dead darlin' sons.

The members of the interrupted tea party show little sympathy for Mrs. Tancred and resume their jollifications till the passage of the funeral procession in the street below calls them to the windows to look on. At this point we get a clear indication of the ultimate fate of Johnny. An Irregular Mobilizer summons him to a meeting to offer explanations as to his supposed connection with the death of Tancred, and he refuses to go.

In Act III two months later, we see the tragic downfall of the family fortunes. Bentham has deserted Mary, who is going to have a child, and her appeal to her former lover, Jerry Devine, is in vain; the legacy has fallen through owing to Bentham's clumsiness in drafting the will; tradesmen and neighbours call to collect their debts or recover their property; and in the midst of the hurly burly the Irregular Mobilizers come to hurry off Johnny to his doom for betrayal of a comrade. An hour later Mrs. Boyle is summoned by the police to identify her son's body and she goes forth on her terrible errand repeating the words, which, untouched, she has heard from the lips of Mrs. Tancred:

Mother o' God, Mother o' God, have pity on us all! Blessed Virgin, where were you when me darlin' son was riddled with bullets? . . . Sacred heart o' Jesus, take away our hearts o' stone, and give us hearts o' flesh! Take away this murdherin' hate, an' give us Thine own eternal love!

But immediately upon her exit comes the entrance of the Paycock and Joxer, both very drunk, and it is the Paycock, not Juno, who speaks the final word of the play, telling us in his blundering drunken fashion that "the whole world's in a terrible state of chaos."

The representation of Irish life in this play provoked a good deal of discussion but no public protest. St. John Ervine, who, having missed the first performance in London, went to see a later one, not to criticize, but to enjoy a holiday, could not forbear from putting pen to paper, with the following result:

I doubt if any people, except, perhaps, Russians, will be able to witness this play without being made to laugh at passages which an Irishman can only observe with poignance or shame. Juno makes me feel that even in the depth of that squalor and debasement there is beauty which may yet emerge and transfigure the most squalid and the most debased; but how do I know that this feeling does not spring from my own desire and not from the thought provoked by Mr. O'Casey? An English lady—and it is to state her opinion of the play that I am writing this article—said to me after we had seen it, "If I were a patriotic Irishman I should refuse to act in that play outside Ireland!" I inquired why, and she replied in a tone of horror, "Such people! *Such* people! I'd hate to expose my country like that!" This is not a point of view that I can easily understand. I am not willing to tell the truth to the extent of causing the heavens to fall, because the truth would then be pointless, but I think it should be told up to the edge of disaster. I commonly hear English people saying, "Why do the Irish dramatists and novelists write so bitterly about their own countrymen?" and I always reply, "There is no one so bitter as the disillusioned romantic, no one who drops so deeply into despair as the idealist whose ideals have been destroyed!" How swiftly the English authors responded to the despair of their race after the disasters and humiliations of the Boer War! It is the same sort of reaction which is moving Irish authors to-day. Many of them, indeed, believe that there can be

no revival of hope in their country until Irishmen have shed all
their vain illusions about themselves and have been steeped in the
waters of self-disgust. Is there a race in the world so romantically deceived about itself as the Irish? Can a people hope to
walk in any certitude until they have learned how to stand up?
If a man is covered with dirty deceptions how can he be made
clean until he has first been stripped bare? I do not say that
every Irish author consciously writes to that end, but there is a
consciousness outside ourselves which compels us to acknowledge
our sins and to humiliate ourselves even to the point of exposure;
and we are now under that compulsion. There will not always be
"Paycocks" and "Joxers" in Ireland. The waters of Marah will
surely submerge them for ever. But there will be Junos to soften
these hearts of stone and dissolve our hatreds in love and charity.
Mr. O'Casey's play is at once Russian in its bitter truthfulness
and Elizabethan in its mingling of the pitiful and the comic;
but it is Irish, too, in its recollection of the spark of beauty to be
found even in the heart of despair. When I am asked to remember "Joxer," I remember Juno, and, remembering her, am no
longer ashamed.

The storm broke over the play dealing with the Easter
Rising of 1916, *The Plough and the Stars*; it had probably *The Plough*
been gathering during the performances of the preceding *and the*
plays, for to the detached observer there seems nothing to *Stars*
distinguish the third play in temper and purport from the
two that had gone before. There is the same richly
humorous setting enveloping and often overwhelming
tragic issues and the same realistic treatment of political
movements and the people who take part in them. Instead
of two loquacious tenement types we have four—one of
them a charwoman, Mrs. Gogan, whose lively gossip in the
opening scene introduces us to the other characters.
Fluther Good, the successor to the Paycock and equally
bibulous and loquacious, differs from him in being more
industrious and more quarrelsome. He is a carpenter, and

when the curtain goes up he is admiring a door he has just repaired, "openin' an' shuttin' now with a well-mannered motion, like a door of a select bar in a high-class pub." To him Mrs. Gogan discourses on the peculiarities of the Clitheroes, who are the occupants of the front and back drawing-rooms of a fine old Georgian house, now fallen from its high estate, which form the scene. Nora Clitheroe, the young wife, is ambitious for better things, though to Mrs. Gogan it seems "that her skirts are a little too short for a married woman. An' to see her sometimes of an evenin' in her glad-neck gown would make a body's blood run cold." But Nora is a good housekeeper and does well out of her two lodgers. "An' she has th' life frightened out o' them; washin' their face, combin' their hair, wipin' their feet, brushin' their clothes, thrimmin' their nails, cleanin' their teeth—God Almighty, you'd think th' poor men were undhergoin' penal servitude." One of the lodgers, Nora's uncle Peter Flynn, is in white whipcord knee-breeches dressing himself up to appear as an officer of the Foresters in a patriotic procession with plumed hat and sword and ruffled shirt; just now he is struggling with a stiffly-starched collar which he tries in vain to get round his neck and eventually flings on the floor with a curse. Mrs. Gogan describes him as "like somethin' you'd pick off a Christmas Tree. . . . When he's dressed up in his canonicals, you'd wondher where he'd been got. God forgive me, when I see him in them, I always think he must ha' had a Mormon for a father." Uncle Peter is the butt for everybody's scorn and ridicule, and especially for his fellow lodger, the Socialist orator, Young Covey, who after teasing and tormenting him with minor pricks, goes off with the taunt that he looks "like th' illegitimate son of an illegitimate child of a corporal in th' Mexican army!" Nora herself

comes in and innocently contributes to the uproar by a
quarrel with Bessie Burgess, the tenant of the top story,
who objects to Nora's uppish ways, but at last the stage
is cleared for a charming love scene between Nora and her
young husband, who has been dissuaded from his devotion
to the Citizen Army, partly by Nora's entreaties, partly
by disappointment of his expectation to be made Captain.
Mrs. Gogan has already informed us that "he was so cock-
sure o' being made one that he bought a Sam Browne belt,
an' was always puttin' it on an' standin' at th' door showing it off, till th' man came an' put out the street lamps on
him. God, I think he used to bring it to bed with him!"
But the endearments of the young couple are interrupted
by a message from the Commander of the Citizen Army
that he has been appointed not only Captain but Commandant, and that he is to lead the eighth battalion that
night. Nora admits that she burnt the letter informing
him of his appointment as Captain, and in a rage he flings
her from him, puts on his Sam Browne belt, and goes off to
the army. So the Act ends with a premonition of tragedy
and the significant question from a minor character, "Is
there anybody goin' with a titther o' sense?"

To all this the demonstrators at the Abbey Theatre
offered no objection; it was the second Act that aroused
their violent indignation. The scene is the bar of a cor-
ner public house with a large window at the back through
which may be seen and heard the orator on the platform on
the other side of the window, addressing the patriotic
demonstrators and the assembled troops. When the curtain goes up, the Barman is in conversation with Rosie
Redmond, who is leaning over the counter in an attitude
and dress suggestive of her profession. "Nothin' much
doin' in your line tonight, Rosie?" says the Barman, and

she replies, "Curse o' God on th' haporth, hardly, Tom. There isn't much notice taken of a pretty petticoat of a night like this. . . . They're all in a holy mood. Th' solemn-looking dials on th' whole o' them an' they marchin' to th' meetin'. You'd think they were th' glorious company of th' saints an' th' noble army of martyrs thrampin' through the sthreets of paradise. They're all thinkin' of higher things than a girl's garters."

Uproar at the Abbey Theatre

Immediately the theatre was in an uproar, with cries of "put that woman off." From the gallery Mrs. Sheehy Skeffington, a well-known Republican leader, endeavoured to make a speech. She said: "The Free State Government is subsidizing the Abbey to malign Pearse and Connolly (leaders executed in 1916). We have not come here as rowdies. We came to make a protest against the defamation of the men of Easter Week." A young man sought to follow her example, but the din was so great that he could hardly be heard. "We fought in Easter Week," he shouted, "and we don't want any more of this play. It is a slander on the Citizen Army." The actors went on with the play amid considerable disorder. The words of the orator, heard through the window, are words which, according to Padraic Colum, "might have been spoken by Padraic Pearse," one of the leaders of the insurrection, but they are interspersed with the humours of the bar room, a drunken quarrel between Mrs. Gogan and Bessie Burgess, another between Fluther and the Covey; and the Republican section of the audience was particularly offended by the bringing in of the banners of The Plough and the Stars and the Tri-colour, under the folds of which Clitheroe and his comrades, as they drink, pledge themselves to imprisonment, wounds, and death for the Independence of Ireland.

When the curtain went up for the third act the disorder reached its climax in a scene which is thus described by the Dublin correspondent of the *Manchester Guardian:*

Twenty women rushed from the pit to the stalls. Two of them succeeded in reaching the stage, where a general mêlée took place. The invading women were thrown bodily back into the orchestra. A young man then tried to reach the stage, but was cut off by the lowering of the curtain. This he grabbed, swinging out of it in a frantic endeavour to pull it down. Women rushed to aid him in his project, but he was suddenly thrown into the stalls by a sharp blow from one of the actors. The pandemonium created a panic among a section of the audience, who dashed for the exits and added to the confusion.

As soon as the curtain was raised again, up dashed another youth to the stage and got into grips with two actresses opening the next scene. Immediately a couple of actors rushed from the wings and unceremoniously pushed off the intruder. Another man had got on the stage by this time and was attacked by a number of the players. He retaliated vigorously, and after several blows were exchanged a hardy punch on the jaw hurled him into the stalls.

Meanwhile altercations were going on among the two sections of the audience. For several minutes the players calmly walked up and down the stage, but the performance was not resumed. A change came over the troubled scene when a party of detectives and uniformed police arrived and quickly distributed themselves through different parts of the house.

Senator W. B. Yeats, the well-known poet and dramatist, who is a director of the theatre, came forward to the accompaniment of a torrent of boos and hisses. What he said was quite inaudible to a large section of the audience, who knew he was speaking only by the movement of his lips and the waving of his hands in dramatic gesture. This was his speech: "I thought you had got tired of this. It commenced fifteen years ago. You have disgraced yourselves again. Is this to be an ever-recurring celebration of the arrival of Irish genius? Once more you have rocked the cradle of genius. The news of this will go from country to country.

You have once more rocked the cradle of a reputation. The fame of O'Casey is born tonight. This is apotheosis."

As Senator Yeats retired, shouts of "We want the play," mingled with cries of "Up the Republic!" Over a dozen women demonstrators seized a number of front row seats, vacated by people who had rushed away in panic. The women began to sing the "Soldier's Song," and the chorus was quickly taken up in the gallery. Three or four police approached the women and ejected a number of them, while others fled to the pit.

The removal of these demonstrators marked the beginning of the defeat of the disturbers. Mrs. Sheehy Skeffington rose and announced that "we are now leaving the hall under police protection. I am," she added, "one of the widows of Easter Week. It is no wonder that you do not remember the men of Easter Week because none of you fought on either side. The play is going to London soon to be advertised there because it belies Ireland. All you need do now is to sing 'God save the King.' " She then left.

Most of the demonstrators left with her, and if they had stayed, they would have seen little to content them. It is Easter Week, 1916, and we see the insurrection in progress, but always from the tenement point of view. The Nationalist Fluther and the Socialist Covey, the Catholic Mrs. Gogan and the Protestant Bessie Burgess, are engaged in looting the unguarded stores and bringing home characteristic spoil: Fluther jars of whisky, Covey a sack of flour, and the two women very unsuitable finery, which they propose to wear after lifting "th' bodices up a bit higher, so as to shake th' shame out o' them, an' make them fit for women that hasn't lost themselves in th' nakedness o' th' times." Amid all this Mrs. Gogan's daughter is dying of consumption and Nora is in the throes of a premature confinement brought on by the strain of her last parting from her husband, who is now in the thick of the fighting. It is her old enemy, Bessie Burgess, who braves the rifle shots to go for the doctor with the prayer,

"Oh God, be Thou my help in time o' throuble. An' shelter me safely in th' shadow of Thy wings."

It is upon the attic of Bessie Burgess that the curtain goes up for Act IV. Mrs. Gogan's daughter is dead and Nora's still-born child is to be buried in the same coffin; it is Fluther who has dared the rifle shots to go for the undertaker, but he is now busy drinking and playing cards with Peter Flynn and the Covey in the same room with the coffin. Nora, out of her mind with grief and pain, is being cared for by the faithful Bessie in the adjoining room. A Republican fugitive comes with the message that Commandant Clitheroe's end was "a gleam of glory. Mrs. Clitheroe's grief will be a joy when she realizes that she has had a hero for a husband." Bessie retorts, "If you only seen her, you'd know to th' differ," and Nora appears in her nightdress, her eyes glimmering with the light of incipient insanity. Unconsciously, thinking she is in her own home, she gets tea ready for her husband's return, and is taken back to the bedroom by Bessie, who sings "Lead, kindly light." Upon this scene of poignant suffering there enters a British Corporal on the hunt for snipers and orders off the men, who carry out the coffin, with Mrs. Gogan, as Fluther says, "in her element now, mixin' earth to earth an' ashes t' ashes an' dust to dust, an' revellin' in plumes an' hearses, last days an' judgments." Nora returns singing the song she and her husband had sung together in the first Act and persists in going to the window to watch for him. Bessie drags her away, but in doing so is shot from the street by the British soldiers, who are on the look-out for snipers, and rush in to find that they have killed a woman by mistake. "Well," says the Sergeant, "we couldn't afford to toike any chawnces," and they drink the tea Nora has prepared. They hear the voices of their

247

comrades in the street advancing to the attack on the Post Office, occupied by the rebels, and singing "Keep the Home fires burning," and join in the chorus as the final curtain comes down.

O'Casey's pacifism

Padraic Colum, though he praises the compact and well-ordered construction of the play and its fine dramatic invention, points out, no doubt with justice, that O'Casey in all three plays is anti-militarist and a partisan for pacifism; he contrasts this attitude with that of O'Casey's first book, written to celebrate the doings of the Citizen Army in the insurrection. But O'Casey may well have felt, in the years of murderous disorder that followed the insurrection, that Ireland had had enough of bloodshed and was in need of peace. Commandant Clitheroe was certainly no hero but he was also no coward—simply a poor human being torn in opposite directions by a genuine patriotism and his love for his young wife. Even the treacherous Johnny of *Juno and the Paycock* is an object of pity rather than of contempt; and there are other Irish soldiers in the plays, single-minded to the point of fanaticism, but less interesting because they are less complex. O'Casey's real sympathies are with the women—with the brave Minnie Powell of the first play, who sacrifices her life for the man she loves; with the infinite pity and courage of Juno; and with the torn heart and broken mind of Nora. These are unforgettable figures, and will be treasured as O'Casey's tribute to Irish womanhood when time has taken the sting out of the memory of embittered political differences.

Another thought beside and beyond the mere desire for peace lies at the back of these extraordinary plays. These slum dwellers, with all their humour and poetic phraseology, are living in the midst of ignorance and squalour, driven to drink by sheer apathy and discouragement. No

one has asserted that O'Casey's pictures of the degradation of the Dublin tenements are exaggerated; and it is
upon these social evils that he would have his countrymen
concentrate their attention rather than upon the rankling
memories of political discord. He would have done the
Ireland of today no service by a romantic apotheosis of
the comrades with whom he served in the Citizen Army; it
required far more courage to tell the truth as he saw it
and to invite his Dublin fellow citizens to be courageous
and clearheaded enough to face the facts. The hostile dem-
onstration recorded above was natural enough, but on the
whole the audiences at the Abbey Theatre have stood the
test—and it was a severe one—with dignity and self-
restraint.

From the wider point of view of artistic achievement
O'Casey's work has met with cordial appreciation from
Irish men of letters of such different opinions as W. B.
Yeats, St. John Ervine, Lennox Robinson, James Stephens
and Padraic Colum. The London critics, though sometimes confessedly puzzled by the unfamiliarity of the material and the rapid changes from comedy to tragedy and
back again, have been generous in praise; and a French
critic, Raymond Brugère, has an appreciative article on
O'Casey in a recent number of the *Revue Anglo-Améri-
caine*. An American critic, apropos of the disturbance at
the Abbey Theatre production of *The Plough and the
Stars*, remarked: "Dear, dear, but the Irish are quare.
They consistently produce genius and as consistently rot-
ten-egg it." The allusion is to the more serious riot at the
production of Synge's *Playboy of the Western World*,
which left the interior of the Abbey Theatre almost in
ruins. It was to the same event that W. B. Yeats alluded
in the speech quoted above. If O'Casey finds for himself

a permanent place in literature by the side of Synge, his countrymen may well forget that his presentations of Dublin life were not to their liking in the thought that he has added another name of distinction to the long roll of Irish genius.

AFTER-WAR PLAYWRIGHTS

PLAY LISTS

A. A. MILNE

1917 *Wurzel-Flummery.*
1918 *Belinda.*
1919 *The Camberley Triangle.*
     Mr. Pim Passes By.
1920 *The Romantic Age.*
1921 *The Truth About Blayds.*
     The Lucky One.
1922 *The Dover Road.*
1923 *The Great Broxopp.*
1924 *Success.*
1925 *Ariadne.*

C. K. MUNRO

1915 *Wanderers.*
1921 *At Mrs. Beam's.*
1922 *The Rumour.*
1924 *Progress.*
     Storm.
1926 *The Mountain, or the Story of Captain Yevan.*

NOEL COWARD

1920 *I'll Leave it to You.*
1923 *The Young Idea.*
1924 *The Rat Trap* (pub.)*.*
     The Vortex.
1925 *Fallen Angels.*
     Hay Fever.
1926 *Easy Virtue.*
     The Queen was in the Parlour.
     This Was a Man.

SEAN O'CASEY

1923 *The Shadow of a Gunman.*
1924 *Juno and the Paycock.*
1926 *The Plough and the Stars.*

A WORD IN REVIEW

We have seen that in the first half of the nineteenth century the traditions of Elizabethan tragedy, romantic drama, and polite comedy were alike exhausted and impotent for the creation of any new work of permanent significance; the only *genre* which showed signs of any vigorous life was popular or rhetorical melodrama; the stage was in general disrepute with the more intelligent public and held of little account by men of letters and serious critics. In the second half of the century comedy awoke to new and rather hesitating life in the hands of Robertson, Gilbert, Jones, Pinero and Wilde; their efforts and those of talented actors, stage managers, and critics served to make a better state of things possible, and foreign influences, especially that of Ibsen, contributed to restore the drama to public confidence as a mode of entertainment worthy of respectable and intelligent people. But it was not until Shaw, Barrie, and Galsworthy obtained access to the stage that the English drama established its claims for serious artistic consideration, at home and abroad. It is chiefly owing to their efforts that it has won a place of honour in European drama, and though the work of several of their contemporaries and successors has been of great interest, there seems at present no one likely to maintain their high level of achievement. Their attention has been, in the main, absorbed by the London stage, but there are now important centres of dramatic interest in Ireland, Scotland, and the English provinces from which, it may be, the dramatist of the future will spring. The outlook, if not brilliant, is at any rate much more promising that it was a hundred years ago: there is a public eager to welcome good dramas and willing to pay for them; a successful dramatist can count on a useful and honourable career; the talented actor receives his (or her) meed of public recognition and pecuniary reward. There is every ground for faith that in the twentieth century the drama as a form of art will not fall back into the slough out of which it was pulled, with so much difficulty, during the last fifty years.

BOOKS OF GENERAL REFERENCE

AGATE, JAMES, *The Contemporary Theatre, 1923,* 1924.
AGATE, JAMES, *The Contemporary Theatre, 1924,* 1925.
AGATE, JAMES, *The Contemporary Theatre, 1925,* 1926.
ARCHER, WILLIAM, *English Dramatists of Today,* 1882.
ARCHER, WILLIAM, *About the Theatre,* 1886.
ARCHER, WILLIAM, *The Old Drama and the New,* 1923.
ARCHER, WILLIAM, and BARKER, H. G., *Scheme and Estimates for a National Theatre,* 1908.
BANCROFT, SIR SQUIRE, *Recollections of Sixty Years,* 1909.
BRERETON, AUSTIN, *The Life of Sir Henry Irving,* 1908.
CALVERT, ADELAIDE HELEN, *Sixty-eight Years on the Stage,* 1911.
CARTER, HUNTLY, *The New Spirit in Drama and Art,* 1912.
CARTER, HUNTLY, *The New Spirit in the European Theatre, 1914-24,* 1925.
CHANDLER, F. W., *Aspects of Modern Drama,* 1914.
CLARK, BARRETT H., *British and American Dramatists of Today,* 1915.
CLARK, BARRETT H., *A Study of the Modern Drama,* 1925.
COLEMAN, JOHN, *Players and Playwrights I Have Known,* 1888.
COLEMAN, JOHN, *Fifty Years of an Actor's Life,* 1904.
COOK, DUTTON, *A Book of the Play: Studies and Illustrations of Histrionic Story, Life, and Character,* 1876; rev. ed. 1881.
COOK, DUTTON, *Hours with the Players,* 1881.
COOK, DUTTON, *Nights at the Play,* 1883.
DICKINSON, T. H., *The Contemporary Drama of England,* 1920.
DUKES, ASHLEY, *Modern Dramatists,* 1912.
ERVINE, ST. JOHN, *The Organized Theatre,* 1924.
FILON, A., *Le Théâtre Anglais; hier, aujourd'hui, demain,* Paris, 1896; trans. by F. Whyte, *The English Stage. Being an Account of the Victorian Drama,* 1897.
FITZGERALD, PERCY H., *The Kembles,* 1871.

BOOKS OF GENERAL REFERENCE

FITZGERALD, PERCY H., *The Book of Theatrical Anecdotes*, 1874.

FITZGERALD, PERCY H., *The Romance of the English Stage*, 1874.

FITZGERALD, PERCY H., *The World behind the Scenes*, 1881.

FITZGERALD, PERCY H., *Henry Irving, a Record of twenty years at the Lyceum*, 1893; rev. ed. 1895.

FITZGERALD, PERCY H., *The Garrick Club*, 1904.

FITZGERALD, PERCY H., *Sir Henry Irving: a Biography*, 1906.

FORBES-ROBERTSON, SIR JOHNSTON, *A Player under three Reigns*, 1925.

GREIN, J. T., *The New World of the Theatre, 1923-24*, 1924.

HALE, E. E., *Dramatists of Today*, 1911.

HENDERSON, ARCHIBALD, *The Changing Drama*, 1914.

HOWE, P. P., *The Repertory Theatre, a Record and a Criticism*, 1910.

HOWE, P. P., *Dramatic Portraits*, 1913.

HUNEKER, JAMES, *Iconoclasts: a Book of Dramatists*, 1905.

JAMESON, M. STURM, *Modern Drama in Europe*, 1920.

JONES, H. A., *The Renascence of the English Drama*, 1895.

JONES, H. A., *Foundations of a National Drama*, 1912.

LEWISOHN, LUDWIG, *The Modern Drama*, 1915.

LEWISOHN, LUDWIG, *The Drama and the Stage*, 1922.

MARSTON, JOHN WESTLAND, *Our Recent Actors*, 1888.

MAUDE, CYRIL, *The Haymarket Theatre*, 1903.

MODERWELL, H. K., *The Theatre of Today*, 1914.

MONTAGUE, C. E., *Dramatic Values*, 1911.

MORGAN, A. E., *Tendencies of Modern English Drama*, 1924.

MORLEY, HENRY, *The Journal of a London Playgoer from 1851 to 1866*, 1866.

NICOLL, ALLARDYCE, *British Drama*, 1925.

OLIVER, D. E., *The English Stage: its origin and modern developments*, 1912.

PHELPS, WILLIAM LYON, *The Twentieth Century Theatre*, 1918.

PHELPS, WILLIAM LYON, *Essays on Modern Dramatists*, 1919.

PALMER, JOHN, *The Future of the Theatre*, 1913.

SCOTT, CLEMENT W., *The Drama of Yesterday and Today*, 1899.

SHARP, ROBERT FARQUHARSON, *A Short History of the English Stage, from its Beginnings to the Summer of the Year 1908*, 1909.

MODERN ENGLISH PLAYWRIGHTS

SHAW, GEORGE BERNARD, *Dramatic Opinions and Essays,* 1907.
SUTTON, GRAHAM, *Some Contemporary Dramatists,* 1926.
WALBROOK, H. M., *Nights at the Play,* 1911.
WALKLEY, A. B., *Drama and Life,* 1908.
WALKLEY, A. B., *Pastiche and Prejudice,* 1921.
WALKLEY, A. B., *More Prejudice,* 1923.
WALKLEY, A. B., *Still more Prejudice,* 1925.
WATSON, ERNEST BRADLEE, *Sheridan to Robertson. A Study of the Nineteenth Century London Stage,* 1926.
WYNDHAM, H. S., *The Annals of Covent Garden Theatre from 1732 to 1897,* 1906.
YATES, EDMUND, *Recollections and Experiences,* 1885.

INDEX

Titles of plays are printed in italics

INDEX

INDEX

INDEX

THE END